ADVANCES IN INFORMATION SYSTEMS RESEARCH, EDUCATION AND PRACTICE

T0180654

IFIP – The International Federation for Information Processing

IFIP was founded in 1960 under the auspices of UNESCO, following the First World Computer Congress held in Paris the previous year. An umbrella organization for societies working in information processing, IFIP's aim is two-fold: to support information processing within its member countries and to encourage technology transfer to developing nations. As its mission statement clearly states,

> IFIP's mission is to be the leading, truly international, apolitical organization which encourages and assists in the development, exploitation and application of information technology for the benefit of all people.

IFIP is a non-profitmaking organization, run almost solely by 2500 volunteers. It operates through a number of technical committees, which organize events and publications. IFIP's events range from an international congress to local seminars, but the most important are:

• The IFIP World Computer Congress, held every second year;
• Open conferences;
• Working conferences.

The flagship event is the IFIP World Computer Congress, at which both invited and contributed papers are presented. Contributed papers are rigorously refereed and the rejection rate is high.

As with the Congress, participation in the open conferences is open to all and papers may be invited or submitted. Again, submitted papers are stringently refereed.

The working conferences are structured differently. They are usually run by a working group and attendance is small and by invitation only. Their purpose is to create an atmosphere conducive to innovation and development. Refereeing is less rigorous and papers are subjected to extensive group discussion.

Publications arising from IFIP events vary. The papers presented at the IFIP World Computer Congress and at open conferences are published as conference proceedings, while the results of the working conferences are often published as collections of selected and edited papers.

Any national society whose primary activity is in information may apply to become a full member of IFIP, although full membership is restricted to one society per country. Full members are entitled to vote at the annual General Assembly, National societies preferring a less committed involvement may apply for associate or corresponding membership. Associate members enjoy the same benefits as full members, but without voting rights. Corresponding members are not represented in IFIP bodies. Affiliated membership is open to non-national societies, and individual and honorary membership schemes are also offered.

ADVANCES IN INFORMATION SYSTEMS RESEARCH, EDUCATION AND PRACTICE

IFIP 20th World Computer Congress, TC 8, Information Systems, September 7-10, 2008, Milano, Italy

Edited by

David Avison
Essec Business School
France

George M. Kasper
Virginia Commonwealth University
USA

Barbara Pernici
Politecnico di Milano
Italy

Isabel Ramos
University of Minho
Portugal

Dewald Roode
INBEKON Management Institute
South Africa

 Springer

*Advances in Information Systems Research, Education
and Practice*

Edited by David Avison, George M. Kasper, Barbara Pernici,
Isabel Ramos and Dewald Roode

p. cm. (IFIP International Federation for Information Processing, a Springer Series in Computer Science)

ISSN: 1571-5736 / 1861-2288 (Internet)

ISBN: 978-1-4419-3515-1   eISBN: 978-0-387-09682-7

Printed on acid-free paper

9 8 7 6 5 4 3 2 1

springer.com

IFIP 2008 World Computer Congress (WCC'08)

Message from the Chairs

Every two years, the International Federation for Information Processing hosts a major event which showcases the scientific endeavours of its over one hundred Technical Committees and Working Groups. 2008 sees the 20th World Computer Congress (WCC 2008) take place for the first time in Italy, in Milan from 7-10 September 2008, at the MIC - Milano Convention Centre. The Congress is hosted by the Italian Computer Society, AICA, under the chairmanship of Giulio Occhini.

The Congress runs as a federation of co-located conferences offered by the different IFIP bodies, under the chairmanship of the scientific chair, Judith Bishop. For this Congress, we have a larger than usual number of thirteen conferences, ranging from Theoretical Computer Science, to Open Source Systems, to Entertainment Computing. Some of these are established conferences that run each year and some represent new, breaking areas of computing. Each conference had a call for papers, an International Programme Committee of experts and a thorough peer reviewed process. The Congress received 661 papers for the thirteen conferences, and selected 375 from those representing an acceptance rate of 56% (averaged over all conferences).

An innovative feature of WCC 2008 is the setting aside of two hours each day for cross-sessions relating to the integration of business and research, featuring the use of IT in Italian industry, sport, fashion and so on. This part is organized by Ivo De Lotto. The Congress will be opened by representatives from government bodies and Societies associated with IT in Italy.

This volume is one of fourteen volumes associated with the scientific conferences and the industry sessions. Each covers a specific topic and separately or together they form a valuable record of the state of computing research in the world in 2008. Each volume was prepared for publication in the Springer IFIP Series by the conference's volume editors. The overall Chair for all the volumes published for the Congress is John Impagliazzo.

For full details on the Congress, refer to the webpage http://www.wcc2008.org.

Judith Bishop, South Africa, Co-Chair, International Program Committee
Ivo De Lotto, Italy, Co-Chair, International Program Committee
Giulio Occhini, Italy, Chair, Organizing Committee
John Impagliazzo, United States, Publications Chair

WCC 2008 Scientific Conferences

TC12	**AI**	Artificial Intelligence 2008
TC10	**BICC**	Biologically Inspired Cooperative Computing
WG 5.4	**CAI**	Computer-Aided Innovation (Topical Session)
WG 10.2	**DIPES**	Distributed and Parallel Embedded Systems
TC14	**ECS**	Entertainment Computing Symposium
TC3	**ED_L2L**	Learning to Live in the Knowledge Society
WG 9.7 TC3	**HCE3**	History of Computing and Education 3
TC13	**HCI**	Human Computer Interaction
TC8	**ISREP**	Information Systems Research, Education and Practice
WG 12.6	**KMIA**	Knowledge Management in Action
TC2 WG 2.13	**OSS**	Open Source Systems
TC11	**IFIP SEC**	Information Security Conference
TC1	**TCS**	Theoretical Computer Science

IFIP

- is the leading multinational, apolitical organization in Information and Communications Technologies and Sciences
- is recognized by United Nations and other world bodies
- represents IT Societies from 56 countries or regions, covering all 5 continents with a total membership of over half a million
- links more than 3500 scientists from Academia and Industry, organized in more than 101 Working Groups reporting to 13 Technical Committees
- sponsors 100 conferences yearly providing unparalleled coverage from theoretical informatics to the relationship between informatics and society including hardware and software technologies, and networked information systems

Details of the IFIP Technical Committees and Working Groups can be found on the website at http://www.ifip.org.

Preface

Introduction

The International Federation for Information Processing (IFIP) is a non-profit umbrella organization for national societies working in the field of information processing. It was founded in 1960 under the auspices of UNESCO. It is organized into several technical committees. This book represents the proceedings of the 2008 conference of technical committee 8 (TC8), which covers the field of information systems. TC8 aims to promote and encourage the advancement of research and practice of concepts, methods, techniques and issues related to information systems in organisations. TC8 has established eight working groups covering the following areas: design and evaluation of information systems; the interaction of information systems and the organization; decision support systems; e-business information systems: multi-disciplinary research and practice; information systems in public administration; smart cards, technology, applications and methods; and enterprise information systems. Further details of the technical committee and its working groups can be found on our website (ifiptc8.dsi.uminho.pt).

This conference was part of IFIP's World Computer Congress in Milan, Italy which took place 7-10 September 2008. The occasion celebrated the 32nd anniversary of IFIP TC8. The call for papers invited researchers, educators, and practitioners to submit papers and panel proposals that advance concepts, methods, techniques, tools, issues, education, and practice of information systems in organizations. Thirty one submissions were received. All submissions were rigorously refereed by at least three reviewers and following the review and resubmission process, less than half of the submissions were accepted. The current proceedings reflect not only the breadth and depth of the work of TC8, but also the international nature of the group - the authors come from 10 countries and 5 continents.

The Information Systems discipline has often reflected about the issues addressed in this conference. This has been most noticeably undertaken by TC8's WG8.2 – for example, at its 2000 Working Conference on <u>Organizational and Social Perspectives on Information Technology</u>, and, more recently, in 2004 at its 20th year retrospective, <u>Relevant Theory and Informed Practice</u>. This is, however, is the first time that TC8 as a whole is addressing issues of research, education, and practice, and therefore, a milestone in its own right. It is the hope of the organizers that this conference responds to the call of Hirschheim and Klein in their 2000 paper on "Information Systems at the Crossroads: External versus Internal Views," where they pointed out that "the current publication culture of narrowly focused, highly specialized papers is one of the major impediments to making our research more relevant to practitioners. We simply must attempt the difficult, but invaluable, syntheses that pull together research results from the various sub-communities into broader analyses of potential interest to practitioner communities."

The 15 papers in this volume cover a broad spectrum, and in order to provide a structure for the presentation of the papers at the conference itself, we made an attempt to classify the papers, and we followed this classification in this volume. We realise that it is never straightforward to classify a set of papers. Any classification imposes a certain mental compartmentalisation of the material at hand, and (potentially) destroys the relationships between the component parts of the whole. We ask the reader to discover the integrated whole of the proceedings as an exercise in hermeneutical analysis! Our classification of the papers is as follows: Information systems education; New perspectives on information systems development; Defining, modelling and diffusing information systems projects; Knowledge management and business intelligence; and Applications and emerging technologies.

Before introducing the papers in the proceedings, we would like recognize our two very special keynote speakers. Both look at our conference theme with the overall umbrella of professionalism. Information systems is no longer 'the new kid on the block,' and we no longer have the luxury of "beginner's errors." We must attain professional standards in our research, education, and practice commensurate with societies' dependence on the systems we build. Bill Olle exemplifies this professionalism and indeed he has every right to be seen as the 'organizational knowledge' of TC8 as he was an early pioneer in our field as well as being a consistent contributor to the group's work over the years. His keynote paper is entitled *reflections on 50 years of computing: impact of professionalism on teaching, practice and research* and these reflections form an ideal base on which to build our conference.

Our second keynote speaker turns our attention to the future with his vision of tomorrow's IS professional. As chair of the IFIP International professional practice partnership, Charles Hughes is leading an effort to build a global standard of IT knowledge, experience, competency, and integrity. His talk is entitled *The IFIP International professional practice partnership: Transforming and informing IT professional practice.*

Information Systems Education

Our first group of three papers have been categorized as IS education, though the papers can be seen also as covering the discipline of information systems as a whole as they discuss the links between teaching, research, and practice. The first paper by Jorma Riihijärvi and Juhani Iivari is entitled *the practical relevance of IT education: skill requirements and education expectations of practitioners.* This paper suggests two interpretations of the practical relevance of IT education at the university level: the congruence between skill requirements of IT experts and the skills provided by the education on the one hand and the practitioners' expectations concerning these skills on the other. A questionnaire study shows significant differences between what is provided compared to what is expected.

The second paper by Juhani Iivari, Rudy Hirschheim and Heinz K. Klein is entitled *challenges of professionalization: bridging research and practice through a body of knowledge for IT specialists.* This paper suggests that the interpretation and development of IT occupations as knowledge work might provide a more realistic avenue to proceed towards more professional practice in the IT field than the ambition of trying to establish them as true professions. The idea of knowledge work leads the authors to focus on a distinct body of knowledge for IS professionals. The paper discusses how the gap between research and practice could be bridged by making IT research more sensitive to practice.

The final paper in this category is *mapping research questions to research methods* by Pertti Järvinen. In information systems there is a wide range of research methods available. Yet selection of a research method appropriate to the research question remains a problem. The author supplements the well-accepted IS research methods with some important amendments like mathematical approaches, theoretical studies and the dissensus and consensus views, and he presents instructions on how to select a suitable research approach given a research question.

New Perspectives on Information Systems Development

Our second category of papers, that of new perspectives on IS development has sometimes been seen as the core of the discipline and has been a main concern of two of TC 8's most well-established working groups, on the design and evaluation of information systems (WG 1), and the interaction of information systems and the organization (WG 2).

The paper of Jan Pries-Heje, Linda Levine, Richard Baskerville and Bala Ramesh entitled *advances in information systems development: from discipline and predictability to agility and improvisation* discusses how the process of IS development has changed over the years. When information systems development (ISD) was coined as a term and evolved into a research area we lived in a largely industrial economy. This traditional universe placed high value on discipline and predictability for its own sake. In the 1990s several new trends began to question and challenge the traditional view. Specifically, Internet marketplaces created a new environment for information systems development, and novel approaches such as agile methods emerged. In their paper, these authors present an analysis of empirical findings showing how new principles and practices have come to exist in a parallel economic universe with increased emphasis on agility and improvisation.

The paper by Jens-Magnus Arndt, Thomas Kude and Jens Dibbern, *the emergence of partnership networks in the enterprise application development industry: a global corporation perspective,* points out that within the IS development industry, incumbent system developers (hubs) are increasingly embracing partnerships with less well established companies acting in specific niches (spokes). This paper seeks to develop a better understanding of the motives for this strategy. Relying on existing work on strategic alliance formation, three categories of capabilities are identified and analyzed through a single-case study. The case represents a market leader in the global IS development industry, which fosters a network of smaller partner firms. The study reveals that temporal dynamics between the identified factors exist in these networks. A cyclical partnership model is developed that attempts to explain the life cycle of partnerships within such a network.

In the paper by Tuure Tuunanen, Michael Myers and Harold Cassab entitled *challenges of consumer information systems development: the case of interactive television services,* the authors suggest that a new type of information system appears to be increasing in importance, that of consumer information systems. Compared with traditional information systems development approaches, where the focus is on improving the efficiency and effectiveness of organizational processes, the design of consumer information systems focuses more on the enjoyment, pleasure and purchases of the consumer. The authors argue that the shift in focus from users to consumers in consumer information systems calls for a significant re-appraisal of our current information systems development methods. Hence, this paper proposes a new research agenda for IS researchers using design science research and enabling a more holistic evaluation of consumer information systems.

Defining, Modelling and Diffusing IS Projects

Ronell Alberts and Vreda Pieterse assert that diffusion of information technology in a developing world context is difficult due to the fact that most of the targeted communities are in market neglect environments. In their paper, *improving diffusion of Information Technology in communities in a developing world context,* they characterize market neglect environments as those that fail to make a economic market and have an economic impact because the prospect for immediate or even intermediate return on investment is low given that the client base is small or with little economic power. Software development for market neglect areas face a number of unique challenges while at the same time needing (perhaps more than in developed economies) to produce products of high quality, on budget and on time. In their paper, the authors' aim to identify the unique problems experienced when developing for market neglect environments and to identify tools and methods needed in for software development methodology to address these problems in order to improve the diffusion of information technology in market neglect economies.

The next paper in this category is entitled *'Driving' IS projects* by Marta Fernández-Diego and Julián Marcelo-Cocho. This paper begins with a discussion of complexity and uncertainty as determinants of IS project success and the relation to 'right' and 'left' brain notions of problem solving. The authors then review different auto racing circuits as methaphors for 'driving' an IS project to completion and dealing with the accompanying complexity and uncertainty. For example, drivers on an oval track have a very different support structure and exposure to risk and complexity than do drivers on off-road rallies. These metaphors provide interesting perspectives for IS project development and management.

The paper by Viera Rozinajova, Marek Braun, Pavol Navrat and Maria Bielikova, *bridging the gap between service-oriented and object-oriented architectures in information systems development,* is the last paper in this grouping. Service-oriented architecture is currently one of the most promising technologies in the area of information systems development, whereas the most popular development methodology of the last decade was object-oriented. The goal of this paper is to investigate the possibility of enhancing object-oriented methodology with service-oriented architecture.

Knowledge Management and Business Intelligence

During the last few years much emphasis in organisations has been given to the capture and retention of knowledge and business intelligence, and this forms the fourth of our conference themes. Our first paper in this grouping is *requirements elicitation in data mining for business intelligence projects* by Paola Britos, Oscar Dieste and Ramon Garcia-Martinez. The authors argue that there are no suitable data mining methodologies for business intelligence. They argue that the classical software engineering approach is not completely suitable for data mining for business intelligence because it neglects the requirements specification aspects of the project. The authors propose a data mining business intelligence elicitation process and show how requirements can be educed by their proposal.

William Dixon argues that little is known about how people, contexts, and tools impact decisions to use a Knowledge Management System (KMS) in his paper *social networks and knowledge management systems use in US IT services.* The purpose of his study is to understand information retrieval better when solving difficult problems. Key research questions focus on social structure, interpersonal relationships, and the nature of the KMS. In this sequential exploratory study, semi-structured interviews were conducted and questionnaires distributed in a large accounting firm. Social structure analysis showed fewer structural holes within networks among routine KMS users. Contrary to social resource theory, information was rarely sought from supervisors. Reciprocal information exchange accompanied asking for help, but not when information was retrieved from the KMS. The KMS facilitated the distribution of information and enabled learning, but was not uniformly adopted. Recommendations for practice include the strategic designation of experts and refinement of mechanisms available for information retrieval.

Business Intelligence (BI) remains one of the top priority issues for CIOs and investment in BI technologies continues to grow. Derek Smith and Maria Crossland in their paper *realizing the value of business intelligence* attempt to understand how an organization can realize and measures the business value derived from their investment in BI. A single, in-depth case study was undertaken in a major South African financial services organization. The study found that the realization of business value from BI is highly dependent on activities that occur in all stages of the process model – from the alignment of the BI and organizational strategy to the way the business measures the benefits of BI.

Applications and Emerging Technologies

Information systems is about how the new technology fits in with people, organizations and society, and it is fitting that our last theme looks at emerging technologies that will impact us in the next few years. Lisa Seymour, Emma Lambert-Porter and Lars Willuweit discuss one such technology in their paper *towards an RFID adoption framework: a container supply chain analysis.* While the benefits of RFID (radio frequency identification) in supply chains have had extensive press, there are few publicised cases showing poor returns on investment. This qualitative study in the South African port community refines and extends an RFID adoption framework and provides insight into the factors potentially affecting the adoption of this new technology as well as the probability of adoption in that community. Four new factors not previously mentioned in research were identified: related initiatives; the integrated structure of the industry; organisational dominance with the supply chain and the supply chain culture. The research reveals that cost, the absence of a universally-adopted standard and the supply chain culture are currently the major impediments to RFID adoption in the South African port community.

The deliberations of our working group on information systems in public administration (WG8.5) is well represented in the two papers on e-government. Ilse Baumgartner and Peter Green report on a case study which focuses on the question: what are the critical factors that influence IT professionals' intention to adopt the Service Oriented Computing (SOC) paradigm? Their paper, *adoption of service oriented computing from the IT professionals' perspective: an e-Government case study,* examines the e-Government initiative in a middle-sized European city. It uses an initial SOC adoption model developed through a proceeding interview-based exploratory study. The current study has two principle aims. The first aim is to "shed some light" on the IT professionals' acceptance of such complex technological approaches as Service-Oriented Computing in the e-Government sector and to report key learning factors that emerge from the case study. Their case study also aims to bring further credibility to their first study and to validate its assertions. As such, some of the major findings of the study are the replacement of the complexity variable by the variable of maintainability, and the replacement of the trust and dependency variables (both of inter-personal rather than of technical nature) by the variable of external involvement. The results of the study also suggest the introduction of the "champion" of the approach variable.

John Krogstie looks at the reasons why the introduction of the Internet Marketplace – eHandel.no – has thus far failed to be a success in the County Municipality of Sør-Trøndelag, as compared to the original ambitions regarding usage volume for this channel. In his paper, *introduction of a public sector e-procurement solution: lessons learned from disappointing adoption,* he uses various acceptance theories to analyze why users fail to accept eHandel.no. The theories were utilized prior to the interviews in order to formulate interview questions. Afterwards the same theories were used to analyze the results. The results indicate that good product catalogues, motivated users, compulsory use of the system, and renegotiation of contracts with the suppliers are some of the most important prerequisites in order to achieve success using eHandel.no.

Further Reflections

In organizing an international conference many people put in a great deal of time and effort in ensuring its success. We first wish to recognize two colleagues, Bill Olle and A. Min Tjoa, members of IFIP Technical Committee 8 who helped us greatly in the early stages and we are very grateful for this support. The Chairs and Committee Members of the various working groups within IFIP TC8 acted as associate editors and we would particularly like to mention the help of this group and the following individuals. Neither this conference nor the proceedings can happen without the commitment of these individuals to the profession.

Frederic Adam
(University College Cork, IE)

Roger Clarke
(Xamax Consultancy, AU)

Yves Deswarte
(LAAS, FR)

Josep Domingo-Ferrer
(Universitat Rovira i Virgili, ES)

Vivienne Farrell
(Swinburne University of Technology, AU)

Andreas Gadatsch
(Bonn-Rhein-Sieg University of Applied Sciences, DE)

Lucia Garcia
(London School of Economics, GB)

Shirley Gregor
(The Australian National University, AU)

Helle Zinner Henriksen
(Copenhagen Business School, DK)

Patrick Humphreys
(London School of Econ. & Political Sciences, GB)

Robert Johnston
(University of Melbourne, AU)

Karl Kautz
(Copenhagen Business School, DK)

Michael D. Myers
(University of Auckland, NZ)

Pierre Paradinas
(CNAM, FR)

Joachim Posegga
(University of Hamburg, DE)

Erik Proper
(Radboud University, NL)

Gerald Quirchmayr
(University of Vienna, AT)

Jean-Jacques Quisquater
(DICE, BE)

Nancy Russo
(Northern Illinois University, US)

Jochen Scholl
(University of Washington, EUA)

Alexandra Steinberg
(EM Lyon, FR)

Manoj Thomas
(Virginia Commonwealth University, US.)

A Min Tjoa
(Vienna University of Technology, AT)

David Wastell
(Nottingham University, GB)

John Krogstie
(NTNU, NO)

Linda Levine
(Carnegie Mellon University, US)

Vladimir Marik
(Czech Technical University, CZ)

Maria Wimmer
(University of Koblenz, DE)

Li D Xu
(Old Dominion University, US)

Mahmood Shafiee Zargar
(ESSEC Business School, FR)

Table of Contents

THE PRACTICAL RELEVANCE OF IT EDUCATION: SKILL REQUIREMENTS AND EDUCATION EXPECTATIONS OF PRACTITIONERS

Jorma Riihijärvi and Juhani Iivari

Department of Information Processing Science, University of Oulu, P.O. Box 3000, FIN-90014 Oulun yliopisto, FI

Abstract: This paper suggests two interpretations of the practical relevance of IT education at the university level, as the congruence between the skill requirements of IT experts and the skills provided by the education, and as the congruence between practitioners' education expectations concerning the skills to be taught and the skills provided by the education. The paper analyzes these two interpretations empirically based on a questionnaire study and shows that the two interpretations differ significantly, lead to quite different conclusions about the practical relevance of the curriculum and education, and differ in their stability when background variables such as the gender, age, job category and year of graduation of the respondents are taken into consideration.

1. INTRODUCTION

The university-level education of IT experts has been of a considerable interest during the last ten years when developing curricula in the areas of Computing Engineering, Computer Science, Software Engineering, Information Systems and Information Technology (Computing Curricula 2005a), work that has resulted in curricular specifications at the undergraduate level in each of these areas. Concurrently, there have been some attempts to investigate empirically what

Please use the following format when citing this chapter:

Riihijärvi, J. and Iivari, J., 2008, in IFIP International Federation for Information Processing, Volume 274; *Advances in Information Systems Research, Education and Practice*; David Avison, George M. Kasper, Barbara Pernici, Isabel Ramos, Dewald Roode; (Boston: Springer), pp. 1–13.

industry and the practitioners themselves expect from the education of future IT practitioners (Lethbridge 2000, Kitchenham et al. 2005).[1]

Curriculum development in IT faces difficult challenges as to what to teach. One challenge is to decide to what extent to emphasize theoretical topics even though practitioners do not see them as important. Teaching mathematics is a good example. Both Lethbridge (2000) and Kitchenham et al. (2005) report that software engineers believe that mathematical topics are not very important for them. Does this imply that mathematics and formal methods should not be taught in SE curricula? A second major challenge in an extremely dynamic field such as IT is to what extent to emphasize immediate practical, job entry-level needs and to what extent to teach more invariant material that might support the life-long career development of future IT experts. Studies of job advertisements tend to reflect the former (Surakka 2005), although Gallivan et al. (2004) end up in their analysis of job advertisements with an emphasis on skills for life-long learning.

Another question concerns national differences. Although the computing disciplines are inherently international, there may be significant differences between countries that justify different curricula. The five Computing Curricula reflect mainly the North American perspective, although the overview report (Computing Curricula 2005a) does recognize some international differences, among which the idea of each discipline having its own core, prevalent the US, is the most significant from the viewpoint of the content of curricula. More from the practitioner perspective, one should note that countries differ in their industrial structure and in the range of IT specialists that they need.

The purpose of the present paper is to analyze the practical relevance of IT education both theoretically and empirically. The paper suggests two major interpretations of this practical relevance, as the congruence between the skill requirements of IT experts and the skills provided by the education, and as the congruence between practitioners' education expectations concerning the skills to be taught and the skills provided by the education.

---

[1] In general, we use the term "Information Technology" (IT) in a broader meaning than in the Computing Curricula, Information Technology Volume (2005).

The empirical comparison of the two interpretations of the practical relevance of IT education in this paper comes from one country, Finland, which is fairly advanced in applying IT in various spheres of life and which also has a fairly strong IT industry, especially in the telecommunications sector.

2. PRACTICAL RELEVANCE OF IT EDUCATION

The practical relevance of IT education is a significant concern, since IT experts are educated to work competently in different IT occupations in practice. One can identify two major interpretations of this practical relevance in current empirical evaluations of the education of IT experts. The first anchors it to the skills required in practice. Focusing on Information Systems, Leitheiser (1992) analyzed IS managers' perceptions of the importance of 54 skills for systems developers and 26 skills for technical specialists, while Trauth et al. (1993) compared an IS faculty's perceptions of the importance of a number of items describing the tasks IS practitioners perform, their technical skill requirements and interpersonal and business skills with those of the IS practitioners themselves. Lee et al. (1995) conducted quite a similar study of the critical skills for IS practitioners, but excluding IS faculty respondents. Tye et al. (1995) targeted their questionnaire study at all computing degree students who had graduated from one department in Hong Kong in 1988 to 1993, asking them to evaluate the importance of the 54 IS skills identified by Leitheiser (1992) and the extent to which these skills were emphasized in the curriculum. Among other things, the analysis included a comparison between the importance of the skills and the emphasis placed on them in the curriculum.

The second approach anchors the practical relevance to the respondent's career development. The central theme of the surveys conducted by Lethbridge (1998, 2000) was to ask respondents to evaluate how useful the material they learned at university or college has been for their career as software developer or software managers. Kitchenham et al. (2005) essentially replicated Lethbridge's survey in the UK, although they expanded the number of topics from 57 in Lethbridge

(1998) and 75 in Lethbdridge (2000) to 78. The idea of Lethbrdige (1998, 2000) was obviously to capture the relevance of the education for the respondents' actual careers in the field. If their careers since graduating have not yet been very long (4-7 years in Kitchenham et al. 2005), the respondents may be able to evaluate the usefulness of the material they learned over their career up to that time. One should note, however, that the question does not concern what the students were taught but what they learnt, so that the answers are extremely subjective – their subjective perceptions of the value of their personal learning experience for their personal career.

One central problem in curriculum design is that a curriculum cannot cover all potentially relevant material. Curriculum designers must choose how to emphasize different bodies of material, and in the case of electives and optional studies the students must decide what material to choose. The studies of practical skill requirements reviewed above do not include this problem of choice and weighting. It may well be that the practitioners themselves accept that IT departments cannot teach them all the skills they need in practice but must concentrate on some core topics.

Recognizing this, we suggest a third interpretation of the practical relevance of IT education, as the congruence between practitioners' expectations concerning the skills to be taught and the skills provided by the education.

The present paper will focus on two interpretations of the practical relevance of IT education, one anchored in the skills required in practice and the other in expectations regarding the education. The paper has two purposes:
1.   To analyze empirically how the two interpretations differ.
2.   To analyze the stability of the two interpretations.

As reviewed above, there is some empirical research that addresses the first interpretation, although it is from the early 1990's and therefore not necessarily valid any longer. To our knowledge, the second interpretation is a totally new idea, and consequently there is no prior research that addresses it.

3. RESEARCH METHOD

To answer the above questions, we conducted a questionnaire study targeted at graduates of the Department of Information Processing Science, University of Oulu. Established in 1969, the department has a M.Sc. program in IT with a number of possibilities to specialize.[2] The first students graduated at the M.Sc. level in 1973, and the number of graduates by the end of June 2006 was 749. The questionnaires were sent to 680 of these.[3]

The questionnaire consisted of three major categories of items:

1. The importance of skills in 130 topics from the viewpoint of the respondent's current job, ranging from "no skill requirements" (0) to "very high skill requirements" (5).

2. The skills provided in the curriculum of the Department of Information Processing Science in each of the 130 topics, ranging from "no skills provided" (0) to "very high skills provided" (5).

3. Respondents' views of the percentage of the teaching that should be allocated to each of the 130 topics.

The last question was to be answered hierarchically. First, the respondents were asked to allocate teaching between 10 topics within each of 13 knowledge areas to be introduced below, reaching a total of 100%. They were then asked to allocate teaching between the six technical knowledge areas and separately between the seven non-technical knowledge areas, in each case to a total of 100%, and finally, they were to allocate teaching between the technical and non-technical areas to a total of 100%. The weight given to each of the 130 topics was then calculated as a product of these three percentages.

---

[2] The department's M.Sc. curriculum can best be characterized as a 4-year programme of full-time studies, although there have been nation-wide changes in M.Sc. programmes in Finland over the years. At the beginning, the main focus of the curriculum was on Information Systems, but it was expanded in the 1980's to include Software Engineering and during the last ten years to comprise digital media, mobile computing and software business.

[3] Of the 749 graduates, 54 had refused to give their addresses, 5 had died and 10 participated in the pilot questionnaire and were therefore excluded.

The identification of the 130 topics started out from the classification of the Body of Knowledge (BoK) for IS experts into technical knowledge, application knowledge, application domain knowledge, organizational knowledge and system development knowledge as proposed by Iivari et al. (2004) but expanded to include "communication and co-operation skills" and a category "miscellaneous". Technical knowledge as defined in Iivari et al. (2004) was then further divided into six areas: 1) Hardware, operating systems and telecommunications; 2) Programming and program languages, 3) Implementation technologies, 4) Databases and data modelling, 5) User interfaces and usability, 6) Computer security. Correspondingly, systems development knowledge was decomposed into two areas: Systems development approaches and Systems development process models. This gave the total of 13 knowledge areas. The detailed list of the 130 skills was based on previous research (especially Lethbridge 2000) and the Computing Curricula reports (Computing Curricula 2001, 2002, 2005b, Software Engineering, 2004).

To answer all the three categories of questions would have led to a long questionnaire, which would probably have had an effect on the response rate. To shorten the questionnaires, we developed three versions, each including two categories of questions, targeted as follows:

1. Version 1, focusing on the importance of the 130 skill requirements (category 1 questions) and the respondents' views regarding the percentage of teaching that should be allocated to these (category 3 questions), was targeted at the 320 graduates from 1973-1994.

2. Version 2, focusing on the importance of the 130 skill requirements (category 1 questions) and the skills provided by the curriculum of the Department of Information Processing Science (category 2 questions), was targeted at a randomly selected half of the graduates from 1995-2006, i..e. 180 graduates.

3. Version 3, focusing on the respondents' views regarding the percentage of teaching that should be allocated to the 130 skills (category 3 questions) and the skills provided by the curriculum of the Department of Information

Processing Science (category 2 questions), was targeted at the other half of the graduates from 1995-2006, i.e. 180 graduates.[4]

The questionnaires were mailed to the respondents in May-June, 2007, with a request to return them in the enclosed prepaid envelopes. Eight of the 680 questionnaires were returned unopened because of a mistaken address. Altogether 210 replies were received, 90 from **respondent group 1** (response rate 28.1%), 87 from **group 2** (response rate 48.3%) and only 33 from **group 3** (response rate 18.3%). Sixteen of the replies were so incomplete that we were forced to reject them, leading to 194 completed questionnaires. A likely reason for the lower response rates in groups 1 and 3 is that their questionnaires included the weighting questions, which were more complicated to answer. Because of practical problems in mailing, we cannot safely use the return date to evaluate the non-response bias.

Table 1: Profiles of the respondents

Gender		Age		Specialization		Job category	
Male	135	25-29	30	Digital media	30	Teacher &	28
Female	55	30-39	51	Information systems	100	researcher	
		40-49	39	Mobile services	7	Analyzer & designer	62
Miss-ing	7	50-59	61	Software business	5	Lower management	51
		60-	6	Software engineering	49	Higher management	26
		Miss-ing	7	Missing	3	Other	14
						Missing	13

The profiles of the respondents are described in Table 1. There were 28 respondents with the job category "Teachers and researchers". We tested whether this category differed from the rest, but as we did not find any significant differences in either skill requirements or education expectations in any of the 13 knowledge areas we decided not to exclude them from the data set.

---

[4] The reason for the above grouping was that we did not see any point in presenting category 2 questions to the oldest graduates. We also anticipated that the response rate among the oldest graduates would be lower. This was why we targeted the first version at a higher number of graduates than the other two.

4. RESULTS

The results of respondent group 1, contrasting skill requirements and education expectations at the level of the 13 knowledge areas, are described in Table 2. The detailed 130 skills requirements of each respondent were converted into weighted requirements using the formula weighted importance = importance $*100/m$, where m is the sum of the importance scores attached to the 130 skills by the respondent. The weighted importance of the skills and the weights of the education expectations in each of the 13 knowledge area are calculated as the sum of the corresponding values for the ten detailed knowledge units.

Table 2: Weighted skill requirements vs. education expectations (n = 90)

Knowledge area	Weighted skill requirements	Education expectations
Hardware, operating systems, telecomm's	7.00	6.12*
Programming and programming languages	6.48	7.79*
Implementation technologies	4.88	5.33
Databases and data modelling	7.51	8.65*
User interfaces and usability	6.26	8.50*
Computer security	7.42	6.93
Systems development approaches	7.33	10.60**
Systems development process models	9.97	10.25
Application knowledge	6.82	6.28
Application domain knowledge	5.17	5.97
Organizational and business knowledge	10.32	9.42
Communications and co-operation skills	14.59	11.73**
Miscellaneous	6.04	4.54*

* $p \leq 0.05$ ** $p \leq 0.01$ *** $p \leq 0.001$

As seen in Table 2, there are significant differences between the weighted skill requirements and education expectations when tested using the paired-samples t test. Education expectations concerning "Hardware, operating systems and telecommunications" are significantly lower than the weighted skill requirements, one explanation for which may be that much of this knowledge is changing so fast that practitioners do not see any reason for investing too much education effort in it. In the case of "Programming and programming languages", "Databases and data modelling" and "User interfaces and usability" the situation is just the opposite, i.e. it may be that the practitioners regard these as core areas that must be taught in any case. The respondents' expectations concerning "Systems development approaches" are clearly higher than the weighted skill requirements, while the reverse is true of "Communication and co-operation skills", where the (weighted) requirements are clearly higher than education expectations, and of "Miscellaneous" skills.

In the case of respondent group 2 (n = 81) we contrasted the skill requirements with the skills provided by calculating the gap between the two. The paired-samples t-test identified seven significant negative gaps where the Department of Information Processing Science had failed to satisfy the practitioners' skill requirements and only two significant positive gaps where the skills provided had exceeded those required.

We also contrasted education expectations with the skills provided by the curriculum, by converting the skills provided as indicated by each respondent (measured on the scale 0-5) to weighted skills provided using the formula: weighted skills provided = skills provided * 100/m, where m is the sum of scores on skills provided given by the respondent. Because of the low number of valid responses obtained from group 3 (n = 24) we decided to test the gap by contrasting the education expectations expressed by groups 1 and 3 combined (n = 114) with the skills provided as reported by groups 2 and 3 combined (n = 105) and assessing its significance using the independent samples t-test.[5] The essential finding in the comparison between the gaps (skills provided – skills required vs. skills provided – education expectations) was that the latter gap gives quite a different picture from the former gap, as there were three significant negative gaps and four significant positive ones between education expectations and skills provided.

The influence of background variables on the skills requirements is examined separately for each knowledge area in Table 3. The results are based on regression

---

[5] Note that in the second case the samples are not independent, since respondent group 3 (n = 24) belongs to both.

analyses of respondent groups 1 and 2 combined (n = 171). Note that the job categories "Teachers & researchers" and "Others" were deleted from these analyses so that the variable described the organizational level of the respondent.

Table 3: Relationships between background variables and skill requirements

Knowledge area	Gender	Age	Graduation year	Job category	R2
Hardware, operating systems, telecommunications				0.25*	0.11
Programming and programming languages	0.40***			-0.33*	0.19
Implementation technologies		0.38*			0.15
Databases and data modelling		0.45**			0.17
User interfaces and usability					0.03
Computer security		0.38**		0.43***	0.32
Systems development approaches	0.21*	0.38*			0.22
Systems development process models					0.08
Application knowledge		0.43**		0.26*	0.24
Application domain knowledge		0.52***		0.32**	0.41
Organizational and business knowledge				0.53***	0.32
Communication and co-operation skills	-0.28*			0.45***	0.19
Miscellaneous		0.51**	0.32*	0.24*	0.25

$* \ p \leq 0.05$ $** \ p \leq 0.01$ $*** \ p \leq 0.001$

As seen in Table 3, the skill requirements are highly dependent on the background variables. Male respondents reported higher skill requirements in programming and programming languages and in systems development approaches than their female colleagues did, while female respondents reported higher communication and co-operation skill requirements. Age influenced skill requirements in seven knowledge areas – in the sense that *ceteris paribus* skill requirements tend to rise with age, but skills were significantly related to the year of graduation only in one knowledge area. Skill requirements were also closely related to job category. While skill requirements in programming and programming languages tend to decrease as one proceeds in one's career, those in application domain knowledge, organizational and business knowledge and communication & co-operation in particular tend to rise. Similarly skills in security issues tend to rise with age and job category.

When we performed a similar regression analysis to examine the relationships between background variables and education expectations in respondent groups 1 and 3 combined (n = 114) we found only one significant regression coefficient, between job category and application knowledge (ß = -0.24, p ≤ 0.05). Comparison of the results regarding education expectations with those in Table 3 clearly shows that skill requirements are highly dependent on the respondents' background variables while education expectations are virtually independent of these. This suggests that the education expectations expressed by seasoned practitioners are much more stable than their skill requirements.

5. DISCUSSION AND CONCLUSIONS

The above analysis compared two interpretations of the practical relevance of IT education, showing that these differ significantly, lead to quite different con-clusions regarding the practical relevance of the case curriculum, and differ in their stability when different background variables are taken into consideration.

One explanation for the finding that, even though skill requirements differ de-pending on the background variables, education expectations remain very much same might be that the education that the respondents have received has indoctrinated them into expecting certain topics. One should note, however, that the respondents (in groups 1 and 3) who expressed their education expectations had graduated between 1973 and 2006, so that it is unlikely that the education provided could alone explain this consistency of expectations.

The above results have clear practical implications for curriculum design. We conceive of it as a two-stage process:

1. The design of the obligatory studies, informed by the education expecta-tions expressed by practitioners.
2. The design of elective and optional studies, informed by the skill re-quirements of practitioners.

The phrase "informed by" above points out that we do not see that the curriculum design should be entirely based on the education expectations and skill requirements of practitioners, as the curriculum may also reflect the structure, themes and research topics of the respective discipline. Nevertheless, it is important to note that the fact that the respondents' education expectations were independent of the background variables implies a certain consensus among practitioners about what should be taught in university IT curricula. It seems natural to design the core of the curriculum – especially the obligatory studies – so that they reflect these consensual education expectations.

As emphasized several times, we cannot expect IT curricula to provide all the skills required in practice. Yet, we regard the skill requirements of practitioners as informative when designing elective and optional studies, which can complement the core of the curriculum so that they focus on knowledge areas and topics where the weighted skill requirements are clearly higher than either the education expectations or the skills actually provided.

The present paper has its limitations. Its empirical results are based on responses received from graduates of one department in one country. The findings concerning the skills provided in particular inevitably reflect the curriculum in force and education provided from 1990 onwards, since the majority of the respondents had graduated from the department between 1995 and 2006. It is beyond the scope of the present paper to describe the department's curriculum or its various versions in detail.

One of the starting points for the present paper was that each country may have its specific features - such as its industrial structure and the variety of IT specialists needed – which justify different points of emphasis in the education of IT experts. This paper reports results from one country that is fairly advanced in the development and application of IT, but it would be interesting to see comparable data and analyses from different countries. We therefore hope that the present paper will stimulate similar studies in other countries.

REFERENCES

Computing Curricula 2001, Computer Science Volume. Final Report. The Joint Task Force for Computing Curricula

Computing Curricula 2002, Information Systems Volume. Model Curriculum and Guidelines for Undergraduate Degree Programs in Information Systems. The Joint Task Force for Computing Curricula

Computing Curricula 2005a, The Overview Report. Covering Undergraduate Degree Programs in Computing for Computer Engineering, Computer Science, Information Systems, Information Technology and Software Engineering The Joint Task Force for Computing Curricula 2005.

Computing Curricula 2005b, Information Technology Volume. Version: October 2005. The Joint Task Force for Computing Curricula 2005.

Gallivan, M., Truex, D. & Kvasny, L. 2004. Changing Patterns in IT Skill Sets 1988-2003: A Content Analysis of Classified Advertising, *The Data Base for Advances in Information Systems*, 35(3), 2004, pp. 64-87

Lee, D.M., Trauth, E.M. and Farwell, D., Critical skills and knowledge requirements of IS professionals: A joint academic/industry investigation, *MIS Quarterly*, 19(3), 1995, pp. 313-340

Leitheiser, R. L., MIS Skills for the 1990s: A Survey of MIS Managers' Perception, *Journal of Management Information Systems,* 9(1), 1992, pp. 69-91

Software Engineering 2004, *Curriculum Guidelines for Undergraduate Degree Programs in Software Engineering*, A Volume of the Computing Curricula Series, August 23, 2004

Surakka, S., Analysis of technical skills in job advertisements targeted to software developers, *Informatics in Education*, 4(1), 2005, pp. 101-122

Trauth, E.M., Farwell, D.W. and Lee, D., The IS expectation gap: Industry expectations versus academic preparation, *MIS Quarterly*, 17(3), 1993, pp. 293.307

Tye, E.M.W.N., Pooh, R.S.K. and Burn, J.M., Information systems skills: Achieving alignment between the curriculum and the needs of the is professionals in the future, *Data Base*, 26(4), 1995, pp. 47-61

CHALLENGES OF PROFESSIONALIZA-
TION: BRIDGING RESEARCH AND
PRACTICE THROUGH A BODY OF
KNOWLEDGE FOR IT SPECIALISTS

Juhani Iivari[1], Rudy Hirschheim[2] and H.K. Klein[3]

[1] Department of Information Processing Science, University of Oulu, P.O. Box 3000, FIN-90014 Oulun yliopisto, FI

[2] E. J. Ourso College of Business, Louisiana State University, Baton Rouge, LA 70803, US

[3] School of Management, SUNY-Binghamton, Binghamton, NY 13902, US

Abstract: This paper suggests that the interpretation and development of IT occupations as knowledge work might provide a more realistic avenue to proceed towards more professional practice in the IT field rather than the ambition of trying to establish them as true professions. The idea of knowledge work leads us to focus on the body of knowledge possessed by it specialists, which is the hallmark of all professions. The on-going debate about the practical relevance of IT research suggests that there is a significant gap between research and practice in the IT field. The paper discusses how the gap could be bridged by making IT research more sensitive to practice.

1. INTRODUCTION

A joint project of the ACM and IEEE Computer Society to define Software Engineering (SE) as a profession is perhaps the most serious attempt to professionalize an IT occupation.[1] The project proposed a guide for the SE body of

---

[1] There is no standard definition of IT occupations (Kaarst-Brown and Guzman 2004). Without any formal definition IT occupations are exemplified by jobs such as programmer, telecommunication specialist, database specialist, software engineer, human-computer specialist, systems designer, systems analysts, systems support, help desk, (IT) team leader,

---

Please use the following format when citing this chapter:

Iivari, J., Hirschheim, R. and Klein, H.K., 2008, in IFIP International Federation for Information Processing, Volume 274; *Advances in Information Systems Research, Education and Practice*; David Avison, George M. Kasper, Barbara Pernici, Isabel Ramos, Dewald Roode; (Boston: Springer), pp. 15–27.

knowledge (SWEBOK 2004) as well as a code of ethics and professional practices (SWECOE 2000). More recently, IFIP has also started a program to promote professionalization. The IFIP Professional Practice Task Force recommends that IFIP should initiate a vigorous activity to promote professionalism worldwide (IFIP 2007). The Task Force also emphasizes that the voice of the IT practitioner should be clearly and powerfully expressed alongside other competing groups.

Whilst these goals are laudable, IFIP is somewhat silent on how to effect such professionalization, in particular when it is still an open question if the aforementioned ACM/ IEEE project will manage to establish SE as a profession with associated accreditation, certification and licensing practices.

This paper takes a positive position to "professionalization" of IT occupations as far as the enhancement of ethical principles, knowledge and expertise is concerned. However, we are much more circumspect with the enforcement aspects of professionalization, i.e. certification and licensing which would establish SE and IS as true professions. Instead, we propose that IT occupations may be developed in a professional direction by viewing themselves as knowledge work and by strengthening their underlying bodies of knowledge (BoK).

The literature on professionalization (e.g. Abbott 1988) suggests that a scientifically grounded body of knowledge is a necessary, but not sufficient condition for any profession. There should also be demand for that knowledge in practice (Collins 1990). The present paper especially focuses on the question of demand for the knowledge produced by IT research institutions. The gap between research and practice in the IT field (e.g. Osterweil, 1996; Benbasat and Zmud 1999) implies that the demand is not self-evident. So, while we encourage the IT communities to take active steps towards creating such professional bodies of knowledge, we also see it as important that the knowledge will be made more relevant for practice. Therefore our special focus is in how to bridge research and practice when specifying bodies of knowledge for IT specialists.

(IT) project manager, CIO, etc. These are often referred to as 'IT specialists'. We also assume that IT specialists earned at least an undergraduate degree in a relevant subject.

2. PROFESSIONS AND PROFESSIONALIZATION

Professions and professionalization are widely discussed in sociology. Sociologists have been particularly interested in how certain occupational groups have managed to persuade society to grant them a privileged position as a profession. Following Abbott (1988) one can identify three major traditions in the literature on professions, strands which are clearly relevant in the current efforts to professionalize IT. The first tradition refers to the early literature on professions dominated by traits of professions such as a service ideal, professional culture and associations, and what the profession stands for. The second tradition focuses on the professionalization process as a sequence of events such as establishing formal education, licensing, founding a national association, developing a code of ethics and school accreditation (Wilensky 1964). The third tradition centers on power (Larson 1977), looking at how a profession is able to achieve its privileged position and maintain it.

But what is a profession? Although there is no consensus on the necessary traits of professions, a system of characteristics such as a unique BoK, code of ethics, lengthy education, control of the entry to the profession, and high autonomy are often associated with professions. Among these the BoK is central (e.g. Abbott 1988; Macdonald, 1995).

There are a few attempts to analyze IT occupations as possible professions. Ensmenger (2000) shows that professional efforts in the computer fields have a long history, starting already in the 1950's and 1960's. Orlikowski and Baroudi (1989) claim that IS specialists (including operators, programmers, analysts and various technical specialists) cannot be considered professions. Ford and Gibbs (1996) conclude that SE as an occupation does not fulfill the traits of a profession.

It is clear that the SE professionalization project has insufficiently discussed the project from the power perspective. It is widely accepted that professionalization efforts have an ideological and political aspect of increasing the status of the occupation in question. Abbott (1988) interprets professionalization as competition between different occupational groups for jurisdiction. Professional autonomy, emphasized by Freidson (1988), includes the right to serve as the best experts on affairs related the BoK and to decide about it, to control the education and accreditation of new entrants, and autonomy over the practical aspects of their work (Freidson 1994). Accordingly, professionalization means building 'exclusionary shelters in the market' and providing a market monopoly (Freidsonn 1988; Collins 1990; Macdonald 1995).

Professionalization as standardization of skills provides companies with one coordination mechanism (Minzberg 1983). The rise of outsourcing and especially offshore software development may also play an important role in professionalization, although at this point it is not clear whether it would be pro or con (*cf.* Sahay et al. 2003). Yet, it is questionable if companies employing IT experts are ready to support professionalization, since the exclusionary shelters may influence the labor market in a way that is not beneficial to employing companies.

In this paper, however, we do not wish to discuss the political side of professionalization of the IT occupations nor do we wish to become strong advocates for professionalization. Instead we focus on analyzing IS as knowledge work, suggesting that this is a more realistic avenue to enhance the expertise of IT specialists and thereby their "professionalism". The advantage of a knowledge work perspective is that it focuses attention on the BoK of IT specialists and the gaps between research and practice without getting involved in the political battle of professionalization, which is considered to lie beyond the scope of this paper.

3. IT OCCUPATIONS AS KNOWLEDGE WORK

One possibility for avoiding the political battle of professionalization is to have a more modest goal: to have the IT occupations recognized as knowledge work. This would have the effect of directing attention to the bodies of knowledge of IT specialists. As discussed above a scientifically grounded BoK is a necessary, but not sufficient condition for any profession.

3.1 Knowledge work

Knowledge work (KW) is difficult to define precisely because all work requires knowledge to some extent (Beyerlein et al. 1995, Pyöriä 2005) and because the concept of knowledge is ambiguous (Schultze 2000). Despite the difficulty to define KW there are a number of attempts (see Kelloway and Barling 2000). We propose four criteria to characterize KW (Iivari and Linger 1999):

(i)   KW is based on a demonstrable body of knowledge (BoK),
(ii)   entails working on representations (data) of the objects of work,
(iii) stipulates a deep, theoretical understanding of the objects of work, and
(iv)   KW produces results, which entail knowledge as their essential ingredient.

The first characteristic emphasizes the significance of a BoK, often codified, as a resource in KW. This is consistent with Stehr's (1992) emphasis of the relational structures of knowledge-based occupations, i.e. their relation to socially constructed forms and stocks of knowledge. This underscores that knowledge workers "are not isolated individuals but derive and defend their expertise by virtue of their memberships and standing in communities of" knowledge workers.

The second characteristic emphasizes the abstract and detached nature of KW. Working indirectly through the representation of the object of work requires intellective skills (Zuboff 1988), in contrast to action-centered skills.

The third characteristic, a deep, theoretical understanding of the object of work, means that knowledge work typically requires several years' training, usually through formal high-level education. This theoretical understanding may help the knowledge worker to deal with new and exceptional cases, but in particular to adapt to changes in the objects of work, to accommodate changes in the BoK, and to adopt technologies allowing new representations of the object of work.

The fourth characteristic does not stipulate that the output of KW is perceived primarily as knowledge but that the output includes knowledge as an essential ingredient. Overall, our conception of KW views it primarily as knowledge applying work rather than as creative, knowledge producing work (Machlup 1962; Schultze 2000). Note, however, that much of the creative knowledge producing work is also knowledge applying work, and that our interpretation does not deny that knowledge workers and even their employer organizations are learning through their work. In that sense, KW is producing knowledge, but it is not necessarily the primary purpose of the work.

Referring to the topic of the present paper, it is apparent that software and information systems development satisfies characteristics (ii) and (iv) above. The question is whether IS development is based on a systematic BoK and whether the development requires any deep, theoretical understanding of software/information systems as the objects of that work.

3.2   Bodies of Knowledge for IT specialists

A body of knowledge is knowledge of the relevant phenomena associated with KW as an activity. To our knowledge, the Software Engineering Body of Knowledge (SWEBOK) is the most ambitious attempt to define a BoK for one IT occupation. SWEBOK (2004) identifies ten knowledge areas: software requirements, software design, software construction, software testing, software maintenance, software configuration management, software engineering management, software engineering process, software engineering tools and methods, software quality.

To broaden our vision of the required potential scope of the BoK to be considered as relevant for IT specialists, we note the following recent computer curricula which have specified bodies of knowledge for five 'computing disciplines': Computer Engineering, Computer Science, Software Engineering, Information Systems, and Information Technology (Computing Curricula 2005).

Iivari et al. (2004) suggests five broad knowledge areas for IS specialists: technology knowledge, application domain knowledge, organizational knowledge, IS application knowledge, and systems development process knowledge. *Technology knowledge* refers to knowledge associated with understanding the types of hardware and software available and how and where they might be applied. *Application domain knowledge* refers to knowledge about the application domain for which an IS is built. For example, in the case of accounting information systems, the application domain knowledge relates to accounting concepts and principles. *Organizational knowledge* is knowledge "about the social and economic processes in the organizational contexts in which the IS is to be developed and used" (Jones and Walsham, 1992). *IS application knowledge* is the knowledge about typical IS applications, their structure, functionality, behavior and use, in a given application domain. It includes the knowledge of possibilities to support activities in the intra- and inter-organizational context by IS applications in a specific application domain. *Systems development process knowledge* refers to the tools, techniques, methods, approaches and principles used in systems development.

Iivari et al. (2004) go on to describe how these five knowledge areas form a nascent BoK for IS development. In this paper, we now wish to take these five knowledge areas and see how they differ from the perspective of research and practice. In particular, we see knowledge generated through research to be more general in nature, while the knowledge used in practice is more contextual. It is apparent that there exists gaps between the general and contextual knowledge; and it is in these gaps that a more professional BoK could be of help.

4. THE RELATIONSHIP BETWEEN RESEARCH AND PRACTICE

The on-going debate about the practical relevance of IS research (see Schauer 2007 for a review) suggests that there is a significant gap between research and practice in the IS field. The SE community has also suffered a similar dilemma (e.g. Osterweil 1996).

Often the assumption in the debate is that academic knowledge does not sufficiently influence practice. This section reverses the view and looks at how practice could better influence research, contending that we in academia should pay more attention and give more respect to the experience-based knowledge of practitioners when attempting to specify a BoK for IT specialists. Indeed, Klein and Hirschheim (2008) offer a number of change strategies for academia to better take into account the knowledge possessed by practitioners. Yet, if one considers the continued problems and failures of information systems and software development, it is obvious that we cannot accept the current practice and its underlying knowledge uncritically. To this end, we offer a framework for thinking about a BoK which embraces the knowledge generated from both research ('general' or 'theoretical' knowledge) and practice ('contextual' or 'experiential' knowledge).

4.1 Academic and practical knowledge

One of the reasons for the chasm between academia and practice is the different nature of knowledge on which they focus. Classical Greek epistemology illustrates the difference by distinguishing *episteme, techne, phronesis,* and *metis* (Baumard 1999). *Episteme* is abstract and general theoretical knowledge, while *techne* describes the practical knowledge in craft and art covering techniques and artifacts which provide methods and means to accomplish tasks.

The practice of developing and applying IT normally takes place in an organizational or inter-organizational context. *Phronesis* refers to social knowledge required in our everyday interaction with other people. Hirschheim and Klein (2003) characterize *phronesis* (or applicative knowledge as they call it) as closely related to a person's identity, emotions and interests, and rooted in one's lived experience and especially the tradition into which someone is born and into which he/she has chosen to integrate. They also point out how critical applicative knowledge is for achieving mutual understanding and consensus when developing information systems.

The practice of developing and applying IT also takes place in a dynamic context. Every situation is potentially new and unique. To address these new and unique situations successfully one needs knowledge that ancient Greeks called *metis*. Baumard (1999) translates it into "conjectural knowledge" and Spender (1996) characterizes it as cunning and shrewdness. *Metis* can be interpreted to include improvisation as situated performance where thinking and action emerge simultaneously at the spur of the moment (Ciborra 1999).

While theoretical knowledge (*episteme*) is considered the most valuable knowledge produced by research, practitioners presumably are more interested in *techne*, i.e. effective means to achieve their goals, than *episteme* as abstract theories do not inform them about effective action. Yet, to apply technology successfully, practitioners need *phronesis* and *metis*. One should note, however, that *phronesis* and *metis* are highly situated and therefore difficult to separate from the concrete context in which they are rooted and where they emerged.

4.2. How to bridge the gap between research and practice?

We believe the challenge for the IT field is to develop a BoK which embraces both research-originated and practice-originated IT knowledge and bridges the gaps between the two. Referring to the contextuality of practice-originated knowledge (*phronesis* and *metis*) we do not see any short-term solutions to bridge the two, as it requires profound changes on both sides that can only be addressed with a long time perspective.

Schauer (2007) analyzes the relevance vs. rigor debate in IS and distills a number of recommendations from that literature. Table 1 is a partial summary of the recommendations from her work, but extends them in many ways. We note that many of the recommendations in Table 1 are not particularly novel, and that different communities as well as different regional areas and countries differ in the degree and extent to which they already follow the recommendations. The point of Table 1 is that one should be as comprehensive and systematic in the measures to bridge research and practice as possible.

5. CONCLUSIONS

Several authors have recommended that IT should emulate established professions to bridge the gap between research and practice (*cf.* Davenport and Markus 1999). While we agree that the analogy between IT and more established professions such as engineering or medicine and law is informative, one must also be conscious of essential differences between these professions and the IT field. One must keep in mind that, although medicine has become ever more dependent on technology it is ultimately concerned with the human body which has remained essentially the same for hundreds of thousands of years. The IT field on the contrary deals with a constantly evolving artificial world of IT artifacts, which are developed and applied in the artificial worlds of organizations and societies. Law is also concerned with a socially constructed artificial world, but the law profession is lucky in the sense that it actively constructs the artificial world called "law", i.e. the system of legal procedures, codes and precedents (Collins 1990). In the IT field, the IT experts cannot control which IT artifacts are developed and how they are applied. In fact, the IT field probably resembles engineering more than anything else. If so, it is worthwhile realizing that engineering has been much less successful in its professionalization than medicine and law (Collins 1990).

The case of engineers illustrates that the existence of a BoK and the demand for that knowledge in practice is not enough for professionalization. It requires the capability to monopolize that knowledge. The gap between research and practice in the IT field led us to wonder if there is real demand for the knowledge that the discipline provides. Therefore, in our view it is not sufficient that we specify a BoK for the IT disciplines but that knowledge should also have practical relevance. In this paper, we have specifically focused on the issue of how to bridge the gap between research and practice by making research more sensitive to practice. In conclusion, while the professionalization model might inform us on how to bridge the gap between research and practice in the IT field, the very same gap also hinders all professionalization efforts in our field.

Although we support stronger sensitivity to practice, one should not interpret this to imply that the current practice should have the right to decide research directions. From the standpoint of practice and society, research needs to have autonomy for at least two reasons. One is to play its intellectual role of fundamental criticism as defined by Etzioni (1968) and discussed in more detail in Klein and Myers (2007). The other is that research as an institution needs to develop its ideas freely so that it can be a productive contributor to the global marketplace of ideas. Yet, we believe that researchers should also always seriously assess if their research projects have any chance of producing knowledge that could affect practice. Therefore, it is extremely important that we do not bring in rigidities that jeopardize the freedom of research and its potential innovativeness when attempting to develop the IT field towards more professionalization.

Table 1: Recommendations for how to bridge research and practice

Category	Recommendations
Improve conditions for relevant IT research	Promote mobility between academia and industry - recruit more faculty with industry experience in universities - provide university faculty with opportunities to have sabbaticals at business organizations - have more IT PhDs working in industry
	Change doctoral education to address better industry interests - recruit doctoral students from industry - create special doctoral programs for practitioners interested in doctoral studies - provide funding for doctoral students from industry
	Foster joint university and industry research projects - provide special funding for joint projects - simplify the bureaucracy with funding
	Encourage responsible consulting by faculty members
Conduct more relevant IT research	Strive for relevant research questions and results - joint university and industry research projects - make sure that the joint projects also have high scientific ambitions - integrate joint projects with a research program that has a longer time frame - focus on applied theory research, evaluation research, policy research and design science research
	Apply research methods that support industry participation and enable the capitalization of practical experience of researchers - emphasis on qualitative research methods - action research and constructive (design science) research
	Produce better consumable research articles - publish in both academic publication forums and practitioner-oriented outlets - write in a way that is more targeted to practitioners - organize the results in a way that is action-oriented
Increase the academic acceptance of relevant research	Reward publications in practitioner outlets Establish new publication outlets Change academic journal policies Broaden acceptable dissertation research

REFERENCES

Abbott, A., *The System of Professions: An Essay on the Division of Expert Labor*, The University of Chicago Press, Chicago, 1988

Benbasat, I. and Zmud, R., Empirical Research in Information Systems: The Practice of Relevance, *MIS Quarterly*, 23(1), 1999, pp. 3-16.

Beyerlein, M.M., Johnson, D.A. and Beyerlein, S.T. (eds.), *Knowledge Work in Teams*, JAI Press, Greenwich, CT, 1995

Ciborra, C., Notes on improvisation and time in organizations, *Accounting, Management and Information Technology*, 9, 1999, pp. 77-94

Collins, R., Changing conceptions in the sociology of the professions, in Tortsnedahl, R. and Burrage, M., *The Formation of Professions: Knowledge, State and Strategy*, SAGE Publications, London, 1990, pp. 11-23

Computing Curricula 2005, The Overview Report Covering Undergraduate Degree Programs in Computing for Computer Engineering, Computer Science, Information Systems, Information Technology and Software Engineering. The Joint Task Force for Computing Curricula, 2005

Davenport, T. and Markus, M. L., Rigor vs. Relevance Revisited: Response to Benbasat and Zmud, *MIS Quarterly*, 23(1), 1999, pp. 19-23.

Etzioni, A., *The Active Society,* Collier-McMillan, The Free Press, 1968.

Ensmenger, N.L. The question of professionalism´ in the computer fields, *IEEE Annals of the History of Computing*, October-December 2001, pp. 56-74

Ford, G. and Gibbs, N.E., *A mature profession of software engineering*, Technical Report CMU/SEI-96-TR-004, Software Engineering Institute, Carnegie Mellon University, Pittsburgh, 1996

Freidson, E., *Professions of Medicine: A Study of the Sociology of Applied Knowledge*, The University of Chicago Press, 1988 (First published 1970)

Freidson, E., *Professionalism Reborn*, Polity Press, 1994

Hirschheim, R. and Klein, H. K., Crisis in the IS Field? A Critical Reflection on the State of the Discipline, *Journal of the Association for Information Systems*, 4(5), 2003, pp.237-293

IFIP, First Report of the IFIP Professional Practice Task Force, January 2007

Iivari, J., Hirschheim, R. and Klein, H.K., Towards a distinctive body of knowledge for information systems experts: coding ISD process knowledge in two IS journals, *Information Systems Journal*, 14(4), 2004, pp. 313-342

Iivari, J. and Linger, H., Knowledge Work as Collaborative Work: A Situated Activity Theory View, *Proceedings of the 32nd Hawaii International Conference on System Sciences*, 1999

Jones, M. and Walsham, G., The limits of the knowledge: Organizational and design knowledge in systems development, in Kendall, K.E. (ed.), *The Impact of Computer Supported Technologies on Information Systems Development*, Elsevier Science Publishers B.V (North-Holland), Amsterdam, 1992, pp. 195-213

Kaarst-Brown, M.L. and Guzman, I.R., Who is the 'IT workforce'? Challenges facing policymakers, educators, management, and research, *Proceedings of the 2005 ACM SIGMIS CPR Conference,* Atlanta, 2005, pp. 1-8

Kelloway, E.K. and Barling, J., Knowledge work as organizational behavior, *International Journal of Management Reviews,* Vol. 2, No. 3, 2000, pp. 287-304

Klein, H. K. and Hirschheim, R., The Structure of the IS Discipline Reconsidered: Implications and Reflections from a Community of Practice Perspective, *Information and Organization,* forthcoming

Klein, H. K. and Myers, M., A set of principles for conducting and evaluating critical field studies in information systems, submitted, Nov. 2007.

Macdonald, K.M., *The Sociology of the Professions,* Sage Publications, London, 1995

Machlup, F., *The Production and Distribution of Knowledge in the United States,* Princeton University Press, Princeton, NJ, 1962

Maclaughlin, J. and Webster, A., Rationalizing knowledge: IT systems, professional identities and power, *Sociological Review,* 46(4), 1998, pp. 781-802

Minzberg, H., *Structure in Fives: Designing Effective Organizations,* Prentice Hall, Englewood Cliffs, NJ, 1983

Orlikowski, W. and Baroudi, J., The information systems profession: Myth or reality, *Office: Technology and People,* 4(1), 1989, pp. 13-30

Osterweil, L., Strategic Directions in Software Quality, *ACM Computing Surveys,* 28(4), 1996, pp. 738-750

Pyöriä, P., The concept of knowledge work revisited, *Journal of Knowledge Management,* 9(3), 2005, pp. 116-127

Sahay, S. Nicholson, B. and Krishna S., *Global Software Work: Micro-Studies Across Borders,* Cambridge University Press, 2003

Schauer, C., *Relevance and Success of IS Teaching and Research, An Analysis of the "Relevance Debate",* ICB-Research Report No. 19, Universität Duisburg-Essen, Essen, Germany, 2007

Schultze, U., A confessional account of an ethnography about knowledge work, *MIS Quarterly,* 24(1), 2000, pp. 1-41

Spender, J.-C., Making knowledge the basis of a dynamic theory of the firm, *Strategic Management Journal,* 17, 1996, pp. 45-62

Stehr, N., Experts, counselors and advisers, in Stehr, N. and Ericsson, R.V. (eds.), *The Culture and Power of Knowledge,* Walter de Gruyter, Berlin, 1992, pp. 107-155

SWEBOK, *Guide to the Software Engineering Body of Knowledge, 2004 Version,* February IEEE, 2004 (www.swebok.org)

SWECOE, *Software Engineering Code of Ethics and Professional Practice,* (www.cs.etsu.edu/seeri/secode.htm)

Wilensky, H.C., The professionalization for everyone, *American Journal of Sociology,* 7, 1964, pp. 137-158

Zuboff, S., *In the Age of the Smart Machine, The Future of Work and Power,* Heineman, Oxford, 1988

Mapping Research Questions to Research Methods

Pertti Järvinen
University of Tampere, FI
Department of Computer Sciences
pj@cs.uta.fi

Abstract: In Information Systems (IS) research, there is a wide range of research methods available. Yet the selection of a suitable research method remains a problem. March and Smith (1995) proposed a classification of research methods. Instead of their great merits, for example, differentiation between design science and natural science, we would here like to supplement them with some important amendments like mathematical approaches, theoretical studies and the dissensus and consensus views. In particular, we demonstrate how to select a suitable research approach in light of the research question.

1. Introduction

In this paper we prepare the taxonomy of research approaches in such a way that a junior researcher can find a suitable research approach to her research question. Sometimes the selection of a proper research method is simple, but sometimes the junior researcher at least may find it difficult. At the beginning of the research process the formulation of the research problem may well undergo a slight change, likewise the research method. Junior researchers may then utilize the taxonomy of research methods, if it is properly constructed.

Galliers and Land (1987) proposed the first taxonomy of information systems (IS) research taxonomy. It was based on "the *object* of which the research effort is focused and the *mode* by which the research is carried out are differentiated" (p. 901). They identified the following object categories: Society, organization (group), individual, technology, and methodology. The latter refers to the IS development approaches (Galliers 1985). The research approaches were divided into two classes: Modes for traditional empirical approaches (observations) consisting of theorem proof, laboratory experiment, field experiment, case study, survey, forecasting and simulation; and modes of newer approaches (interpretations) consisting of game/role playing, subjective/ argumentative, descriptive/interpretive and action research. Galliers and Land used the expressions: yes, possibly, and no, when they evaluated whether a certain mode was suitable for a particular object. We give two examples of research modes. First, according to their recommendation, theorem proof is suitable for research on technology, but not for research on

Please use the following format when citing this chapter:

Järvinen, P., 2008, in IFIP International Federation for Information Processing, Volume 274; *Advances in Information Systems Research, Education and Practice*; David Avison, George M. Kasper, Barbara Pernici, Isabel Ramos, Dewald Roode; (Boston: Springer), pp. 29–41.

society, organization, individual or methodology. Secondly, laboratory experiment is suitable for individual, technology, and possibly for small groups, but not for society, methodology or organization. Galliers and Land's taxonomy shows that organization and individual as research foci can be approached by all the other modes but theorem proof. Hence, we conclude that the object categories do not efficiently guide a researcher in the choice of mode of research approach.

Next, we turn to consider whether the form of research question could help. In his case study textbook Yin (1989) gives a proposal for how some determinants (Table 1) could be used to select a suitable research strategy.

Table 1: Relevant situations for different research strategies (Yin (1989, p.17)

Strategy	Form of research question	Requires control over behavioral events?	Focuses on contemporary events?
Experiment	how, why	yes	yes
Survey	who, what*, where, how many, how much	no	yes
Archival analysis (e.g. economic study)	who, what*, where, how many, how much	no	yes
History	how, why	no	no
Case study	how, why	no	yes

* "What" questions, when asked as part of an exploratory study, pertain to all five strategies

The table above shows that survey and archival analysis rows are identical, i.e. Table 1 cannot give instructions when we should use survey or archival analysis as a research strategy. The other three research strategies have the same forms of research question, but they can be distinguished by using the required control over behavioral events and whether we are concerned with contemporary or past events. Yin does not include such research strategies as theorem proof, grounded theory, ethnography, action research, and design research in his classification. Hence, it is reasonable to seek a better taxonomy.

According to March and Smith (1995), "scientific interest in IT reflects assumptions that these phenomena can be explained by scientific theories and that scientific research can improve IT practice. Note, however, that there are two kinds of scientific interest in IT, descriptive and prescriptive. Descriptive research aims at understanding the nature of IT. It is knowledge-producing activity corresponding to natural science. Prescriptive research aims at improving IT performance. It is a knowledge-using activity corresponding to design science." (p. 252)

March and Smith (p. 253) continue that "IT research studies artificial as opposed to natural phenomena. It deals with human creations such as organizations and information systems. This has significant implications for IT research which is discussed later. Of immediate interest is that fact that artificial phenomena can be both created and studied, and that scientists can contribute to each of these activities. This underlies the dual nature of IT research. Rather than being in conflict, however, both activities can be encompassed under broad notion of science that includes two distinct species, termed natural and design science. Natural science is concerned with explaining how and why things are. Design science is concerned with 'devising artifacts to attain goals' (Simon 1981, p. 133)."

Our main purpose is to help a junior scientist to find the most suitable research method by analyzing the research question. The distinction between natural and design sciences may be based either on the object under study (the use of an IT system vs. the construction of a new IT artifact) or on the form of the research question (how and why things are vs. devise an artifact) or on the verb used in the formulation (understand vs. improve) of the question. March and Smith clearly concentrate on research problems in the real world, and they propose that we should distinguish between natural science and design science studies.

March and Smith (1995) describe these two sciences as follows: "Research activities in natural science are parallel: discover and justify. Discover, or more appropriately for IT research, theorize, refers to the constructions of theories that explain how and why something happens. In the case of IT research this is primarily an explanation of how or why an artifact works within its environment. Justify refers to theory proving. It requires scientific evidence that supports or refutes the theory.

Research activities in design science are twofold: build and evaluate. Build refers to the construction of the artifact, demonstrating that such an artifact *can* be constructed. Evaluate refers to the development of criteria and the assessment of artifact performance against those criteria.

We *build* an artifact to perform a specific task. The basic question is, does it work? Building an artifact demonstrates feasibility. These artifacts then become the object of study. We build constructs, models, methods, and instantiations. Each is a technology that, once built, must be evaluated scientifically.

We *evaluate* artifacts to determine if we have made any progress. The basic question is, how well does it work? Recall that progress is achieved when a technology is replaced by more effective one. Evaluation requires the development of metrics and the measurement of artifacts according to those metrics. Metrics define what we are trying to accomplish. They are used to assess the performance of an artifact. Lack of metrics and failure to measure artifact performance according to established criteria result in an inability to effectively judge research efforts." (p. 258)

These descriptions of natural sciences and design sciences provide a preliminary taxonomy of different studies (Figure 1).

A junior IS researcher can use Figure 1 in such a way that she first tries to distinguish whether she seeks to understand the nature of IT or to improve IT performance, i.e., to distinguish between natural sciences and design sciences. In the latter case she wants to ascertain whether she is building a new IT artifact or evaluating an existing one, i.e. measuring how good a new artifact is or if it is better than the best of all possible artifacts for a given task. For the natural science case, a junior scientist can discover whether or not there is in the literature prior knowledge about her research topic (cf. Edmondson and McManus 2007). If the prior knowledge exists, she can develop a theoretical framework to be justified, and if it does not exist, she must herself theorize this new topic.

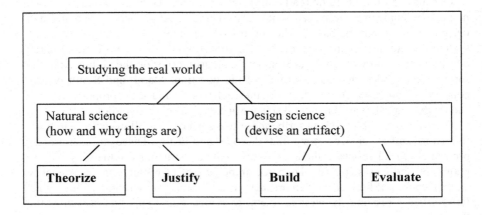

Figure 1. Preliminary taxonomy of different studies (cf. March and Smith 1995)

Figure 1 describing the broad structure and classification of the most commonly occurring studies does not, however, include all the studies and research methods needed. For example, critical studies are lacking. Further, I should like to point out that such abstract research objects as formal languages and general systems having no reference to the real world are also lacking. March and Smith (1995) do not pay much attention to purely conceptual studies, although in the classic survey by Ives et al. (1980) the second common research strategy was already "non-data" studies (30.5 %). For these reasons we can state our research problem in this paper: *How can we develop such a taxonomy of studies that is as exhaustive as possible?*

In the rest of the paper we first develop a more exhaustive taxonomy. Thereafter we propose which research methods are suitable for each class of studies, and how a junior scientist could find the correct class by analyzing her research question. Finally we discuss various implications of our study.

2. Towards a more exhaustive taxonomy of studies

In order to emphasize the exhaustiveness of our taxonomy (Bunge 1967) we select the top-down approach. We first consider all the studies and distinguish such research objects as formal languages, algebraic units etc., in other words, symbol systems having no direct reference to the real world. Gregor (2006) developed the taxonomy of 5 types of theory in IS. She poses the question and giver her own answer (p. 631): "Do some theory types belong to particular paradigms? An unequivocal 'no' is the answer to this question. ... Theory Types II to V require some form of realist ontology, as constructs in theoretical statements can refer to entities in the real world. Type I theory does not necessitate reference to real-world entities, but could be purely analytic, as in mathematics and logic"

From the remaining studies concerning reality, we pay attention to the use of values in differing between natural and design science studies. March and Smith (1995, p. 260) already write that "research in the build activity should be judged based on *value* or utility to a community of users". In the build and evaluation activities the utility of an innovation (IT artifact) is most often stressed, but van der Heijden (2004), studying hedonic (pleasure-oriented) systems, and Iivari (2007) paying attention to entertaining, artisticizing and accompanying IT systems, demonstrated other values in IT studies ("value-laden"). In addition to technical artefacts or innovations, we also accept that there may also be social and informational innovations. Therefore we use the term innovation instead of artefact.

Those studies that do not emphasize values ("value-free"), i.e., studies that are interested in "how and why things are" in understanding the phenomenon under study may be either theoretical or empirical. Empirical studies may be concerned with either theorizing (theory-developing studies) or justifying (theory-testing studies). In theory-testing studies we can a priori assume either dissensus or consensus (Burrel and Morgan 1979; Deetz 1996). In theory-creating studies we recognize whether dissensus or consensus holds at the research site. We adopt Deetz's (1996) taxonomy of discourses and cite Sanford and Rose (2007, p. 408): "Although developed in the context of organizational science, it provides a well-known and reasonably transferable account of different research styles suitable for use in most socially oriented literatures."

To summarize earlier distinctions we present Figure 2 below. To give a more concrete view of our classes we enumerate research approaches in mathematical, theoretical, theory-testing and theory-developing, innovation-building and innovation-evaluation studies.

3. Research methods are suitable for each class of studies

We use the term 'research approach' as an umbrella expression to refer to similar research methods. *Mathematical* studies, e.g., general systems theory, can also be utilized in some IS studies. For example, Aulin (1989) mathematically developed the classification of dynamic systems that can help IS researchers to differentiate IT artifacts from the information systems where people play a central role.

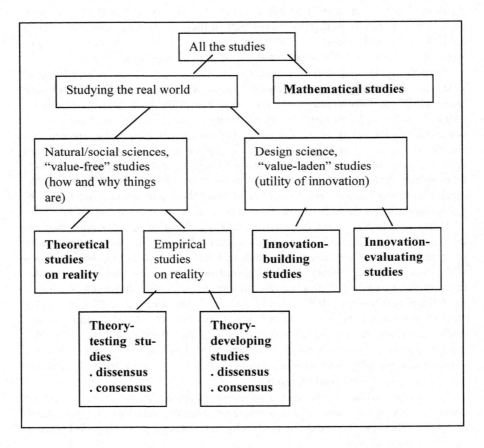

Figure 2. Our taxonomy of different studies

By using set theory Aulin (1982) also developed an actor model where three constructs (beliefs, values and procedural norms) can to a great extent explain human behavior. He argued that, if something (for example, self-steering) cannot be directly observed, it can sometimes be studied indirectly, mathematically. In mathematical studies a certain theorem, lemma or assertion is proved to be true.

In *theoretical* studies on reality the basic assumptions (for example, Wand and Wang 1996) underlying constructs are first analyzed; theories, models and frameworks used in previous empirical studies are identified, and logical reasoning is thereafter applied.

When we empirically study the past and present, we can use theory-testing or theory-developing methods depending on whether we have a theory, model or theoretical framework guiding our research or whether we are developing a new theory grounded on the raw data gathered.

In *theory-testing* studies such methods as laboratory experiment, survey, field study, field test etc. are used. Lee (1989) presented a particular version of the case study, which should be classified as a theory testing approach, but has had a marginal effect so far. Some longitudinal study methods belong to this category. In a study using the theory-testing method the theory, model or framework is either selected from the literature after a comparison of those available or developed or refined for the study at hand. In many IS studies, consensus is tacitly assumed. But if dissensus is assumed, as in an activity theory (Kuutti 1991), a critical study is then performed (cf. Richardson and also Robinson 2007).

Among the *theory-developing* studies we include "normal" case study (Yin 1989, Eisenhardt 1989), multiple case study (Eisenhardt and Graebner 2007), content analysis, ethnographic method, grounded theory (Glaser and Strauss 1967; Strauss and Corbin 1990; Suddaby 2006)), phenomenography, contextualism (Pettigrew 1985), discourse analysis, some longitudinal study methods, phenomenological study, hermeneutics etc. In the theory-developing study, an attempt is made to create one story or tentative theory and the consensus is then implicitly presupposed. But if the case cannot be described with one story only, and two, three, even four stories are needed as in Buchanan (2003), then dissensus holds.

In *building* an innovation the utility or other aspects (that can be collected into a goal function (Järvinen 2007b)) are pursued and a particular (information systems) development method and/or the design theory is applied or developed (Gregor and Jones 2007). In the *evaluation* of the innovation, e.g. an information system, some criteria or a certain goal function are applied and some measurements performed.

4. From research question to research methods

To demonstrate how from the research question we can arrive at a suitable research approach in mathematical, theoretical, theory-testing and theory-developing, innovation-building and -evaluation studies we present some examples. Aulin (1989) could state his research question as follows: What is an exhaustive classification of general systems theories? The latter as research objects do not refer to real world entities. Hence *mathematical* approaches can be recommended.

Albert et al. (2004, p. 163) state that "our goal is to propose an operational framework for continuous redesign, especially for non-transactional sites". The verb 'redesign' refers to innovation-*building* studies. Gregor (2006) also assigned the paper by Albert et al. to her Type V theory (design and action). Albert et al. (p. 164) continue that "as suggested in Hevner et al. (2004), we use an observational *evaluation* method to evaluate the design". In this class [design research] we try to answer the questions: Can we build a certain innovation and how useful will it be? We may also ask what a certain innovation ought to be like, and how we could build it? For example, how could we improve our human-computer interface so as to reduce the number of errors? If our research question contains the following verbs: build, change, improve, enhance, maintain, extend, correct, adjust, introduce, etc., our study might belong to design science research.

Gefen et al. (2003, p. 53) have two objectives in their study. "The first objective of this study is *to integrate trust-based antecedents and the technological attribute-based antecedents found in TAM into a theoretical model. ... Examining how customer trust can be maintained in an e-vendor* is accordingly, the second objective of this study." Gefen et al. clearly study a part of the real world. Their first objective concerns *theoretical* part of their study. The second objective emphasizes their empirical part of the study where their theoretical model is *tested*. In this class [theory-testing studies] we try to answer the question: Does a particular theory, model or framework aptly describe a certain part of reality? In a more detail, do our experiments, field or case studies confirm or refute our theory, model or framework?

Lamb and Kling (2003, p. 198) regret that "within several research disciplines related to IS studies, there is a growing realization that ICTs, such as online information services, have achieved only limited success as useful information systems, in part because they are based on models that reflect this user concept". They later (p. 202) continue that "in order to develop a better understanding of ICT use, and to develop an alternative to the user concept, we designed a study to examine online information services from the perspective of the people who were actually using or not using them. Mindful of the main criticism of the user concepts that have informed its critiques, we focused our qualitative research on the organizational contexts of situated use." Lamb and Kling study a part of the real world, and develop a new user concept. Hence, their study belongs to the *theory-developing studies*. They used on-site interviews to assemble their raw data and they mainly followed the rules of grounded theory (Glaser and Strauss 1967) in their analysis. Miles and Huberman (1994) refer to Tesch's (1990) book with 27 research approaches and classify those theory-developing research methods into more detailed classes. In this class [theory-developing studies] we try to answer the question: What kind of theory, model or framework best describes or explains a part of reality? In more detail, what kinds of theories, models or frameworks can we use to describe and explain our observations from case studies, content analyses, ethnographic, phenomenological, hermeneutic, phenomenographic etc. studies?

To summarize, we have given examples and guidelines for how to arrive at a suitable research approach from the research question. My personal experience (Järvinen, 2004) as a supervisor of doctoral students, especially students coming from industry, supports my claim that our taxonomy (Figure 2) can guide junior scientists to choose a suitable research approach for their studies. Next, we move on to consider the implications of our taxonomy for science.

5. Implications

March and Smith (1995) placed much emphasis on design science with two activities, build and evaluate. It is interesting to note that Susman and Evered (1978) described *action research* as a repetitive performance of the following cycle: Diagnose, plan, implement, evaluate and learn. The three first phases in the cycle (diagnose, plan and implement) resemble the information systems development method when the so-called phase approach is applied, i.e. when a new system is built. Hence, action research seems to contain both the build and evaluate activities (cf. Järvinen 2007a). This may resolve the problem of how to categorize action research. Ives et al. (1980) included action research studies in the category of "unknown research strategy", Iivari (1991) assigned action research to idiographic methods, and Orlikowski and Baroudi (1991) had one action research article in their set of 155 article studies, which they classified as either positivist or interpretive but not as critical philosophy. Our result that action research is a combination of the build and evaluation activities, and hence belongs to design science concurs with the fact that in every action research project some utility is emphasized and some improvement is stressed. Our taxonomy seems to evince more evidence for Järvinen's (2007a) tentative consideration.

It is significant that March and Smith (1995) write "natural science uses but does not produce methods. Design science creates the methodological tools that natural science uses." The distinction between natural science and design science concerning method corresponds to the distinction between *positive* and *normative* (prescriptive) views, where the positive view proclaims what reality *is*, and the normative view what reality *ought to be*. The positive methods are included in a certain (positive) theory describing a part of reality, its structure and action. For example, Hann and Weber (1996) assume that the research object (in a part of reality) have reached a stable state. The normative methods demonstrate how to build an IT artifact, for example, and an information system (van Aken 2004; Gregor and Jones 2007).

Concerning instantiations the difference between natural science and design science is that natural science describes why and how a particular instantiation is as it is, its structure and action, and this description is then value-neutral. But at the beginning of the building process design science emphasises the problematic initial situation, i.e. a low utility or a low value of the goal function, and during the building process design science stresses the expected utility of the desired state of the new system. During the evaluation of the ready-made instantiation its final state (or more exactly its goal function) is compared with the expected state (its goal function). Hence, values play a crucial role in design science research.

Deetz (1996) proposed two dimensions to contrast Burrell and Morgan's (1979) dimensions. The first new dimension (local/emergent vs. elite/ a priori) focuses on the origin of concepts and problem statement as part of the constitutive process in research. The second "consensus-dissensus" dimension draws attention to the relation of research to existing social orders. This dimension is similar to Burrell and Morgan's use of the traditional sociological distinctions between an interest in "change" or "regulation", but enables some advantages. The first dimension (local/emergent vs. elite/ a priori) supports March and Smith's distinction between theory-developing (theorizing) and theory-testing (justifying) activities. Deetz calls the combination of a priori theory and dissensus the discourse of *critical studies,* where some conflicts are pre-supposed in the theoretical framework or theory to be tested. Orlikowski and Baroudi (1991) recommended "ethnographic studies of organizational processes and structures" when the critical philosophy of information systems research will be applied. But in light of the foregoing we cannot agree with them. Their recommendation is rather valid for Deetz' discourse of dialogic studies, where the local or emergent theory and dissensus were assumed. The class of dialogic studies and its special methods (Buchanan 2003) are new.

We totally agree with Lee (1989), who found that his consideration for assessing the analytical rigor of case studies recognized *no differences between quantitative and qualitative approaches.* Lee concluded that any distinctions between quantitative and qualitative approaches are artificial and inconsequential. Neither type of research is inherently more rigorous than the other. In other fields of academic research, the perceived differences between quantitative and qualitative approaches have, unfortunately, become institutionalized into opposing camps. Some of the methodological concepts in Lee's article may prove helpful in avoiding a similar fate in the academic field of MIS. Deetz' article (1996) used in our taxonomy also supports the same view.

Concerning *mathematical approaches* we would like to pay attention to Aulin's (1982, 1989) studies on dynamic systems. Aulin differentiates nilpotent systems with a rest point or equilibrium from four types of dynamic systems with a continuous goal function g(t). Self-steering dynamic systems seem best imitate human behaviour. One of the most interesting features of self-steering systems is that the same state never recurs. This may explain why repetitive studies with people have not been successful. From the continuous goal function in time we can conclude that we are able to change our minds in the course of time. This may explain in part why maintenance activities (especially perfective maintenance) play as a central role as they do in information systems (Lientz et al. 1978). It seems that the self-steering system is a more realistic model of the human being and of an organization than a machine or an organism, which are frequently evinced as metaphors for that purpose, e.g., Huy (2001). A detailed analysis of our class of mathematical approaches provided self-steering systems, the new and more realistic model of human being. Aulin himself argues for his mathematical approach saying that if we cannot directly observe and measure something we could try to model and study it mathematically.

To summarize, mathematical approaches clearly can provide new applications like self-steering systems. Action research is close to design research, where values play a central role. Concerning methods it is reasonable to distinguish between positive and normative methods. A new class of dialogic studies emerged. Instead of quantitative and qualitative studies we should speak about theory-testing and theory-developing studies. Hence, our taxonomy as such or its immediate corollaries really mean progress in IS.

6. Discussion

In supplementing Figure 1 with some amendments like mathematical studies and consensus-dissensus alternatives, we did not stipulate any conditions or restrictions that a certain study must concern information systems. On the contrary, we even extended our innovations from technical ones to social and informational ones. Hence, our taxonomy (Figure 2) is also equally applicable to other disciplines like engineering, education, social work, etc.

Webster and Watson (2002) give advice on how to conduct a literature review. They also describe how fields of inquiry develop. Their theories are often placed on a hierarchy from ad hoc classification systems (in which categories are used to summarize empirical observations), to taxonomies (in which the relationships between the categories can be described). Two higher level constructions are conceptual frameworks (in which propositions summarize explanations and predictions), and theoretical systems (in which laws are contained within axiomatic or formal theories). To our mind, earlier classifications of research methods (Ives et al. 1980, Galliers 1985, Galliers and Land 1987) as linear lists are ad hoc classifications. Figure 1, based on March and Smith (1995), has some relationships between its constituents. Our tree-like structure in Figure 2 better fulfills the requirements of taxonomy than any other classifications of research methods.

March and Smith (1995) provide some universal criteria for every research output type. "Evaluation of constructs tends to involve completeness, simplicity, elegance, understandability, and ease of use." To demonstrate the *completeness* of our taxonomy we refer to pairs: 1. real/abstract, 2. value-free/value-laden (natural-social science/design science), 3. theoretical/empirical, 4. develop/test, 5. dissensus/consensus, 6. build/evaluate. All the six pairs consist of exhaustive classifications. Concerning *simplicity*, the mental capacity of human short-term memory is restricted to 5 ± 2 observational units (von Wright 1979), and those six pairs are within the limits. The *elegance* of our taxonomy is difficult to evaluate, because elegance is normally "in the eye of the beholder". To measure understandability we must consider how easily we can differentiate these six pairs. Most terms in them are fundamental scientific concepts. A person cannot perform any study if she does not *understand* these terms. Ease of use may depend on the complexity of relationships. Our concepts in Figure 2 do not form any network, but rather a tree-structure. The latter is normally *easier to use* than the former. Hence, according to the universal criteria presented by March and Smith our taxonomy (Figure 2) is a 'good' construct.

References

Albert T.C., Goes P.B. and Gupta A. (2004). GIST: A model for design and management of content and interactivity of customer –centric web sites. *MIS Quarterly*, 28(2), 161-182.
Aulin A. (1982). *The cybernetic laws of social progress*. Oxford: Pergamon Press.
Aulin A. (1989). *Foundations of mathematical system dynamics: The fundamental theory of causal recursion and its application to social science and economics*. Oxford: Pergamon Press.
Buchanan D.A. (2003). Getting the story straight: Illusions and delusions in the organizational change process. *Tamara Journal of Critical Postmodern Organization Science*, 2(4), 7-21.
Bunge M. (1967). *Scientific research I. The search for system*. Berlin: Springer-Verlag.
Burrell G. and Morgan G. (1979). *Sociological paradigms and organizational analysis*. London: Heinemann.
Deetz S. (1996). Describing differences in approaches to organization science: Rethinking Burrell and Morgan and their legacy. *Organization Science*, 7(2), 191-207.
Edmondson A.C. and McManus S.E. (2007). Methodological fit in management field research. *Academy of Management Review*, 32(4), 1155-1179.
Eisenhardt K.M. (1989). Building theories from case study research. *Academy of Management Review*, 14(4), 532-550.
Eisenhardt K.M. and Graebner M.E. (2007). Theory building from cases: Opportunities and challenges. *Academy of Management review*, 50(1), 25-32.
Galliers, R.D. (1985). In search of a paradigm for information systems research. In E. Mumford, R. Hirschheim, C. Fitzgerald and T. Wood-Harper (Eds.), *Research methods in information systems* (pp. 281-297). Amsterdam: North-Holland.
Galliers, R.D. and Land F.F. (1987). Choosing appropriate information systems research methodologies. *Communications of ACM*, 30(11), 900-902.
Gefen D., Karahanna E. and Straub D.W. (2003). Trust and TAM in online shopping: An integrated model. *MIS Quarterly*, 27(1), 51-90.
Glaser B. and Strauss A. (1967). *The discovery of grounded theory: Strategies of qualitative research*. London: Wiedenfeld and Nicholson.
Gregor S. (2006). The nature of theory in information systems. *MIS Quarterly*, 30(3), 611-642.
Gregor S. and Jones D. (2007). The anatomy of a design theory. *Journal of the Association for Information Systems*, 8(2), 312-335.
Hann J. and Weber R. (1996). Information systems planning: A model and empirical tests. *Management Science*, 42(7), 1043-1064.
Hevner, A.R., March, S.T., Park J. and Ram S. (2004). Design science in information systems research. *MIS Quarterly*, 28(1), 75-105.
Huy Q. N. (2001). Time, temporal capability, and planned change. *Academy of Management Review*, 26(4), 601-623.
Iivari J. (1991). A paradigmatic analysis of contemporary schools of IS development. *European Journal of Information Systems*, 1(4), 249-272.
Iivari J. (2008). A paradigmatic analysis of Information Systems as a design science. Forthcoming in *Scandinavian Journal of Information Systems*, draft 27p, ask the newest version from the author juhani.iivari@oulu.fi .
Järvinen P. (2004). *On research methods*. Tampere, Finland: Opinpajan kirja.

Järvinen P. (2007a). Action research is similar to design science. *Quality & Quantity*, 41(1), 37-54.

Järvinen P. (2007b). On reviewing results of design research In proceedings of ECIS2007. In http://www.cs.uta.fi/reports/sarjad.html D-2007-8.

Kuutti K. (1991). Activity theory and its applications to information systems research and development. In H.-E. Nissen, H. Klein and R. Hirschheim (Eds.), *Information systems research: Contemporary approaches and emergent traditions* (pp. 529-549). Amsterdam: Elsevier.

Lamb R. and Kling R. (2003). Reconceptualizing users as social actors in information systems research. *MIS Quarterly*, 27(2), 197-235.

Lee, A.S. (1989). A scientific Methodology for MIS case studies. *MIS Quarterly*, 13(1), 33-50.

Lientz E.P., Swanson E.B. and Tompkins G.E. (1978). Characteristics of application software maintenance. *Communications of ACM*, 21(6), 466-471.

March S.T. and Smith G.F. (1995). Design and natural science research on information technology. *Decision Support Systems*, 15(4), 251-266.

Miles M.B. and Huberman A.M. (1994). *Qualitative data analysis*, 2nd ed. Thousand Oaks, Ca: Sage Publications.

Pettigrew A.M. (1985). Contextualist research and the study of organisational change processes, In E. Mumford, R. Hirschheim, C. Fitzgerald and T. Wood-Harper (Eds.), *Research methods in information systems* (pp. 53-78). Amsterdam: North-Holland.

Richardson H. and Robinson B. (2007). The mysterious case of the missing paradigm: A review of critical information systems research 1991-2001. *Information Systems Journal*, 17(3), 251-270.

Sanford C. and Rose J. (2007). Characterizing eParticipation. *International Journal of Information Management*, 27(6), 406-421.

Simon H.A. (1981). *The sciences of the artificial*. Cambridge, Mass: MIT Press.

Strauss A. and Corbin J. (1990). *Basics of qualitative research - Grounded theory procedures and techniques*. Newbury Park, Ca: Sage Publications.

Suddaby R. (2006). From the editors: What grounded theory is not. *Academy of Management Journal*, 49(4), 633-642.

Susman G.I. and Evered R.D. (1978). An assessment of the scientific merits of action research. Administrative Science Quarterly, (23), 582-603.

Tesch R. (1990). *Qualitative research: Analysis types and software tools*. New York: Falmer.

van Aken J.E. (2004). Management research based on the paradigm of the design sciences: The quest for field-tested and grounded technological rules. *Journal of Management Studies*, 41(2), 219-246.

van der Heijden H. (2004). User acceptance of hedonic information systems. *MIS Quarterly*, 28(4), 695-704.

Wand Y. and Wang R.Y. (1996). Anchoring data quality dimensions in ontological foundations. *Communications of ACM*, 39(11), 86-95.

Webster J. and Watson R.T. (2002). Analyzing the past to prepare for the future: Writing a literature review. *MIS Quarterly*, 26(2), xiii – xxiii.

Wright J. (1979). Ihmisen tiedonkäsittelykyvyn rajoituksia (On the limitations of human information processing). *Academia Scientiarum Fennica, Vuosikirja - Year Book*, 163-171.

Yin R.K. (1989). *Case study research – Design and methods*. Newbury Park, Ca: Sage Publications.

REFLECTIONS ON 50 YEARS OF COMPUTING: IMPACT OF PROFESSIONALISM ON TEACHING, PRACTICE AND RESEARCH

T. William Olle

T. William Olle Associates, GB

1.   Introduction

Fifty five years ago, in 1953, many aspects of computing were not even invented. Even the idea of making a career out of computing was essentially unknown. There were no formal courses for students to attend, no lecturers to teach the courses, practitioners were mainly researchers in universities and government establishments, and programming was a tool for researchers in subjects other than computing. In other words, there were no computer professionals.

In 2008, computing – be it teaching, practice or research – is a major employer of many skilled persons. It is recognized that computers play a significant role in all facets of human endeavour, from toys to jumbo jets, from corner shop businesses to multinational corporation and from children to senior citizens.

This paper examines the dimensions of the "impact of professionalism" and attempts to stimulate more attention on professionalism from the various communities involved, but particularly from the research community.

Please use the following format when citing this chapter:

Olle, T.W., 2008, in IFIP International Federation for Information Processing, Volume 274; *Advances in Information Systems Research, Education and Practice*; David Avison, George M. Kasper, Barbara Pernici, Isabel Ramos, Dewald Roode; (Boston: Springer), pp. 43–51.

2.   Dimensions of professionalism in computing

Professionalism in computing has many dimensions. One is the simple trichotomy - practitioners, teachers and researchers, although many would subsume the last two under the first.

A perspective on sibling professions (namely other than computing) is very important.

Lawyers and doctors have been around a long time and their professional status is centuries old. Accountancy and engineering are more recent.

Another dimension is based on some kind of taxonomy of the total field. The body of knowledge in computing is ever changing and at the same time ever increasing. Emphasis on specialisms which can be a basis for professionalism is needed.

Next, the problem of grading (within a specialism, within each of the three above referenced parts of the trichotomy) must also be considered.

Each of these four "dimensions" will now be discussed in turn.

3.   Simple trichotomy

The trichotomy of practitioner, researcher, teacher (sequence deliberately alphabetical) is useful when considering the impact of professionalism. A practitioner in the computing field might always claim he or she is a professional – possibly only in the sense of a sports person that the person is not an amateur. Anyone who expects remuneration for their work might regard themselves as professional.   However, the question of recognized qualifications is surely paramount here. If the qualification claimed comes from a university then the issue can be interpreted as to whether that qualification is recognized.

The problem of acceptability of a qualification for a professional recognition even goes further.   Some practitioner employment positions may well require no more than a secondary school qualification.   Should such positions and those holding them be regarded as "professional" or should some other term be used?

Moving from practitioner to researcher, it seems appropriate to assert that a researcher should have at least the qualifications of a professionally recognized practitioner.   Since research into computing related topics should really have some kind of practical link, it may be unnecessary to consider professionalism for researchers as different from professionalism for practitioners.

The final member of the trichotomy is teachers, arguably the most critical when it comes to consideration of professionals.

Teachers are required to train practitioners to become professionals in the computing field.   Therefore the teachers themselves must have reached at least the same professional standards as those they are trying to inculcate into their students.

Finally, it should be noted that in tertiary education generally, researchers are expected to teach although the converse may not always be true.

For convenience, this paper refers to all members of this trichotomy as "computing practitioners".

4.   Sibling professions

4.1 Legal profession

It is not clear which branch of professionalism should be noted as the pioneers but it is probably the legal profession. The London Law Society was founded in 1825 [1].   It may well have been formed following a lead established in other countries.

The American Bar Association has published a 21 item list of the "model rules of professional conduct" [2].   It is not clear that this list could serve as a basis for rules in the computer profession.

4.2   Medical profession

Computing is a fairly recent arrival in the world of professionalism. The British Medical Association claims it was established in 1832 [3].

The following extract from paper by David Morell in the February 2003 edition of the Catholic Medical Quarterly [4] is of interest to any consideration of professionalism.

1. The professional has skills or expertise proceeding from a broad knowledge base.

2. The professional provides a service based on a special relationship with those whom he or she serves. This relationship involves a special attitude of beneficence tempered with integrity. This includes fairness, honesty and a bond based on legal and ethical rights and duties authorised by the professional institution and legalised by public esteem.

3. To the extent that the public recognises the authority of the professional, he or she has the social function of speaking out on broad matters of public policy and justice, going beyond duties to specific clients.

4. In order to discharge these functions, professionals must be independent of the influence of the State or commerce.

5. The professional should be educated rather than trained. This means having a wide cognitive perspective, seeing the place of his or her skills within that perspective and continuing to develop this knowledge and skills within a frame work of values.

6. A professional should have legitimised authority. If a profession is to have credibility in the eyes of the general public, it must be widely recognised as independent, disciplined by its professional association, actively expanding its knowledge base and concerned with the

education of its members. If it is widely recognised as satisfying these conditions, then it will possess moral as well as legal legitimacy, and its pronouncements will be listened to with respect.

The question should be asked whether any part of this definition is irrelevant in the world of computing professionalism.

Another aspect of professionalism in the world of medicine surely comes from the 170 years that they have been organized. This aspect is specifically the breakdown of a vast body of knowledge and associated competence into recognized specialist areas.

A few examples in the medical profession are bacteriology, cardiology, paediatrics, pathology, oncology, orthopaedics.

This illustration of a breakdown of a body of knowledge is of significant interest to professionalism in computing where there is also a vast body of knowledge. However, one can argue that any taxonomy of computing which might have been the cornerstone for a breakdown 20 years ago would today be largely obsolete. Not only is the body of knowledge in computing vast, it is also highly volatile.

This is not intended to argue against a breakdown, but rather to emphasize the importance of choosing the components carefully and to prefer those which will stand the test of time.

4.3 Accounting profession

It is important to distinguish the origins of accounting from the origins of the accounting profession. It is asserted in [6] that accounting can trace its origins to the Italian Renaissance.

The accounting profession is arguably closer to the computing profession than is either the medical or legal professions. For one thing, much of what accountants produce makes use of computing systems and resources and has done so for several of the decades during which computers have been available. The early business uses of computers focussed inevitably on accounting applications. This was preceded by the punched card machinery which pre-dated the advent of stored program computers.

The emergence of a professional accounting society is harder to pin-point than for the legal and medical professions [6]. Apparently, the first professional body in accounting was in Edinburgh Scotland in 1853.

There were clear driving forces for the setting up of the accounting profession. One was the Companies Act passed in the UK in 1852. The literature emphasizes two aspects namely accounting standards and ethics. In the computer field, standards are very important but it would be hard to assert that the computing profession is built around them. Ethics are important in any profession. The accounting profession experienced considerable shock in 2003 in the aftermath of the Enron scandal. This kind of event could easily happen in the computing profession.

5.   Emphasis on specialisms

Each of the three sibling professions considered above is partitioned into a set of specialisms. In the case of accounting and legal professions, to which the practice of the profession applies, such factors for partitioning are the areas of application which are not necessarily specific to the profession. This is best illustrated by identifying some specific areas for the accounting profession as follows:

    Charity and Voluntary,
    Entertainment and Mechanical,
    Health Care
    Tourism and Hospitality
    Public Sector
    Farming and Rural.

One can argue that any application area which needs accounting services, also needs computing services (and may possibly need legal expertise).

This raises the question whether a taxonomy of computing specialisms should include a taxonomy of application areas in which the computing is applied. However, many applications of computers cross specialisms. Some simple examples are

Payroll (varies from country to country according to legislation)
Accounting (or finance generally)
Stock control
Banking
Sales

These examples may be contentious in that the idea of designating computer professionals as trained in one of these fairly common well recognized specialisms may seem too simplistic. The question which needs to be addressed is "how is it possible to package parts of computing in a way which is generally acceptable to those who wish to employ a practitioner in computing?".

Another aspect of computing which merits consideration is the irrefutable fact the computing has evolved during a period in history when communication (and indeed labour movement) between countries has been more prevalent than ever before.

Professionalism in the three sibling areas considered in this paper goes back many decades, in some cases to an era before the availability of the telephone. Computing on the other hand has evolved during an era when travel and labour movement generally have been the norm rather than the exception!

This aspect of the problem presents the following challenge for computing professionals. The formulation and introduction of a computing profession should as far as possible take place in an international milieu rather than a national one. This would certainly make the task harder but the ultimate rewards would appear to justify this kind of approach.

6. Way forward

Even on the basis of this brief paper, it is possible to note a number of steps which are already being followed. It is important to build on the work already undertaken [7] in the IFIP International Professional Practice Programme (I3P). The main thrust of this report has been summarized in a paper by Charles Hughes [8]. These two papers give a clear direction for the role of IFIP in developing what is rapidly (and indeed commendably) being identified as the information technology profession. The term is clearly broader and more apposite than older terms such as

> Data processing
> Information processing
> Computer science
> Informatics

Information technology can be taken as subsuming all of these.

The recent one page article [9] on "Advancing the IT Profession" stresses achieving the prestige associated with the three established professions reviewed briefly in this paper, namely law, accountancy and medicine. It also emphasizes the importance of "raising public awareness of the vital role of IT in our modern world.

One aspect of professionalism which these three references ([7], [8] and [9]) do not touch on is the importance of promoting a workable taxonomy (or classification scheme) for the IT profession. The problem is not that such schemes exist but that there are too many of them. These vary both nationally and linguistically.

Since its early inception, IFIP itself has always had a traditional breakdown into "Technical Committees". However the motivation for this partitioning has been based more on technical interest rather than the promotion of career paths and researchable topics.

The use of Special Interest Groups within many of the larger and more active national societies can be regarded in a similar manner to the breakdown into IFIP technical committees.

It is clear that any taxonomy of IT for professional purposes should at least take into account both application areas (clearly overlapping) such as finance, personnel, manufacturing, science, transport) and inherent IT aspects each of which crosses several application areas.

References

[1] www.lawsociety.org.uk/aboutlawsociety/whoweare/abouthistory.law

[2] www.abanet.org/cpr/mrpc/home.html

[3] www.bma.org.uk/ap.nsf/Content/HubhistoryoftheBMA

[4] www.catholicdoctors.org.uk/CMQ/2003/Feb/what-is-professionalism.htm

[5] www.icaew.com/index.cfm?route=155691

[6] http://acct.tamu.edu/giroux/Shorthistory.html

[7] First Report of IFIP Professional Practice Task force January 2007 profess sional practice programme. C.Hughes. Invited paper WCC2008.

[9] Advancing the IT Profession. IFIP News March 2008.

Advances in Information Systems Development: From Discipline and Predictability to Agility and Improvisation

Jan Pries-Heje[1] , Richard Baskerville, Bala Ramesh[2] , Linda Levine[3]

[1] Roskilde University, DK
[2] Georgia State University, Atlanta, US
[3] Software Engineering Institute, Carnegie Mellon University, Pittsburgh, US

Abstract: When *information systems development* (ISD) was coined as a term and evolved into a research area we lived in a largely industrial economy. This traditional universe placed high value on discipline and predictability for its own sake. In the 1990s several new trends began to question and challenge the traditional view. Specifically, Internet marketplaces created a new environment for information systems development, and novel approaches such as agile methods emerged. In this paper, we present an analysis of empirical findings showing how new principles and practices have come to exist in a parallel economic universe. The traditional universe persists with its foundation in an industrial economic model; and an alternative universe has become apparent corresponding to a knowledge-based economic model. Our findings suggest that, in the future, knowledge-based activity will continue to gain ground with increased emphasis on agility and improvisation. Moreover, the purpose of discipline will be newly understood to serve an underlying role, which is supportive rather than dominant.

1. Introduction

Information systems development (ISD) regards systems development processes and products. Systems development typically unfolds in a series of stages such as analysis, design, coding and testing. These stages do not have to be carried out sequentially but can be performed iteratively and in parallel. Often each stage

Please use the following format when citing this chapter:

Pries-Heje, J., Baskerville, R., Ramesh, B. and Levine, L., 2008, in IFIP International Federation for Information Processing, Volume 274; *Advances in Information Systems Research, Education and Practice*; David Avison, George M. Kasper, Barbara Pernici, Isabel Ramos, Dewald Roode; (Boston: Springer), pp. 53–75.

operates with a defined notation and will results in a prescribed artefact, such as a requirements specification or a computer program.

An ISD methodology is a prescribed way of carrying out the development. The description typically includes activities to be performed, artefacts resulting from the activities, plus some principles for organizing the activities and attaching people to perform the activities. An ISD methodology can be aimed at a specific type of development, e.g. database-intensive applications with less than 10 people involved, or it can be specific to a company. However, many ISD methodologies claim to be of generic use.

Very early ISD methodologies were based on practical experiences, i.e. when veteran practitioners simply described how one could develop new IS. But soon things became rather messy. Structured Analysis and Design, for example (cf. Yourdon, 1989), instilled a discipline focusing on functions and data flow between function. Object-Oriented Analysis and Design (cf. Larman, 2005) modeled a system as a group of interacting objects with each object representing an entity of interest in the system being modeled. The lack of theory was also addressed: for example, Andersen et al (1990) builds on a theory that says that ISD consists of nine distinctly different activities, and Highsmith (1999) builds, in part, on the theory of lean thinking (Womack, Jones, & Roos, 1990).

In 1986 the Software Engineering Institute (SEI) in Pittsburgh was asked by the U.S. Air Force in 1986 about a systematic way to evaluate software contractors. The resulting model was called the Capability Maturity Model (CMM). The CMM is a framework characterizing a path with five maturity levels each composed of one or more key process areas. If the organization develops these areas, the software process is known to improve. "Each key process area identifies a cluster of related activities that, when performed collectively, achieve a set of goals considered important for enhancing process capability" (Paulk, Weber, Curtis, & Chrissis, 1995, p. 32). The perspective behind CMM was that software development is a tumultuous human process (Baskerville & Pries-Heje, 1999). "It entails fast-moving computer technology ... [and] skilled, extremely mobile professional workers. These workers must apply creativity and innovation in their development ...Without careful management, the process will quickly disintegrate into near-chaos" (Baskerville & Pries-Heje, 1999).

In the 1990s, some doubts about discipline and predictability began to surface In many situations where an ISD method was claimed to be used, it could not be proven by researchers (Bødker & Bansler, 1993). Furthermore, the practicality of ISD methods was questioned altogether. A growing number of studies suggested that the relationship of disciplined methodologies to the practice of information systems development was altogether tenuous (Fitzgerald, 1997, 1998, 2000; Wynekoop & Russo, 1993). It seems that methodology, discipline and predictability had become so dominant in our thinking about ISD that the result was a self-fulfilling hypothesis. For example, one alternative viewpoint situates systems development as "amethodical:" the management and orchestration of systems development without the predefined sequence, control, rationality, or claims to universality implied by much of methodological thinking (Truex, Baskerville, & Travis, 2000).

We have set out to answer the following related research questions: How has ISD advanced? Does ISD for the Internet differ from traditional ISD? What roles do discipline and predictability play?

Below, first, we present our research method. Second, we discuss our findings with an emphasis on the parallel, dual economies that currently coexist in information systems development. . Finally, we consider future trends which suggest an increasing emphasis on improvisational design.

2. Research Method

To answer our research questions we undertook three phases of research.

2.1 Phase one: Interview study

The first phase of our research involved nine detailed case studies of Internet ISD companies in two major U.S. metropolitan areas. The objective of this phase was to understand whether ISD for the Internet differs from traditional ISD. This phase identified the practices used for Internet ISD and explored the role of quality in this fast-cycle development environment (Baskerville, Levine, Pries-Heje, Ramesh, & Slaughter, 2001).

Data collection was carried out using open-ended interviewing. We used a grounded theory methodology to analyze the data (Strauss & Corbin, 1990). This methodology allows the development of a theory of a problem under investigation without prior hypotheses. The chosen grounded theory approach is composed of an alternation between three different coding procedures to analyze the collected data: open, axial and selective coding. At the end of the coding we had identified categories, sub-categories and relationships in the data (see Appendix A).

The findings from phase one identified key factors affecting Internet ISD practice. Although the practices used in Internet ISD can also be observed in traditional ISD, the intensity with which they were applied and the way they were applied together in Internet ISD was distinctive (Ramesh, Baskerville, & Pries-Heje, 2002).

2.2 Phase 2: The Discovery Colloquium on Internet ISD

The second phase involved a one-day Discovery Colloquium that we facilitated on Innovative Practices for Speed and Agility in Internet ISD (Baskerville, Levine, Pries-Heje, Ramesh, & Slaughter, 2003; Levine et al., 2002). The objectives of this phase were to synthesize knowledge on best practices for quality and agility in Internet ISD. Grounded in Kurt Lewin's action research model, such search conferences seek to "bring the whole system in the room" to exchange views and learn from one another. Like other forms of action research, participants share observations, engage in collaborative analysis, and logically test discoveries in an interactive debate among experts. Search conferences often produce data and findings coincidently.

The Colloquium was designed to benefit from and extend the findings from Phase 1. Interviewees from the nine Phase 1 companies, as well as selected experts were invited. Participants included software practitioners from entrepreneurial small companies as well as large "brick and mortar" companies, Internet business strategists and leading ISD experts. ISD methodological perspectives also ranged from adherents of agile ISDs to adherents of more traditional ISDs, representing a broad spectrum of stakeholders.

Participants joined one of several breakout groups dedicated to exploration of a core issue. The groups worked through a process of hypothesis testing, identifying linkages, contradictions, and inter-dependencies among the hypotheses. The groups then delved into underlying assumptions to further build dialogue from generative ideas, and to allow for both divergence and convergence of insights, with maximum cross-fertilization. Principles, promising practices and other dynamics of relevance were identified. The Discovery Colloquium's foundations in action research are reflected in the way data collection, analysis and social action are conflated into one flowing exercise. The researchers were included as participant-observers in the Colloquium. All of the Colloquium participants, operating in various groups, explicated the concepts from their individual practical experiences. The groups then operated analytically on these concepts in a socially situated forum. Both data and analysis emerged from the Colloquium in the mode of action learning.

The analysis in the present paper is based on the discussion of one breakout group focused on evaluating Agile ISD. The objective of this group's discussion was to explore whether there is anything different about Agile ISD methodologies, vis-à-vis traditional ISD methodologies.

As a result of our grounded theory analysis we identified a set of practices. See Appendix A for more detail.

3. Two parallel economies with matching ISD methods

Our findings suggest that IS developers in the 21st century environment adopted a considerably different set of practices from those associated with traditional ISD. Firms have developed new ISD principles and have also adapted old principles in the search for best practices for this new environment. These new principles and practices have not replaced former principles and practices, but rather the two sets now exist in parallel economic universes. The traditional universe continues with its foundation in an industrial economic model while the alternative universe corresponds to a knowledge-based economic model. Moreover, the industrial economic model and the knowledge-based economic model can operate in parallel, often within the same firm, driving different forms of ISD organizations, each with dominant principles and practices. A comparative analysis of these economic models and the empirical results from our studies yields an emerging pattern of alignment. This pattern reflects the recent movement of certain sectors of the ISD community from an industrial economy (sometimes called "Fordist") toward a post-industrial (sometimes called "post-Fordist" or knowledge-based) knowledge economy.

The distinction between industrial and post-industrial economics offers several important ideas that are useful in contrasting agile methods with traditional ISD methods. The rationalized and mechanistic production approaches found in industrial economics do not require a highly skilled workforce, whereas post-industrial economies require a new kind of "shop floor;" one that conflates the factory and research and development, focused on the power of human creativity and knowledge. That is to say, the intellectual power of the workforce is considered a critical factor of production. Post-industrial economics recognizes that information industries have assumed a powerful role among consumer societies (Rustin, 1989).

Knowledge-based economics recognizes new elements and modes of production. Knowledge has eclipsed land, labor and capital as economic factors of production and is now believed to be the prime resource for production. This represents a major shift in economic thinking and raises information technologies to a supreme level, as a tool that embodies the efficiency and effectiveness of the prime economic resource for production.

The knowledge economy requires organizations to deal with increasing complexity in their products and processes, to manage a rising inventory of technical and non-technical knowledge, to enable quick learning processes in response to increasing competition with shorter product life cycles, and to organize work done by a flexible workforce.

3.1 Comparative analysis

For a comparative analysis, we will use the key attributes detailed by Rustin (1989) as indicators of the ideal types of industrial and knowledge modes of production (Figure 1).

Industrial Economies	Knowledge Economies
Low technological innovation	Accelerated innovation
Fixed product lines, long runs	High variety of product, shorter runs
Mass marketing	Market diversification and niche-ing
Steep hierarchy, vertical chains of command	Flat hierarchy, more lateral
Mechanistic organization	Organic organization
Central planning, vertical and horizontal integration	Autonomous profit centers, network systems, internal markets
Bureaucracy	Professionalism, entrepreneurialism

Figure 1. Ideal types of production in Industrial (Fordist) and Knowledge (Post-Fordist) Economies (adapted from Rustin, 1989).

Our analysis shows how the principles governing "traditional" ISD align with the key attributes of industrial economies, while the emerging principles governing agile methods align with the key attributes of knowledge economies (Baskerville et al., 2003). Traditional ISD principles are indeed a matter of debate, but one set was rigorously developed using a multi-stage Delphi study involving well-respected ISD researchers and practitioners representing a spectrum of viewpoints, and exemplifies in our view the best attempt to date in defining general principles for ISD (Bourque et al., 2002). It is possible to compare these principles with those that proceeded from the Discovery Colloquium which are known to characterize agile.

Our comparison has three sections: First, the distinctive traditional principles of ISD (those traditional principles with no stated equivalent agile principle); second, the distinctive agile development principles (those agile principles with no stated equivalent traditional principle) and third, the overlapping set of comparable traditional and agile development principles (Figure 2). In each section, we analyze the contrasting economic models that inhabit the comparisons. We then summarize the insights from this analysis.

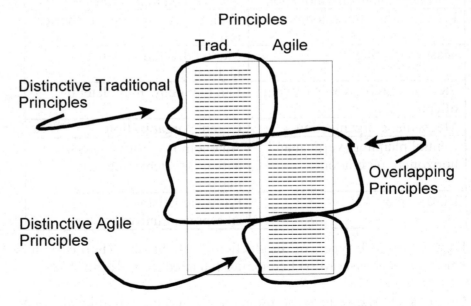

Figure 2. Distinguishing traditional and agile principles of ISD.

3.2 Distinctive Traditional ISD Principles

The distinctive traditional ISD principles (those with no agile counterpart) include quantitative measurement, interchangeable components (reuse), complexity and uncertainty control, rigorous requirements specification, formal quality management, documentation, component coupling, stepwise assembly, and disciplined process. Agile principles may have omitted these traditional ISD principles because they have been inherited from the management of disciplined production processes such as mass production assembly lines. These traditional principles are essential for managing software projects that are large, long, expensive and complex. In contrast, agile developers have scoped their projects using a release approach that keeps the products relatively small, short, cheap and simple. For example one of the Internet software firms we interviewed implemented a new software release every other week. Another firm that was developing a B2B site for transportation told us that customers had asked them to slow down their release speed. Customers simply couldn't cope with major changes every month! The informality of development processes

Industrial Economies	Distinctive Traditional Principles
Low technological innovation	Rigorous requirements specification
Fixed product lines, long runs	Stepwise assembly, component coupling
Mass marketing	Interchangeable components (reuse)
Steep hierarchy, vertical chains of command	Complexity and uncertainty control
Mechanistic organization	Quantitative measurement, documentation
Central planning, vertical and horizontal integration, bureaucracy	Disciplined process, formal quality management

Figure 3. Alignments between key features of ideal type industrial economies and distinctive principles of traditional ISD (adapted from Rustin, 1989).

and the small, frequent releases suggest that agile developers operate in a "job shop" environment rather than in a mass production software "factory" (Fernstrom, Narfelt, & Ohlsson, 1992) .

Figure 3 summarizes the evidence of the alignments between distinctive traditional principles and key features of industrial economies. There is a focus on rigor in the requirements specification process rather than creativity in the design process. Stepwise assembly and coupling of components are techniques that echo the factory model of assembly lines. The reuse of interchangeable components adds an emphasis on broader applications for components: akin to the mass markets of industrial models. Complexity and uncertainty control often introduce project management hierarchies. Quantitative measurement and heavy documentation add a mechanistic tone to project organizations. Principles of disciplining processes and managing quality in formal structures can centralize planning and increase the bureaucratic nature of the project management.

3.3 Distinctive Agile ISD Principles

The distinctive agile principles (those with no traditional counterpart) regard teamwork and on-the-fly software process adaptation. Agile principles emphasize informal knowledge exchange, collaboration, and experience as important elements in ISD, and acknowledge more sensitivity to tailoring project practices to environmental conditions. These principles are essential for managing software projects in volatile settings where fast changing technologies and markets drive fast changing skills and knowledge. Agile developers are more aware of, and learn more quickly about shifts in the environments surrounding their software products. In their view, the 'overhead' required to establish formal processes and mechanisms does not justify their use in a fast changing environment. Thus, agile developers operate in a dynamic and evolving environment rather than in a mature and standardized software market. A developer we interviewed in a large software firm emphasized the importance of being able to dynamically adapt software processes, claiming that "When they [management] start implementing rules and procedures, then I start looking for a new place to work." From his perspective, process rigidity and formality would inhibit the informality and dynamism that was needed in this environment.

Knowledge Economies	Distinctive Agile Principles
Accelerated innovation	On-the-fly software process adaptation
High variety of product, shorter runs, organic organization	Tailoring project practices to environmental conditions
Flat hierarchy, more lateral, professionalism, entrepreneurialism	Teamwork, informal knowledge exchange, collaboration, dependence on experience

Figure 4. Alignments between key features of ideal type knowledge economies and distinctive principles of agile ISD.

Figure 4 summarizes evidence of the alignments between distinctive agile principles and key features of knowledge economies. Agility is focused on incremental innovation, and the principles accordingly allow for an acceleration of development process adaptation. Project practices can be tailored according to the situation. A project may be organized in a certain way for a single product, and the next product may be produced in entirely different way according to its context. Agility embraces teamwork and person-to-person exchange of knowledge and values collaboration and professional experience very highly. These values align well with knowledge economy features like professionalism, entrepreneurialism and flat organizations.

3.4 Overlapping Traditional and Agile ISD Principles

The industrial economy did not end when the knowledge-based economy began. These two modes of production continue in parallel. They overlap. Industrial manufacturing continues to deliver low-cost, mass-produced commodities, while knowledge-based manufacturing delivers reasonably-priced, job-lot commodities. It remains possible to produce software systems in either mode.

Our analysis also yields overlapping principles that characterize both traditional and agile ISD. The overlapping principles include: product flexibility, understanding the functional requirements, responding to change, and learning from experience. In our analysis, the overlapping principles are essential for keeping software products aligned with changing requirements. Agile developers have preserved the principles necessary to support shorter project lifecycles and to respond to complex, fast-moving, and competitive marketplaces. Agile developers have to be as flexible and responsive to change as other software engineers. They must also be just as attuned to the functional requirements and prepared to learn from their own experience. Indeed, as suggested by the distinctive agile principles, agile developers will forego formal structures and exercise extreme adaptive options, such as changing their processes on the fly.

3.5 Insights from Comparative Analysis

Overall, we find a palpable alignment between the attributes of a knowledge economy and the principles that distinguish agile methods. That is, agile ISD occurs in a more informal, dynamic, learning environment rather than a mature and standardized software market. Agile methods support shorter project lifecycles and improvisation in order to respond to complex, fast-moving, and competitive marketplaces. For example, agile methodologies reflect a willingness to use multiple approaches and accommodate change to accelerate innovation for a high variety of products. The use of customer engagement drives market diversification and the development of specialized products that support market niches. An emphasis on teamwork and the opportunistic adaptation of methods and practices rely upon the professional expertise of entrepreneurial developers.

However, our analysis suggests that the new environment for ISD does not appear to be supplanting its predecessor. Rather, the application of traditional ISD principles continues in the traditional software application arenas. This co-existence of parallel development universes is most apparent in large ISD firms that have a broad portfolio of projects. The "back-end" elements of systems, based frequently on large-scale mainframes and database engines, continue to be developed in traditional ways while the "front-end" elements of the systems, based frequently on web-based architectures, employ agile development. For examples, see Cook et al. (2002). The development approaches appear to be selected on the basis of the economic environment of the application rather than its technological environment. In some cases, it is impossible to achieve both speed and the necessary economies of scale and quality. Note, however, that when front-end parts of systems are connected to back-end elements, the different development universes must somehow intersect. Some organizations resolve this potential integration problem by applying agile techniques to the back-end to speed up development of their back-end elements, while other organizations apply traditional methods to the front-end to slow down development of their front-end elements. Still others physically separate the development activities and pause projects while the back-end catches up with the front-end.

This continuation of traditional production approaches in parallel with new innovation-driven production approaches is also supported by theories of organizational innovation. To illustrate, in the Minnesota Innovation Research Program (Van de Ven, Angle, & Poole, 1989), fourteen longitudinal field studies of a variety of innovations revealed that innovation does not arise in a linear sequence of steps or stages, or even in a concurrent set of identifiable events or activities. Rather, these emerge as a splintering of organizational production directions in which innovative new activities occur as new pathways of organizational activities that are distinct in direction from the directions represented by older ongoing activities. Figure 5 shows how the innovation process in organizations shifts and splinters production directions over time. The original direction of the organization's activities ("Old") is joined by a new or reoriented set of activities with a new production direction (towards the right upper corner). The innovation that develops into the new direction arises in an organizational shock, such as a sudden change in the marketplace. New or changing activities tend to proliferate driven by multiple ideas and potential new organizational directions. Not all of these new directions prove fruitful, and some terminate after suffering setbacks. Other new directions will merge and integrate, perhaps merging activities with old and new directions. Early in this process, there is a tendency for top management to intervene in pressing for new-idea activities to merge into old-idea directions. (This is a downward pressure in the figure.) That is, management tends to press for the status quo until or unless it recognizes the value in the new production direction. When this recognition happens, top management engagement will intervene instead to restructure the organization and formalize the new strategic directions. Notably, the original ("old") production directions continue in parallel with the new. These original directions may end after a long term with setbacks, but this distant event is not shown in the diagram.

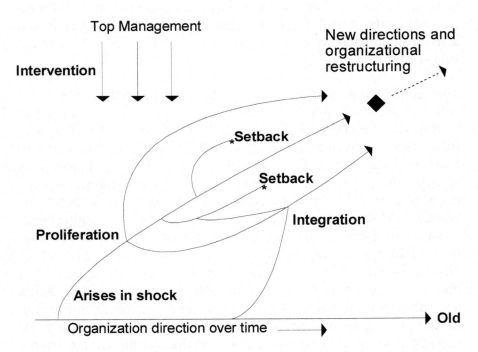

Figure 5. Diagrammatic Elements of the Emerging Innovation Process Model (adapted from Schroeder, Van de Ven, Scudder, & Polley, 1989, p. 131).

This model of emerging innovation explains how and why agile development might appear to be novel to some while to others, agile development is not new at all – as traditional principles of ISD remain valid even when using agile development methods. Agile development functions in a knowledge-based economy that coexists with the traditional economy; that is, there are parallel economic universes that foster different ISD principles. One economic universe has appeared more recently and has demanded innovation. However, it neither eclipses nor supersedes the older, traditional economic universe that continues to demand standard industrial practices.

Using the notation suggested by the Minnesota studies (Schroeder et al., 1989), Figure 6 illustrates how agile development has emerged in parallel with a new software economy. Macro economic forces are pressing both for the continuation of traditional practices and for the development of a knowledge economy. In response, software markets are demanding both traditional practices and agile practices, based on different, but overlapping sets of principles.

The existence of parallel economic universes explains why agile ISD may not lead to any obsolescence of traditional software. Conventional wisdom would expect that the traditional software practices would gradually decline in favour of the new, "better" and more pro-gressive agile practices. While this rival hypothesis appeals to the proponents of agile development, it is likely that these parallel economic universes will preserve a place in ISD for both sets of practices for the foreseeable future. Driven perhaps by the need for quality, economy of scale, and stability, traditional ISD will remain in demand along with the need for agile development.

We see parallels in the literature on organizational ambidexterity refers to the pursuit of conflicting demands on an organization that require tradeoffs (Gupta, Smith, & Shalley, 2006). The development of appropriate processes and systems for a given context that may achieve the desired balance between opposing demands is increasingly recognized as critical for success of organizations (Gibson & Birkinshaw, 2004). Whereas structural ambidexterity emphasizes separation of concerns, contextual ambidexterity emphasizes dual capacities of individuals and systems. While traditional ISD used in industrial economy focus on stability, rigor, and discipline, agile methods focus on flexibility and responsiveness to change. Therefore, achieving ambidexterity involves reconciling the conflicts between practices in traditional ISD and agile methods. Past research on organizational ambidexterity often considers different types of conflicting demands as competing rather than complementary or orthogonal (Katila & Ahuja, 2002), primarily on the basis of constraints on resources available to fulfill both demands.

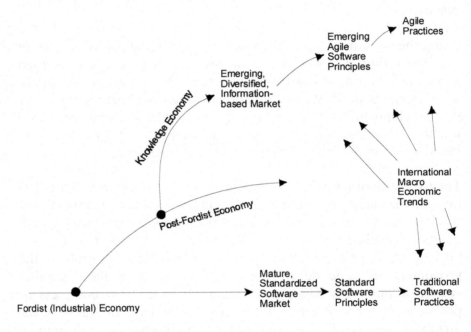

Figure 6. How Agile Methodologies have arisen in Parallel with Traditional Practices.

4. Improvisation: The future challenge

Use of agile methods and agility is consistently associated with software development techniques. But more recently, we have seen fledgling signs of expansion. Ironically, the contracting of the market and the tightening of resources has contributed to an enlarged scope and increased complexity- and a need for balancing at the portfolio and organization levels. This may spur further growth for agile approaches in atypical areas.

That said, the current state for agile methods is still isolated and limited. We have a partial understanding of what agility means for ISD activities. For example, we know that agile methods work well with small teams (especially those that are co-located), where requirements are emergent, and in a turbulent environment of constant change. Agile methods are not recommended in the development of life critical systems; and its use in developing embedded software remains unclear (Ambler, 2004).

We have little understanding of the consequences of agile approaches for technology adoption and implementation activities. Further, within the development and adoption arenas, we have yet to fully grapple with the implications of agility for people, process, and new technology. Our best insights into agility are still achieved through discrete activities—through projects which exist like islands in our organizations. From the development perspective, we have information on different agile methods, where they apply, particular emphases, and some acknowledged limitations. From an adoption perspective, we can speculate that an agile approach would favour pilots, trials, and demonstration projects; and from a knowledge transfer perspective, an agile approach would favour high customer involvement through face-to-face interaction or "body contact."

The challenge for the future is two-part. First, we must optimize the current state with vertical coupling to loosely integrate and propagate agile approaches for development, deployment, and knowledge transfer. This lightweight alignment would allow us to leverage what we know, and to reinforce these otherwise discrete areas of success. Second, and more radically, we must tackle the issue of scaling to investigate options for agile approaches and opportunities that can span organizations. On its face, this might seem contradictory since use of agile methods favours small teams with high contact. But to realize the potential for agile, we must ask how such methods adapt and scale. Perhaps they will do so in entirely new ways.

Austin and Devin (2003) speculate that old production models for ISD are no longer useful. Rather, agile ISD has the potential to be *artful making*. They write: "Artful making (which includes agile software development, theatre rehearsal, some business strategy creation, and much of other knowledge work) is a process for creating form out of disorganized materials. Collaborating artists, using the human brain as their principal technology and ideas as their principal material, work with a very low cost of iteration. They try something and then try it again a different way, constantly re-conceiving ambiguous circumstances and variable materials into coherent and valuable outputs" (pp. xxv-xxvi). Whereas industrial making places a premium on detailed planning, closely specified objectives, processes, and products, artful making is different, fusing iteration and experimentation. Austin and Devin point out that, "if you think and talk about iteration as experimentation, low cost of iteration seems to make business more like science. Its broader effect, though, is to make business more like art" (p. xxv). The authors go on to build an artful framework employing the analogies of theatrical production, extending beyond surface collaboration to the on-cue innovation that theatre companies routinely achieve.

In a similar vein, Stefan Thomke (2003) investigates experi-mentation in innovation, as it "encompasses success and failure; it is an iterative process of understanding what doesn't work and what does" (p. 2). He reminds us that both results are equally important for learning.

Finally, on a related topic, Dee Hock (1999) has characterized the organization of the 21st century organization as a *chaord*. The term chaord was formed out of combining the first three letters of the word chaos, with the first three letters from the word order. Hock and other leading scientists believe that the primary science of the next century will be the study of complex, self-organizing, nonlinear, adaptive systems, often referred to as complexity theory or chaos theory (DeGeus, 1997; Wheatley, 2001). They assert that living systems arise and thrive on the edge of chaos with just enough order to give them pattern, but not so much to slow their adaptation and learning. This is not unlike the challenge for agility in next-generation systems and organizations. We ask: Does this represent the larger paradigm shift of which agile methods are a part?

Some software development organizations achieve structural ambidexterity through separating traditional and agile development into dual structures and by establishing appropriate communication mechanisms across these structures. However, consistent with past literature on contextual ambidexterity (Gibson & Birkinshaw, 2004), organizations may also select systems and processes that define the context in which conflicting demands of traditional ISD and agile methods can be pursued simultaneously. In essence, contextual ambidexterity suggests behavioral orientation towards mixed capacities rather than focusing on any particular concern. This view is consistent with the our argument on the existence of parallel economic universes and the corresponding approaches to software development.

5. Conclusion

The research questions we phrased were:
1. How has ISD advanced?
2. Does ISD for the Internet differ from traditional ISD?
3. What roles do discipline and predictability play?

Through a discovery colloquium and a grounded theory analysis we found that that new principles and practices for ISD have come to exist in a parallel economic universe. The traditional universe persists with its foundation in an industrial economic model and with a focus on structure, discipline and predictability. But in parallel an alternative universe has become apparent corresponding to a knowledge-based economic model.

Our findings suggest that, in the future, knowledge-based activity will continue to gain ground with increased emphasis on agility and improvisation.

Moreover, the purpose of discipline and predictability will in the future be newly understood to serve an underlying role, which is supportive rather than dominant.

References

Ambler, S. (2004). *The Object Primer* (3rd ed.). Cambridge, England: Cambridge University Press.

Andersen, N., Kensing, F., Lundin, J., Mathiassen, L., Munk-Madsen, A., & Sørgaard, P. (1990). *Professional systems development: experience, ideas and action* Upper Saddle River, NJ, USA: Prentice-Hall.

Austin, R., & Devin, L. (2003). *Artful Making: What Managers Need to Know about How Artists Work*. Upper Saddle River, NJ, USA: Pearson Education Inc. Publishing as Financial Times Prentice Hall.

Baskerville, R., Levine, L., Pries-Heje, J., Ramesh, B., & Slaughter, S. (2001). How Internet Software Companies Negotiate Quality. *IEEE Computer, 34*(5), 51-57.

Baskerville, R., Levine, L., Pries-Heje, J., Ramesh, B., & Slaughter, S. (2003). Is Internet-speed software development different? *IEEE Software, 20*(6), in press.

Baskerville, R., & Pries-Heje, J. (1999). Knowledge Capability and Maturity in Software Management. *ACM SIGMIS The Data Base for Advances in Information Systems, 30*(2).

Bødker, K., & Bansler, J. (1993). A reappraisal of structured analysis: design in an organizational context. *ACM Transactions on Information Systems (TOIS), 11*(2).

Bourque, P., Dupuis, R., Abran, A., Moore, J. W., Tripp, L., & Wolff, S. (2002). Fundamental principles of software engineering - a journey. *The Journal of Systems and Software, 62*, 59-70.

Cook, D. L., Benz, J., Pries-Heje, J., Purao, S., & Wareham, J. (2002). Internet Retailing in the United States. In S. Elliott (Ed.), *Electronic Commerce: B2C Strategies and Models.* (pp. Chapter 7). Chichester: John Wiley & Sons.

DeGeus, A. (1997). *The Living Company.* Boston, MA, USA: Harvard Business School Press.

Fernstrom, C., Narfelt, K.-H., & Ohlsson, L. (1992). Software factory principles, architecture, and experiments. *IEEE Software, 9*(2), 36-44.

Fitzgerald, B. (1997). The use of system development methodologies in practice: A field study. *Information Systems Journal, 7*(2), 201-212.

Fitzgerald, B. (1998). An empirical investigation into the adoption of systems development methodologies. *Information and Management,*(34), 317-328.

Fitzgerald, B. (2000). Systems development methodologies: The problem of tenses. . *Information Technology and People, 13*(2), 13-22.

Gibson, C. B., & Birkinshaw, J. (2004). The Antecedents, Consequences, and Mediating Role of Organizational Ambidexterity. *Academy of Management Journal, 47*(2), 209.

Gupta, A. K., Smith, K. G., & Shalley, C. E. (2006). The Interplay between Exploration and Exploitation. *Academy of Management Journal, 49*(4), 693-706.

Highsmith, J. (1999). *Adaptive Software Development*. New York: Dorest House.

Hock, D. (1999). *Birth of the Chaordic Age*. San Francisco, CA, USA: Berrett-Koehler Publishers.

Katila, R., & Ahuja, G. (2002). Something Old, Something New: A Longitudinal Study of Search Behavior and New Product Introduction. *Academy of Management Journal, 45*(6), 1183-1194.

Larman, C. (2005). Applying UML and Patterns - Introduction to OOA/D & Iterative Development. In (3rd ed.): Prentice Hall.

Levine, L., Baskerville, R., Loveland Link, J. L., Pries-Heje, J., Ramesh, B., & Slaughter, S. (2002). *Discovery colloquium: Quality software development @ Internet speed* (No. SEI Technical Report CMU/SEI-2002-TR-020, ESC-TR-2002-020). Pittsburgh, PA: Software Engineering Institute.o. Document Number)

Paulk, M. C., Weber, C., Curtis, B., & Chrissis, M. B. (1995). *The Capability Maturity Model: Guidelines for Improving the Software Process*. Reading, Mass.: Addison-Wesley.

Ramesh, B., Baskerville, R., & Pries-Heje, J. (2002). Internet Software Engineering : A different class of Processes. *Annals of Software Engineering, 14*(1-4), 169-195.

Rustin, M. (1989). The politics of Post-Fordism: or, the trouble with 'New Times'. *New Left Review, 175*(1), 54-77.

Schroeder, R. G., Van de Ven, A. H., Scudder, G. D., & Polley, D. (1989). The development of innovation ideas. In A. H. Van de Ven, H. L. Angle & M. S. Poole (Eds.), *Research on The Management of Innovation: The Minnesota Studies* (pp. 107-134). new York: Harper & Row.

Strauss, A., & Corbin, J. (1990). *Basics of Qualitative Research: Techniques and Procedures for Developing Grounded Theory*. Beverly Hills, CA, USA: Sage Publications.

Thomke, S. (2003). *Experimentation Matters: Unlocking the Potential on New Technologies for Innovation*. Boston, Massachusetts, USA: Harvard Business School Press.

Truex, D., Baskerville, R., & Travis, J. (2000). Amethodical Systems Development: The Deferred Meaning of Systems Development Methods. *Accounting, Management and Information Technology*(10), 539.

Van de Ven, A. H., Angle, H. L., & Poole, M. S. (1989). *Research on The Management of Innovation: The Minnesota Studies*. New York: Harper & Row.

Wheatley, M. J. (2001). *Leadership and the New Science: Discovering Order in a Chaotic World (revised ed.)*. San Francisco, CA, USA Berrett-Koehler Publishers.

Womack, J. P., Jones, D. T., & Roos, D. (1990). *The Machine That Changed The World*. New York: Macmillan Publishing.

Wynekoop, J., & Russo, N. (1993). *System Development Methodologies: Unanswered Questions and the Research-Practice Gap*. Paper presented at the Proceedings of the 14th International Conference Information Systems (ICIS), Orlando, USA.

Yourdon, E. (1989). Modern Structured Analysis. Upper Saddle River, Nj, USA: Yourdon Press.

Appendix A: Grounded theory approach: Three coding procedures

The goal of *open coding* is to reveal the essential ideas found in the data. Open coding involves two tasks: labeling phenomena and categorizing. Labeling discriminates concepts in the data. Each discrete incident or idea receives a representative name or label. These names represent a concept inherent in the observation. Categorizing is the process of grouping related concepts and themes under joint headings.

Axial coding involves two tasks further developing the categories and properties. The first task connects categories in a sequence of relationships. For example, a causal condition or a consequence can connect two categories. The second task is validation of the relationships in the data, yielding the discovery and specification of the differences and similarities among and within the categories. This discovery adds variation and depth of understanding.

Selective coding is the process of determining a core category or story line that explains the categories with minimal contradictions. The core category should be related to most or all other categories, and these relationships must be validated and elaborated. Once settled (called "saturated" in grounded theory methodology), the core category explains all of the other categories.

The grounded theory analysis resulted in the identification of core categories or concepts and relationships among them that explain how and why Internet-speed ISD is different from traditional approaches.

The Emergence of Partnership Networks in the Enterprise Application Development Industry: A Global Corporation Perspective

Jens-M. Arndt, Thomas Kude, and Jens Dibbern

University of Mannheim, Department of Information Systems I, DE
e-mail: jens.arndt|kude|dibbern@uni-mannheim.de

Abstract: Within the IS development industry, incumbent system developers (hubs) are increasingly embracing partnerships with less well established companies acting in specific niches (spokes). This paper seeks to develop a better understanding of the motives for this strategy. Relying on existing work on strategic alliance formation, it is argued that partnering is particularly attractive for hubs if these small companies possess certain capabilities that are difficult to obtain through other arrangements than partnering. Drawing on the literature, three categories of capabilities are identified: the capability to innovate within their niche, the capability to provide a specific functionality that can be integrated with the incumbents' systems, and the capability to address novel markets. These factors are analyzed through a single-case study. The case represents a market leader in the global IS development industry, which fosters a network of smaller partner firms. The study reveals that temporal dynamics between the identified factors exist in these networks. A cyclical partnership model is developed that attempts to explain the life cycle of partnerships within such a network.

Keywords: Software Ecosystems, Inter-Organizational IS Development, Process Theory, Interfirm Partnership Formation

1. Introduction

The structure of the enterprise application systems development industry has been subject to continuous change. While most early systems had been individually developed by software contractors, pre-packaged systems have come to dominate the past decades [6]. However, the integration in-between these systems has proven to be complex and error-prone [27]. Consequently, the trend observable in the industry has been one of consolidation in that existing systems encompassed ever more functionalities, thus reducing the need for integration across

Please use the following format when citing this chapter:

Arndt, J.-M., Kude, T. and Dibbern, J., 2008, in IFIP International Federation for Information Processing, Volume 274; *Advances in Information Systems Research, Education and Practice*; David Avison, George M. Kasper, Barbara Pernici, Isabel Ramos, Dewald Roode; (Boston: Springer), pp. 77–88.

system boundaries [11]. However, currently another paradigm is emerging which potentially reverses this consolidation trend. Fueled by the promise of reduced integration effort through the emergence of service-oriented architectures [17], developers of existing systems are partnering with smaller companies. One of the results of this development is a more intense inter-organizational division of labor, which has already been adopted in many other industries [3], and which has been demanded in the IS context for decades [26]. On the one hand, this division of labor implies that the companies focus on their core competencies, such as a particular software component [38]. On the other hand, these specialized companies have to cooperate with each other in order to ensure that the different parts can be integrated into a coherent system. In order to achieve such a cooperation, a *hub-and-spoke network* has been proposed [33]. In this structure, a core firm inter-connects with all other organizations in a stable network. This central organization takes the role of a platform leader that is assumed to define technologies, markets, strategies, structures, and processes [18].

Contrary to strategic alliances or joint ventures that both imply a certain degree of joint resource deployment, these hub-and-spoke networks can be characterized as loosely coupled systems [31] that rely on a certification of the spokes' solutions by the hub. While the IS industry has widely adopted this loosely coupled structure [28], research is not providing answers to the fundamental questions of *why* the large software vendors abandon their proven strategy of growing through adding functionalities to their own systems. Drawing on the theory of the duality of inducements and opportunities, it is argued that the issue of why hubs form partnerships is equivalent to the question of which capabilities spokes possess that make them attractive partners for the large companies [1]. Analyzing which capabilities should be considered in this context, three broad categories of spoke capabilities are identified [19]. These are further discussed in the light of this study and integrated into a theoretical framework that guides our empirical analysis.

2. Theoretical Foundations

2.1 Access to Dynamic Capabilities as Inducement for Partnering

Previous research has predominantly drawn on the resource-based view (RBV) for understanding why organizations enter into cooperative relationships [21]. By viewing firms as bundles of resources, it has been argued that the main reason why firms partner is to gain access to resources which they currently do not possess, but which the partner is offering [15]. This fact has also been labelled as *duality* of inducements and opportunities, indicating that the propensity to form inter-organizational linkages not only depends on the organizations' willingness to overcome resource gaps, but also on a potential partner's attractiveness, i.e. its ability to close these gaps [1]. In particular, *dynamic capabilities* are assumed to increase an organization's attractiveness. Dynamic capabilities refer to the ability of using resources in a way that enables organizations not only to react to changes in their environment, but to shape it to a certain extent [39]. This ability is particularly relevant in dynamic contexts, such as systems development [30]. Therefore, in order to understand the underlying rationale for the hubs to enter into a partnership with a spoke, it is essential to examine the unique dynamic capabilities that the spokes bring into the network. Dynamic capabilities as success factors for small software firms have been analyzed previously [25]. However, we argue that these dynamic capabilities not only enhance a small software firm's performance, but also increase its attractiveness as a partner for hub organizations.

According to a large scale survey, network formation in high-tech industries such as software development is motivated by three types of capabilities: Speeding the process of innovation, accessing complementary technology, and accessing novel markets [19]. As this study explicitly takes the hubs' perspective, subsequently aspects of these three broad categories are developed that the spokes are assumed to possess and the hubs are assumed to lack. These are proposed as key motivating factors for a hub to enter into partnerships with spokes.

2.1.1 Capabilities to Develop Modular Innovations

Innovativeness plays a key role for organizations in high-tech industries such as the software industry, since they have to constantly cope with new technological advances as well as changing customer requirements [12]. However, while innovativeness clearly constitutes one of the key dynamic capabilities of software firms [25], it is less clear how a hub can benefit from the innovativeness of its small partners. More clarity is achieved through classifying innovations into different categories. As such, for industries that are characterized by a high degree of modularity, the distinction can be made between innovation at the component and the architectural level [20]. While component innovations accrue within the boundaries of specific modules, architectural innovations affect the way or the general structure by which the components are bound together to form a coherent system. In this context, it can be assumed that it is the responsibility of the spokes to engage in these component innovations. This ongoing modular innovativeness of spokes improves the overall system through improving its components.

Another classification divides innovation into being either sustaining or disruptive [7]. Sustaining innovations improve existing products in a way that is valued by mainstream customers, mostly through adding functionality. Contrary, disruptive innovations first appear to be simpler, cheaper or with lower quality than existing products, but might eventually threaten the incumbent products' market position. Within the modular system of the IS industry, spoke companies, on the one hand, provide sustainable innovations by simply adding functionality to the overall system. On the other hand, according to [7], disruptive innovations are most likely to happen in small, flexible companies that serve specific market niches. Thus, by partnering with spokes, hubs ensure that their network disposes of the capability to benefit from and keep control over disruptive innovations.

The reason why smaller firms are assumed to have higher innovative capabilities can be seen in their *entrepreneurial* potential. Both concepts are closely intertwined in that the main characteristic of an entrepreneur is assumed to be innovativeness [4, 14]. However, there is no inevitable connection between entrepreneurial spirit and innovation. Entrepreneurs as profit-seeking individuals are expected to suppress their propensity to innovate if facing adverse conditions [4]. These adverse conditions are supposed to be especially present in large organizations. In contrast, small organizations are assumed to be more suitable for stimulating entrepreneurial spirit. This perception is also shared by [30], who argue that creating value through innovation is best achieved by tapping into the entrepreneurial potential of a network of self-managed firms. Thus, the following relationship is proposed between innovativeness of spokes and their attractiveness as partners.

Proposition I. Large IS producers (hubs) are partnering with small software developers (spokes) in order to gain access to their capabilities to develop modular innovations.

2.1.2 Capabilities to Provide Niche Functionalities

As it has been mentioned above, a key goal of enterprise IS is the coverage of *all* information flows within an organization. However, IS have to be considered an *intellectual* rather than an *industrial* technology [24]. Thus, they are not constrained by physical aspects, but only by the imagination of their users, and therefore IS can be used in a virtually unlimited number of possible domains [8]. Consequently, it is impossible for any single organization, regardless of its size, to cover all these possible domains. A potential, yet limited, way to overcome this drawback is the abundant opportunity to customize standardized IS in order to adapt them to specific customer needs [36]. The here proposed network structure goes beyond this, in that it enables spokes to augment the general purpose platform developed by the hubs with certain complementary niche solutions [2]. The platform thus takes advantage of the mass-marketability of a standardized system, while the specialized components take advantage of the individualized solution quality of bespoke systems [37].

The concept of network externalities indicates that the platform of a central vendor becomes more valuable if more complementary products exist. Hence, complementary solutions are a key necessity for establishing a successful platform. By tying many of these specific niche functionalities to a hub's platform, this platform becomes more attractive for customers, which in turn attracts more partners to the network. A *positive feedback loop* is initiated, which ideally results in this hub's platform becoming a *de facto* standard [32]. Thus, the spokes' capabilities to provide attractive niche functionalities is considered a key motive for hubs to engage in partnerships. Especially those solutions that have a proven track record in the markets and that are complementary to the hub's offering promise to fall into this category. This leads us to the following second proposition.

Proposition F. Large IS producers (hubs) are partnering with small software producers (spokes) in order to gain access to their capabilities to provide complementary niche functionalities.

2.1.3 Capabilities to Access Novel Markets

The final aspect that is promising to be a prime reason for hubs to partner with spokes in such an inter-organizational network is the ability to address novel markets. The existing enterprise IS have been developed out of the striving for seamless integration of information flows in large corporations [11]. In this market segment, they have been highly successful, so that today the market is more and more saturated. Most large corporations either already possess an enterprise IS, or deliberately decided not to implement one [16]. Therefore, the vendors of these systems have to address new markets in order to sustain the growth rates they achieved in the past. Considering the fact that in the past, large IS vendors were selling their systems to the narrow market segment of global corporations, there are still ample opportunities to improve the systems' adequacy for specific requirements of other customer groups [34]. However, as these IS developers are by definition large corporations themselves, they incur considerable overhead costs for addressing these requirements. Thus, depending on the size of a potential market, these large vendors might decide not to develop specific solutions for this market. Contrary, based on the hub's platform, highly focused and efficient niche players are able to develop solutions for markets that the large hubs consider unattractive. Through the joining of forces between the two groups, the overall integrated solution can thus be used in broader markets, benefiting both hubs and spokes.

Another aspect of these niche IS developers is the fact that they can be assumed to have a much closer relationship to their customers, which is assumed to be a key success factor for IS development [35]. It has even been argued that users of these enterprise IS should form a strategic relationship with their developers in order to benefit from seamless future interaction [5]. The reason for this can again be seen in the fact that the customer to a considerable extent depends on the recommendations of the developer, and thus a good relationship between them is imperative for success. As these relationships require considerable time to emerge since they are causally ambiguous and socially complex in that they depend on the people involved in the relationship [23], these also classify for being a key capability of spokes that the hubs attempt to access. Therefore, the following proposition summarizes this market objective from the hubs' perspective.

Proposition M. Large IS producers (hubs) are partnering with small software producers (spokes) in order to gain access to their capabilities to address narrow markets.

2.2 An Integrated Framework for Partnership Formation

The preceding discussion has evolved around the research objective of developing capabilities that act as inducements for joining partnerships in the IS development industry. Three broad factors were identified and refined in the here proposed inter-organizational IS development context. As such, benefits from the spokes' modular innovation capabilities, their capabilities to provide niche functionalities, and their capabilities to access novel markets have been identified. The proposed relationships are illustrated in Figure 1.

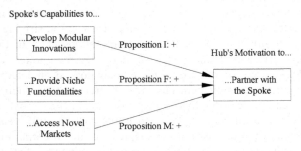

Fig. 1 A Model for Explaining the Partnering Motives of Large Corporations.

3. Empirical Analysis

3.1 Methodology and Data Collection

According to [22], the choice of an appropriate research design is to a large extend determined by the research question that is intended to be answered. This paper deals with the question why global IS development corporations are partnering with small organizations. According to [41], the case study approach is particularly promising to answer such *why* questions about motivations and rationales. As the IS development industry is characterized by an oligopolistic structure, the number of potential cases is limited. However, each one of these large IS development companies can be considered a unique case that is worth being analyzed in detail [41]. Consequently, a single-case study design was chosen [29]. This approach allows for an in-depth investigation of partnership formation, with special consideration of the contextual conditions of this organization [41].

The selected case very well meets the requirements of such a single-case study. The company has a proven track record of developing standardized enterprise IS for over thirty years. With thousands of customers in over one hundred countries worldwide it can be characterized as a truly global company. Finally, with multi-billion dollar revenues, it is one of the leading organizations in IS development. In this case company, several interviews were conducted during spring and summer 2007. Overall, sixteen professionals from various positions in the organization were interviewed in a semi-structured fashion. On average, the interviews lasted about one hour and resulted in a total verbatim transcript of 180 pages with close to 110,000 words. In addition to these interviews, data was collected from multiple other sources, such as secondary material and personal observation. Although the expert interviews were guided by the propositions presented in Section 2, the character of our analysis is rather exploratory.

For data analysis purpose, *codes* were developed for the three discussed propositions by assigning a brief label for each of them: *Innovation, Functionality,* and *Market* [29]. Using this scheme the transcripts of the interviews were then coded by assigning text passages to the three partnership motives proposed in the theoretical framework. These extracted interview fragments were then used for a two-stage analysis. First, a rough estimate of the importance of each of the proposed benefits was assessed by counting the frequencies of the relevant fragments [29]. Then, a second round of analysis was conducted in which the underlying background of each fragment was carefully considered in light of each proposition [13]. In the following, the findings from this two-staged process will be presented.

3.2 Data Analysis

Table 1 provides an overview of the number of relevant interview fragments for each of the proposed partnership motives. As can be inferred from this table, good support was found for all of the proposed motives. The spokes' capabilities to open up new markets for the hubs were most often mentioned as a reason for partnering. From the two other aspects, the capabilities to develop modular innovations seemed to be the second most important. Finally, the capability to provide niche functionalities was mentioned least often. Overall, however, all three were mentioned regularly, giving good support for the proposed assumptions of their importance.

	Innovation	Functionality	Market
Total	39	31	47
Average	2.60	2.07	3.13

Table 1 Relevant Interview Fragments for each Capability

A closer examination of the content of the interview quotes largely confirmed the picture obtained from the frequency counting. Especially the capabilities of spokes to react to customer needs and to establish a good relationship to them was mentioned by the interviewees in the case. Moreover, the large hub corporation was not inclined to address all specific niche markets. Rather, it deliberately decided to partner with small companies in order to provide the necessary solutions for these contexts. Closely related to this broader market reach is the hub's second motive of adding niche functionalities to its platform. Indeed, the choice not to cover all possible domains of an IS was a deliberate one by the hub. Especially for those functionalities that were tightly integrated with other technologies, such as certain machinery, or for those for which a well established de-facto standard existed, partnering was considered attractive. Thus, ample support was found for the proposition that complementary functionalities are motivating partnership formation. Finally, access to innovative capabilities was seen as a main impetus for forming partnerships. Indeed, the hub realized the need for a new innovation model. The interview partners acknowledged that by restricting the sources of innovation to its own organization, the hub would fall behind. By virtue of their smaller size, spoke companies were found to possess the agility and flexibility that the hub was unable to realize. The entrepreneurial spirit of the spokes was deemed necessary to successfully pursue innovative ideas at the modular level.

4. A Process Model of Partnership Formation

The previous section has revealed that all three proposed motives play an important role in the hub's decision to partner. However, further analysis of the data shows that not all motives are equally important for all partners. Rather, different kinds of partnerships can be identified: Some partners are loosely attached to the network, others are tightly connected; some partnerships exist only for a brief time span, others are long lasting. Studying these differences reveals that the static perspective only insufficiently explains the underlying patterns of network formation. Rather, partnerships between hub and spokes go through various stages, which are characterized by these differences in the cooperation. In this context, the above discussed three motives may not only be viewed as drivers for network formation, but also as events that trigger the transition between the stages in this developmental sequence [40].

Essentially, our process model closely resembles the one proposed by [10], who argue that cooperations between hospitals evolve through emergence, transition, maturity, and critical crossroads. Translated to hub-and-spoke networks in the IS development industry, we find five stages that are traversed throughout the process of partnership formation: (0) the initial stage, (1) the awareness stage, (2) the partnership formation and integration stage, (3) the joint market access stage, and (4) the re-evaluation stage, where the partnership can take alternative trajectories from continuation to ending. In the initial stage, both hub and spoke operate independently, developing innovative solutions. This is followed by the awareness stage where hub and spoke become aware of each other's innovations. At this point, it is important to note that innovations of the spokes are perceived as being attractive if they represent existing software solutions that are already sold in the market, rather than concepts or ideas that may potentially become innovations. While in the awareness stage, hub and spoke may build an informal relationship, the next stage is the partnership formation and integration stage, where the hub formally certifies the technical integration capability of the spoke's solution with the hub platform. This requires cooperation between hub and spoke personnel on a technical level. Once solution integration is officially ensured, the next stage is joint market elaboration and access of hub and spoke. This joint addressing of markets is considered a recurring event that ensures the ongoing cooperation between the involved partners. Since the final goal of the hub is revenue generation, innovative ideas not only have to be turned into software solutions that are compatible with the hub platform; they have to be turned into integrated, *marketable* software solutions. Thus, once joined market campaigns are initiated, this leads to the final, ongoing stage, where the success of the partnership is evaluated. This may result in two trajectories. First, the partnership may continue. Second, the hub may decide to take over the functionality of the spoke by either integrating the spoke organization or substituting its solution.

We found the choice between these two trajectories to be dependent on the type of alignment between hub and spoke solution. While we assumed that the hub was looking primarily for complementary functionalities, we also found evidence that the hub was partnering with spokes that were providing supplementary functionalities (i.e., *similar* functionalities brought into the relationship) [9]. As it has been discussed above, the case company had a well developed understanding of what was part of its solution portfolio and what was assumed to be developed by partners. Thus, the parts that were intentionally developed by partners, such as infrastructure components, were indeed complementary. For these, partnership relations were found to be rather stable in that partners were allowed to pursue their own developments.

The large hub was found to also partner with those small companies that were offering functionalities that the case company considered to be within the scope of its system, mainly business functionalities. However, this was only the case for functionalities not covered by any actual solution of the large company. We term this constellation *latent* supplementary or *temporary* complementarity. In such a situation, the partner was providing a solution that the case company was actually willing to provide itself, however, had so far been unable to, for whatever reasons. Those partners had similarly fruitful relationships with the case company as those that provided infinitely complementary functionalities. The situation was found to be entirely different, however, if the small spoke partners provided supplementary functionalities. These were indeed allowed to partner if customers actually demanded their specific niche functionalities. However, these relationships were not found to be very stable. Indeed, the case company actively attempted to integrate these functionalities into its own system.

To sum up, it can be argued that the partnership process is a cyclic one. It starts with an innovation that is developed by a partner. Once it becomes clear that this innovation is attractive for customers, it is technically integrated with the platform of the case company. This integrated solution is then expected to be successfully sold in the market. Once this market success is achieved, the next step depends on the nature of the partner's solution. If it is an infrastructure or niche solution, the partnership continuous to exist as long as it is successful in the market and the solution stays in its niche. If the large hub, however, decides that the solution is supposed to become part of the platform, it either develops its own solution that imitates the functionalities of the existing partner solution, or it outrightly acquires the partner organization. If a partner company's management wants to stay independent, it is then required to come up with a new innovation, and the process begins anew. The overall structure of this partnership process is illustrated in Figure 2.

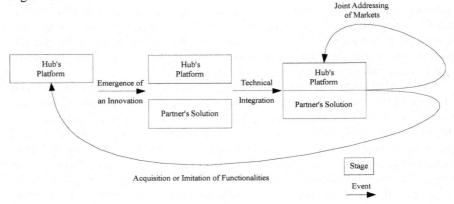

Fig. 2 The Innovation Cycle in IS Development Networks.

5. Conclusions

This paper addressed the question why large IS development companies not only join but even actively foster IS development networks. Drawing from the perspective of the duality of inducements and opportunities, spokes' capabilities were analyzed which were assumed to make them attractive partners for the hubs. Three of these were theoretically developed and further analyzed in a case study of one large IS developer. In this case, indeed all three aspects were found to be important. However, it also became obvious throughout this case that the reasons for this strategy cannot be fully understood from a variance theory perspective. Rather, the entire life cycle of such a partnership has to be examined. A model of this life cycle starts with an innovation of a spoke company, which is then integrated with the overall system, and finally successfully brought to market.

However, what has also been found is that IS development differs from traditional manufacturing in that these relationships are not necessarily stable. Rather, the distinction between complementary and supplementary functionalities has been introduced in order to differentiate those partnerships that are indeed stable from those that are not. Moreover, the novel concept of temporal complementarities has been introduced. These are functionalities that are currently complementary, but which over time can be assumed to turn into supplementarities. Partners that provide such solutions were found to be engaged in an innovation race, which forces them to come up with a novel solution before the hub acquires them or, even worse, imitates their solution.

References

1. Ahuja, G.: The Duality of Collaboration: Inducements and Opportunities in the Formation of Interfirm Linkages. Strategic Management Journal 21(3), 317 – 343 (2000)
2. Arndt, J.M., Dibbern, J.: The Tension between Integration and Fragmentation in a Component-Based Software Development Ecosystem. In: R.H. Sprague Jr. (ed.) Proc. of the 39th HICSS. IEEE Computer Society, Washington (2006)
3. Baldwin, C.Y., Clark, K.B.: Design Rules - Volume 1. The Power of Modularity. The MIT Press, Cambridge (2000)
4. Baumol, W.J.: The Free-Market Innovation Machine - Analyzing the Growth Miracle of Capitalism. Princeton University Press, Princeton (2002)
5. Butler, J.: Risk Management Skills Needed in a Packaged Software Environment. Information Systems Management 16(3), 15 – 20 (1999)
6. Campbell-Kelly, M.: From Airline Reservation to Sonic the Hedgehog: A History of the Software Industry. The MIT Press, Cambridge (2003)
7. Christensen, C.: The Innovator's Dilemma: When New Technologies Cause Great Firms to Fail. Harvard Business School Press, Boston (1997)
8. Curley, K.F., Pyburn, P.J.: "Intellectual" Technologies: The Key to Improving White-Collar Productivity. Sloan Management Review 24(1), 31 – 39 (1982)
9. Das, T.K., Teng, B.S.: A Resource-Based Theory of Strategic Alliances. Journal of Management 26(1), 31 – 61 (2000)
10. D'Aunno, T., Zuckerman, H.: A Life-Cycle Model of Organizational Federations: The Case of Hospitals. The Academy of Management Review 12(3), 534 – 545 (1987)
11. Davenport, T.H.: Putting the Enterprise into the Enterprise System. Harvard Business Review 76(4), 121 – 131 (1998)
12. Denning, P.J.: The Social Life of Innovation. Communications of the ACM 47(4), 15 – 19 (2004)
13. Dibbern, J., Winkler, J., Heinzl, A.: Explaining Variations in Client Extra Costs between Software Projects Offshored to India. MIS Quarterly 31 (Special Issue on IS Offshoring - forthcoming) (2008)
14. Drucker, P.F.: Innovation and Entrepreneurship, Butterworth Heinemann, Oxford (1994)
15. Eisenhardt, K.M., Schoonhoven, C.B.: Resource-based View of Strategic Alliance Formation: Strategic and Social Effects in Entrepreneurial Firms. Organization Science 7(2), 136 – 150 (1996)

16. von Everdingen, Y., van Hillegersberg, J.,Waarts, E.: ERP Adoption by European Midsize Companies. Communication of the ACM 43(3), 27 – 31 (2000)
17. Fan, M., Stallaert, J., Whinston, A.B.: The Adoption and Design Methodologies of Component-Based Enterprise Systems. European Journal of Information Systems 9(1), 25 – 35 (2000)
18. Gawer, A., Cusumano, M.A.: Platform Leadership. Harvard Business School Press, Cambridge (2002)
19. Hagedoorn, J.: Understanding the Rationale of Strategic Technology Partnering: Interorganizational Modes of Cooperation and Sectoral Differences. Strategic Management Journal 14(5), 371 – 385 (1993)
20. Henderson, R.M., Clark, K.B.: Architectural Innovation: The Reconfiguration of Existing Product Technologies and the Failure of Established Firms. Administrative Science Quarterly 35 (Special Issue: Technology, Organizations, and Innovation), 9 – 30 (1990)
21. Ireland, R.D., Hitt, M.A., Vaidyanath, D.: Alliance Management as a Source of Competitive Advantage. Journal of Management 28(3), 413 – 446 (2002)
22. Kerlinger, F.N., Lee, H.B.: Foundations of Behavioral Research, 4th ed., Harcourt College Publishers, Fort Worth (2000)
23. Kumar, K., van Dissel, H.G., Bielli, P.: The Merchant of Prato - Revisited: Toward a Third Rationale of Information Systems. MIS Quarterly 22(2), 199 – 226 (1998)
24. Lee, A.S.: Researching MIS. Oxford University Press, Oxford (1999)
25. Mathiassen, L.,Vainio, A.M.: Dynamic Capabilities in Small Software Firms: A Sense-and-Respond Approach. IEEE TEM 54(3), 522 – 538 (2007)
26. McIlroy, M.D.: Mass Produced Software Components. In: Naur, P., Randell, B. (eds.) Software Engineering, pp. 138 – 156. NATO Science Committee, Garmisch (1969)
27. Mertens, P.: Integrierte Informationsverarbeitung 1, 15th ed., Gabler, Wiesbaden (2005)
28. Messerschmitt, D.G., Szyperski, C.: Software Ecosystem - Understanding an Indispensable Technology and Industry. The MIT Press, Cambridge (2003)
29. Miles, M.B., Huberman, A.M.: Qualitative Data Analysis. Sage, Thousand Oaks (1994)
30. Miles, R.E., Miles, G., Snow, C.C.: Collaborative Entrepreneurship - How Communities of Networked Firms Use Continuous Innovation to Create Economic Wealth. Stanford Business Books, Stanford (2005)
31. Orton, J.D.,Weick, K.E.: Loosely coupled systems: A Reconceptualization. Academy of Management Review 15(2), 203 – 223 (1990)
32. Shapiro, C., Varian, H.R.: Information Rules - A Strategic Guide to the Network Economy. Harvard Business School Press, Boston (1999)
33. Snow, C.C., Miles, R.E., Coleman, H.J.: Managing 21st Century Network Organizations. Organizational Dynamics 20(3), 4 – 20 (1992)
34. Soh, C., Kien, S.S., Tay-Yap, J.: Cultural Fits and Misfits: Is ERP a Universal Solution? Communications of the ACM 43(4), 47 – 51 (2000)
35. Somers, T.M., Nelson, K.G.: A Taxonomy of Players and Activities across the ERP Project Life Cycle. Information and Management 41(3), 257 – 278 (2004)
36. Sommerville, I.: Software Engineering, 7th ed., Pearson Education Limited, Harlow (2004)
37. Sprott, D.: Componentizing the Enterprise Application Packages. Communications of the ACM 43(4), 63 – 69 (2000)
38. Staudenmayer, N., Tripsas, M., Tucci, C.L.: Interfirm Modularity and its Implications for Product Development. Journal of Product Innovation Management 22(4), 303 – 321 (2005)
39. Teece, D.J., Pisano, G., Shuen, A.: Dynamic Capabilities and Strategic Management. Strategic Management Journal 18(7), 509 – 533 (1997)
40. van de Ven, A.H.: Suggestions for Studying Strategy Process: A Research Note. Strategic Management Journal 13 (Special Issue: Strategy Process: Managing Corporate Self-Renewal), 169 – 191 (1992)
41. Yin, R.K.: Case Study Research - Design and Methods, Applied Social Research Methods Series, vol. 5, 3rd ed., Sage, Thousand Oaks (2003)

Challenges of Consumer Information Systems Development: The Case of Interactive Television Services

Tuure Tuunanen, Michael D. Myers, and Harold Cassab

The University of Auckland, NZ

Abstract: We suggest that a new type of information system appears to be increasing in importance, that of *consumer information systems*. Compared with traditional information systems development approaches, where the focus is on improving the efficiency and effectiveness of organizational processes, design for consumer information systems focuses more on the enjoyment, pleasure and purchases of the consumer. We argue that the shift in focus from *users* to *consumers* in consumer information systems calls for a significant re-appraisal of our current information systems development methods. Hence, this paper proposes a new research agenda for IS researchers focusing on the development of consumer information systems. We plan to pursue this agenda by primarily using design science research, supplemented by other research methods as needed. The expected contributions include new insights into effective management processes for service design, a better understanding of issues of integration of information systems development practices used to develop consumer information systems, and the development of methods for requirements discovery for service innovation. These three components aim to contribute to a holistic evaluation of consumer information systems.

1. Introduction

We believe we may be entering a new era of Consumer Information Systems (CIS). Until now most information systems have been developed to improve the efficiency and effectiveness of organizations. However, the rationale for the development of CIS is different: it is to facilitate the enjoyment and pleasure of the consumer. A consumer is defined by the Concise Oxford English Dictionary as:

1. a person or thing that eats or uses something.

Please use the following format when citing this chapter:

Tuunanen, T., Myers, M.D. and Cassab, H., 2008, in IFIP International Federation for Information Processing, Volume 274; *Advances in Information Systems Research, Education and Practice*; David Avison, George M. Kasper, Barbara Pernici, Isabel Ramos, Dewald Roode; (Boston: Springer), pp. 89–100.

2. a person who buys goods and services for personal use (Soanes & Stevenson, 2004).

As can be seen from this definition, the primary meaning of a consumer is of a person who "eats or uses something." The secondary meaning is of person who purchases a service or product. Hence, it is possible for someone to enjoy watching a TV program (consume it) without having to pay for it. In this case, the TV program may actually be "paid for" (indirectly) by advertising. An alternative, of course, is for consumers to purchase TV programs directly (e.g. via a subscription service or pay per view).

It seems to us that the design and development of consumer information systems requires a change in the way we have traditionally thought about users (Lamb & Kling, 2003). Users have been conceptualized as mostly concerned about the effectiveness and efficiency of work processes. Consumers, on the other hand, are mostly interested in the enjoyment or pleasure associated with "consuming" a product or service. Users have been thought of as passive "users" of the system (as compared with "developers"). Consumers, by contrast, can be much more active in their use of a product or system. This is especially the case with the emergence of new internet-enabled multimedia services where consumers can become participants and co-creators of the television experience or "service". Another difference between users and consumers is that of scale: the number of consumers potentially involved in the development process is very large. Finally, the concept of services (Grönroos, 2007; Menor, Takikonda, & Sampson, 2002) takes centre stage (as opposed to the idea of creating a distinct IS software product). The focus shifts to innovating, designing and developing internet-enabled services.

This feature of co-creation of the service is facilitated by the social interaction between consumers and producers of services via different feedback mechanisms (such as Facebook-type services). The IP-Television concept, e.g. Joost.com, is one novel way to use the Internet to distribute on-demand digital programming in this fashion. Another example is Mobile Television that merges cellular phones with digital Television broadcasts and rapid feedback mechanisms, like texting. These technological changes are driving the market toward real Interactive Television systems, which will enable consumers not only to participate, but also to be part of the programming i.e. co-creators of CIS.

In this paper, then, we propose a research agenda to investigate the challenges academics and practitioners are likely to face when developing consumer information systems. Our targeted case domain area will be Interactive Television services. We review requirements discovery, information systems development, and service design literature, in order to develop a preliminary framework to drive the proposed research agenda. Finally, we discuss the potential contributions of this paper to IS research and practice.

2. Consumer Information Systems: Challenges for Research

An information system is often defined as the interplay of technology, software and people with the purpose of storing, distributing and communicating information. Others have described an information systems as a system of communication used by members of some human group (Bastek, Tuunanen, & Gardner, 2008; Beynon-Davies, 2002). Consumer Information Systems have been defined as

> A system that uses information technology to provide consumers with services to access, process, and manipulate data over the Internet (Bastek, Tuunanen, & Gardner, 2008).

Our paper seeks to understand more about CIS: how consumer requirements can be determined; the possible changes required to information systems development processes; and finally, design of consumer targeted services. We review relevant literature and raise a few research challenges below.

2.1 Requirements Discovery

Various disciplines have been dealing with the issues surrounding the problem of recognizing the needs of end-users of services and products. In Information Systems the usual way of trying to solve these problems has been to determine the needs of the organizational end-user and then to analyze the data in order to achieve requirements specification of feasible quality (Byrd, Cossick, & Zmud, 1992; Davis, 1982; Keil & Carmel, 1995). More recently, however, it has been suggested that users should be reconceptualized as "actors" (Lamb & Kling, 2003). In marketing, a specific discussion has emerged regarding the issues of developing new products. In this field, the problems have been approached more from a consumers' point of view, and the new product development discipline has been strongly arguing for involving them in the development process (Thomke & von Hippel, 2002).

Within the software engineering discipline, requirements engineering has been focusing on the issues surrounding the problems in eliciting, analyzing, validating, and managing end-users' requirements (Dubois & Pohl, 2003; Jarke & Pohl, 1994). The requirements phase has traditionally been regarded as a phase to "capture" end-user requirements. However, recently this view has started to change. Jirotka and Goguen (1994) have recommended using the term "elicitation" instead of "capture" so as to avoid the suggestion that requirements are out there to be collected simply by asking the right questions. Bergman et al. (2002) suggest that requirements are defined in a political process between the stakeholders.

Building on this recent work, some IS researchers have suggested that requirements elicitation is a voyage to discovering end-users' needs (Mathiassen, Saarinen, Tuunanen, & Rossi, 2007), modeling them using suitable techniques, and finally finding consensus among stakeholders in their prioritization. They have further characterized specific risks associated with CIS kinds of development projects, such as the availability of requirements. If we consider developing consumer information systems for global markets or even for regional markets, how we can reach these end-users efficiently? Tuunanen et al (2004) have proposed specific features to be considered for requirements discovery methods. Among others they raise context and reach as important features for such methods. Context of the developed systems always affects the user experience. The question remains, according to Tuunanen et al (2004), how we can understand the user context of consumers. Similarly, they point out that the techniques used should be able to reach multitudes of users outside of the developing organization cost-efficiently. This leads us to propose our first research question (RQ):

RQ1: How is it possible to elicit consumers' requirements effectively?

2.2 Information Systems Development

The history of Information Systems development can be characterized as a venture to find solutions for raising the productivity of developers, making systems less defective, or developing systems by techniques that pay more attention to the end-users and their needs (Brooks, 1975). Hirschheim et al. (1995) define information systems development as an "organized collection of concepts, methods, beliefs, values and normative principles supported by material resources". They summarize this as a methodology for Information Systems development. Hence we focus on information systems development (ISD) methods in relation to CIS.

Methods for ISD began with the 'code-and-fix' approach (Boehm, 1988). This method was blamed for many problems, starting with poorly understood requirements and problematical structure of coding and resulting in great expenses when fixes are needed later on (Boehm, 1988). The more structured 'waterfall model' emerged as a systematic, sequential solution to software development problems (Brooks, 1975; Hirschheim, Klein, & Lyytinen, 2003). With this method, the IS artifact was not delivered until the whole linear sequence had been completed. With the waterfall method, researchers also became more focused on requirements. Determining requirements was considered to be essential and it was suggested to collect them at the start of the development process.

As projects became larger and more complex, such problems as stagnant requirements and badly structured programming started to emerge. Through an overlapping of the development phases (Sommerville, 2001) and through the introduction of the more incremental spiral model (Boehm, 1988; Iivari, 1990a,

1990b) it was possible to tackle many of the difficulties mentioned above. Recently, different agile methods (Merisalo-Rantanen, Tuunanen, & Rossi, 2005) have gained recognition. Agile methods return to the idea of focusing on working on the code and minimizing documentation, but at the same time trying to maximize customer satisfaction by involving end-users.

However, there is no agreement in the literature with respect to how users of CIS should be involved in the development process. Participatory design (Clemont & Besselaar, 1993; Smart & Whiting, 2001; Vredenburg, Mao, Smith, & Carey, 2002) and the Scandinavian IS development approach (Iivari & Lyytinen, 1999; Kautz, 2001) have been suggested as answers, but exact ways of connecting these approaches with the required development methods for CIS are not present in the literature (Tuunanen, 2003). Thus we present our second research question:

> RQ2: How is it possible to modify contemporary information systems development methods for consumer information systems?

2.3 Service Design

What is a service? Various definitions exist, but usually the IS research literature concentrates on the difference between physical products and services (Penttinen, 2007). The characteristics of services are often addressed by providing sets of attributes inherent to services as contrasted with products (Bastek, Tuunanen, & Gardner, 2008). Lovelock and Wirtz (2004) capture the essence of services with the notion that a service is any act, performance, or experience that one party can offer to another and that is essentially intangible and does not result in ownership. Traditionally, services have been considered to have the unique characteristics of intangibility, heterogeneity, inseparability of production and consumption, and perishability. Recently, the generalizability of these characteristics has been challenged (Lovelock and Gummeson, 2004), driving the need for contemporary perspectives in service research.

Clearly, it is important to understand consumer requirements in order to deliver a service that meets consumers' needs. Hill et al (2002) suggest that the flow of the service experience and time of flow of the delivered service is important to consumers, as is the emotional responses of consumers to the service. They present a needs-based approach to understand the consumer, which offers a way of conceptualizing consumer evaluations of a service that is different from the usual "met expectations" model (Zeithmal, Parasuraman, and Berry, 1985).

The consumer-based approach thus raises questions about how the service design process should be conducted (Hill et al., 2002; Menor, Takikonda, & Sampson, 2002). Stuart and Tax (2004) have called for an integrative, holistic service design approach, which would tie together all the areas needed for designing a successful service. Menor et al (2002), however, remain uncertain about the actual method needed for new service design. Thus we present our third and final research question:

> RQ3: How is it possible for CIS development and requirements discovery methods to take account of the service nature of consumer information systems?

3. Research Agenda for Consumer Information Systems Development: The Case of Interactive Television Services

We see fascinating possibilities in terms of understanding how to develop Consumer Information Systems and Interactive TV Services in particular. We have proposed three specific research questions drawn from the literature to set the basis for our research agenda (see Table 1). The focus of study will be to understand consumers' requirements and development methods to support the development of a service. The theoretical framework connecting these is presented in Figure 1 below. We see that the interaction between requirements discovery, information systems development, and service design will drive towards a need for a more holistic approach to consumer information systems development. Thus, our main research objective (RO) will be

> RO: The design of a holistic approach to consumer information systems development.

RQ1: How is it possible to elicit consumers' requirements effectively?
RQ2: How is it possible to modify contemporary information systems development methods for consumer information systems?
RQ3: How is it possible for CIS development and requirements discovery methods to take account of the service nature of consumer information systems?

Table 1. Research questions

We will use **Interactive Television Services** as the domain of the study. Interactive Television Services will see the convergence of current IP-TV, mobile and web based services to one distinct service targeted to mainstream consumers of global markets. We define the concept of *interactivity* as anything that lets the consumer engage in a dialogue with the provider of the given service enabling him or her to make choices and take actions to influence the content of the provided service (Bastek, Tuunanen, & Gardner, 2008; Gawlinski, 2003). Currently, the contemporary technology platforms do not support development of such services, although platforms for broadcasting high quality video streams do exist[1]. Figure 2 displays some typical applications available today. These usually include electronic programme guides, chat or email clients, or games.

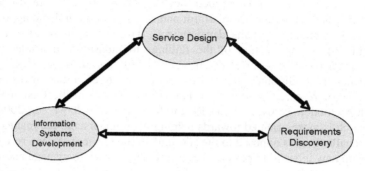

Fig. 1 Challenges of Consumer Information Systems Development

Our vision of Interactive Television Services includes more rich information media, such as two-way video streaming, interaction between participants in real time, and probably a strong social networking context (Peffers & Tuunanen, 2005). One possible application area could be tertiary education with students participating in a classroom, from campus, home or office with live interaction. Another possibility could be a variation of reality television where participants of the service would affect the course of the service, or more traditionally speaking, the programming on a live Television show. This kind of service will more likely also require active participation and understanding of media production from the developers.

Fig. 2 Industry examples of traditional Interactive Television Services, slightly modified from http://www.ortikon.com/press/

---

[1] Such as platforms by provided www.joost.com, www.redlynx.com and www.matrixstream.com

We plan to use Design Science Research to drive the research agenda (Hevner, March, Park, & Ram, 2004; Peffers, Tuunanen, Rothenberger, & Chatterjee, 2008). The framework is summarized in the figure below. The nominal research process is divided into 1) problem identification, 2) objectives, 3) creation of artifact (in this case Interactive TV platform and Services and a holistic approach to Consumer Information Systems development), 4) demonstration, 5) evaluation, and finally 6) communication of the findings to industry and academia. The framework also provides different entry points for the research. Our research agenda takes the traditional approach of problem-centered initiation. In order to answer specific research questions we intend to complement the Design Science Research Methodology with Action Research (Baskerville & Myers, 2004). Action research is more oriented towards helping us to understand the management-oriented challenges (as opposed to the "design" of the service). Action research also so opens up new interesting possibilities to investigate how to manage and use the newly developed platform.

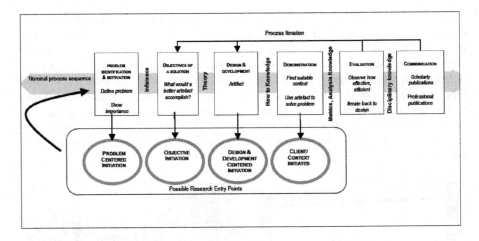

Fig. 3 Design Science Research Methodology, adapted from (Peffers, Tuunanen, Rothenberger, & Chatterjee, 2008)

The proposed research will be conducted in cooperation with industry and New Zealand universities. We are currently working with the University of Otago (Dunedin) and Victoria University (Wellington) to initiate the development of the Interactive Television Services platform. Furthermore, New Zealand industry participants have welcomed the research agenda. One of our first projects has included a case study of major corporate level players in IPTV (Bastek, Tuunanen, & Gardner, 2008) and the New Zealand Wireless and Broadband Forum[2], one of

---

[2] http://wirelessdataforum.co.nz

the largest industry associations in New Zealand, is actively involved in the study. Currently, we are actively recruiting media industry participants with whom we have been in talks e.g., TVNZ and Weta.

4. Research in progress

The proposed research is currently under way and we are at the 'problem identification' stage of design science research methodology (Peffers, Tuunanen, Rothenberger, & Chatterjee, 2008). More specifically, we are in the middle of the requirements discovery process to understand potential end-user requirements for Interactive Television Services for tertiary education. For this purpose we are using an adaptation of wide audience requirements engineering method (Tuunanen, Peffers, & Gengler, 2004), which incorporates an in-depth interviewing technique called laddering.

The laddering technique is based on the Personal Construct Theory (Kelly, 1955). With laddering, analysts can discover the implicit requirements of potential users of innovative products or services (Peffers & Tuunanen, 2005; Tuunanen, 2003; Tuunanen, Peffers, & Gengler, 2004). Laddering uses open-ended questioning with simple probing questions like "what would you like to have in this service" or "why this feature would be important to you" to discover features of the developed artifact. The follow-up questioning in turn opens up the understanding of why these provide value to the users. This process creates chains of ladders, which can be used for analyzing the priority of requirements.

Our current project uses potential lead-users (Rogers, 1995; von Hippel, 1986) of Interactive TV Services for tertiary education, namely first and second year undergraduate students in The University of Auckland Business School. Our initial target is to get approximately thirty laddering interviews done by end of March 2008 and do the preliminary analysis done by April. The pilot study tries to set objectives for a more elaborate way of discovering consumers' requirements and thus creates the basis for providing answers to our first research questions and eventually creation of the new requirements discovery method. We expect to have initial results to report in July-August 2008.

5. Conclusion

The paper has proposed a research agenda for investigating challenges of developing Consumer Information Systems. More specifically, we have focused on understanding how the change in concept of "end-user" in traditional information systems development methods to "consumer" potentially affects the overall design of the more service-oriented aspects of CIS.

We see the intersection of requirements discovery (Mathiassen, Saarinen, Tuunanen, & Rossi, 2007; Tuunanen, 2003), information systems development, and service design (Grönroos, 2007; Menor, Takikonda, & Sampson, 2002; Stuart & Tax, 2004) as a intriguing area of future research. We have suggested a set of research questions in order to understand how to best manage the CIS development process.

We have proposed Design Science Research (Peffers, Tuunanen, Rothenberger, & Chatterjee, 2008) as our primary research method. Our intention is to complement this approach with action research (Baskerville & Myers, 2004). Action research has been considered to be a good complement to Design Science Research (Järvinen, 2007; Rossi & Sein, 2003).

We have chosen one of the emerging application areas of CIS as our research domain. Interactive Television Services are just starting to become available. Our intention is help the TV industry to push the current envelope of provided services and create an Interactive Television Service platform for consumers. Furthermore, we expect that our action research co-operation with New Zealand industry will create further interesting uses for the developed platform.

The main academic contribution of our proposed research agenda lies in its contribution to the development of Consumer Information Systems. We propose integrating Service Design, information systems development, and requirements discovery practices. Furthermore, we see that we will be able to contribute by developing new ways for requirements discovery for consumer markets. Finally, the interactive nature of the developed services opens interesting research possibilities. How the change from passive to active participants, or even co-creation, changes "user" or "consumer" behavior is an interesting question.

Practical contributions for industry and education will emerge from building a test environment and prototype systems. One such possibility would be to use the local student population to build and create content for a national interactive TV IP-based network. After the piloting phase we could extend this nationally in New Zealand. This "live" Interactive TV media laboratory would enable New Zealand firms to trial Interactive TV services.

References

Baida, Z., Gordijn, J., & Omelayenko, B. (2004). *A shared service terminology for online service provisioning*. Paper presented at the 6th international conference on electronic commerce, Delft, The Netherlands.

Baskerville, R., & Myers, M. (2004). Special Issue on Action Research in Information Systems: Making IS Research Relevant to Practice — Foreword. *MIS Quarterly, 28*(3), 329-336.

Bastek, M., Tuunanen, T., & Gardner, L. (2008). Consumer Information Systems Service Families (pp. 10): The University of Auckland Business School.

Bergman, M., King, J. L., & Lyytinen, K. (2002). Large Scale Requirements Analysis Revisited: The Need for Understanding the Political Ecology of Requirements Engineering. *Requirements Engineering, 7*(3), 152-171.

Beynon-Davies, P. (2002). *Information systems - an introduction to informatics in organizations.* Houndmills: Palgrave.

Boehm, B. (1988). A Spiral model of software development and enhancement. *IEEE Computer, 21*(5), 61-72.

Brooks, F. (1975). *The Mythical Man Month: Essays on Software Engineering.* Reading, Mass, USA: Addison-Wesley.

Byrd, T. A., Cossick, K. L., & Zmud, R. W. (1992). A Synthesis of Research on Requirements Analysis and Knowledge Acquisition Techniques. *MIS Quarterly, 16*(1), 117-138.

Clemont, A., & Besselaar, O. (1993). A Retrospective look at PD projects. *Communications of the ACM, 36*(4), 29-39.

Davis, G. (1982). Strategies for information requirements determination. *IBM Systems Journal, 21*(1), 4-31.

Dubois, E., & Pohl, K. (2003). RE 02: A major step toward a mature requirements engineering community. *Ieee Software, 20*(1), 14-15.

Gawlinski, M. (2003). *Interactive television production.* Oxford: Focal Press.

Grönroos, C. (2007). *Service management and marketing - customer management in service competition.* Chichester: Wiley.

Hevner, A. R., March, S. T., Park, J., & Ram, S. (2004). Design Science in Information Systems Research. *MIS Quarterly, 28*(1), 75-105.

Hill, A. V., Collier, D. A., Froehle, C. M., Goodale, J. C., Metters, R. D., & Verma, R. (2002). Research opportunities in service process design. *Journal of Operations Management, 20*(2), 189-202.

Hirschheim, R., Heinzl, K. K., & Lyytinen, K. (1995). *Information Systems Development and Data Modelling*: Cambridge University Press.

Hirschheim, R., Klein, H. K., & Lyytinen, K. (2003). *Information Systems Development and Data Modeling : Conceptual and Philosophical Foundations*: Cambridge University Press.

Iivari, J. (1990a). Hierarchical Spiral Model for Information-System and Software- Development .1. Theoretical Background. *Information and Software Technology, 32*(6), 386-399.

Iivari, J. (1990b). Hierarchical Spiral Model for Information-System and Software- Development .2. Design Process. *Information and Software Technology, 32*(7), 450-458.

Iivari, J., & Lyytinen, K. (1999). Research on Information Systems Development in Scandinavia- Unity in Plurality. *Scandinavian Journal of Information Systems, 10*(1-2), 135-185.

Jarke, M., & Pohl, K. (1994). Requirements Engineering in 2001 - (Virtually) Managing a Changing Reality. *Software Engineering Journal, 9*(6), 257-266.

Jirotka, M., & Goguen, J. (Eds.). (1994). *Requirements Engineering: Social and Technical Issues*: Academic Press.

Järvinen, P. (2007). Action Research is Similar to Design Science. *Quality & Quantity, 41*(1), 37-54.

Kautz, K. (2001). Trends in the Research on Software Process Improvement in Scandinavia. *Scandinavian Journal of Information Information Systems, 13*, 3-6.

Keil, M., & Carmel, E. (1995). Customer Developer Links in Software-Development. *Communications of the ACM, 38*(5), 33-44.

Kelly, G. A. (1955). *The Psychology of Personal Constructs*. New York: W W Norton & Company.

Lamb, R., & Kling, R. (2003). Reconceptualizing Users as Social Actors in Information Systems Research. *MIS Quarterly, 27*(2), 197-235.

Mathiassen, L., Saarinen, T., Tuunanen, T., & Rossi, M. (2007). A Contigency Model for Requirements Development. *Journal of Association of Information Systems, 8*(11), 569-597.

Menor, L. J., Takikonda, M. V., & Sampson, S. E. (2002). New service development: areas for exploitation and exploration. *Journal of Operations Management, 20*(2), 135-157.

Merisalo-Rantanen, H., Tuunanen, T., & Rossi, M. (2005). Is Extreme Programming Just Old Wine in New Bottles: A Comparison of Two Cases. *Journal of Database Management, 16*(4), 41-61.

Peffers, K., & Tuunanen, T. (2005). Planning for IS applications: a practical, information theoretical method and case study in mobile financial services. *Information & Management, 42*(3), 483-501.

Peffers, K., Tuunanen, T., Rothenberger, M., & Chatterjee, S. (2008). A Design Science Research Methodology for Information Systems Research. *Journal of Management Information Systems, 24*(3), 45-78.

Penttinen, E. (2007). *Transition from products to services within the manufacturing business.* Unpublished Doctoral dissertation, Helsinki School of Economics, Helsinki.

Rogers, E. M. (1995). *Diffusion of Innovations* (4th ed.). New York: The Free Press.

Rossi, M., & Sein, M. K. (2003). *Design research workshop: a proactive research approach.* Paper presented at the Conference Name|. Retrieved Access Date|. from URL|.

Smart, K. L., & Whiting, M. E. (2001). Designing Systems that support learning and use: A Customer-centered approach. *Information & Management, 39*(3), 177-190.

Soanes, C., & Stevenson, A. (Eds.). (2004). *Concise Oxford English Dictionary* (11th ed.). Oxford: Oxford University Press.

Sommerville, I. (2001). *Software Engineering* (6th ed.): Addison-Wesley.

Stuart, F. I., & Tax, S. (2004). Toward an integrative approach to designing service experiences Lessons learned from theatre. *Journal of Operations Management, 22*(6), 690-627.

Thomke, S., & von Hippel, E. (2002). Customers as innovators - A new way to create value. *Harvard Business Review, 80*(4), 74-+.

Tuunanen, T. (2003). A New Perspective on Requirements Elicitation Methods. *JITTA : Journal of Information Technology Theory & Application, 5*(3), 45-62.

Tuunanen, T., Peffers, K., & Gengler, C. (2004). *Wide Audience Requirements Engineering (WARE): a Practical Method and Case Study* (No. W-378). Helsinki: Helsinki School of Economics.

von Hippel, E. (1986). Lead Users: A Source of Novel Product Concepts. *Management Science, 32*(7), 791-805.

Vredenburg, K., Mao, J., Smith, P. W., & Carey, T. (2002). A survey of user-centered design practise. *CHI Letters, 12*(2).

Zeithaml, V. A., Parasuraman, A., & Berry, L. L. (1985). Problems and strategies in services marketing. *Journal of Marketing, 49*(2), 33-46.

Improving diffusion of Information Technology in communities in a developing world context

Ronell Alberts[1] and Vreda Pieterse[2]

[1]Meraka Institute, Council for Scientific and Industrial Research, Pretoria, ZA,
ralberts@csir.co.za

[2]University of Pretoria, Department of Computer Science, Pretoria, ZA,
vpieterse@cs.up.ac.za

Abstract: Diffusion of information technology in a developing world context is difficult due to the fact that most of the targeted communities are in market neglect environments. Market neglect environments are characterised by a failure of the market to make an impact. In these environments the client base is marginalised, small or with low economic power. Consequently, the prospect for immediate return on investment or profit in the short or medium term is low in these environments. Software development for market neglect areas faces a number of unique challenges while still needing to produce products of high quality, on budget and on time. Traditional software methodologies have been applied in these areas with limited success, but due to the unique challenges within these areas, it has become apparent that a new or adapted software methodology is needed to ensure the effective diffusion of technology in market neglect communities. In this paper, we aim to pin down the unique problems experienced when developing for market neglect areas and to identify tools and methods required in a software development methodology to address these problems in order to improve the diffusion of information technology in market neglect areas.

1. Introduction

Software development methodologies share the common goals to accurately define requirements, structure the development effort, and deliver systems of high quality within a specific time frame and budget [1, 14, 5, 4]. Market neglect environments (MNEs) are areas where industry is not active due to the uncertain prospect of return on investment such as in developing world countries. Developing software and diffusion information technology interventions in MNEs pose unique challenges that differ from those encountered when developing and deploying software in a corporate setting. The quality of products developed in a MNE is dependent on the processes for knowledge acquisition and internal processes for the assimilation and application of technology and knowledge [22]. This implies that the application of an effective software development methodology, when developing software for the application in a MNE, is an essential factor to ensure that the

Please use the following format when citing this chapter:

Alberts, R. and Pieterse, V., 2008, in IFIP International Federation for Information Processing, Volume 274; *Advances in Information Systems Research, Education and Practice*; David Avison, George M. Kasper, Barbara Pernici, Isabel Ramos, Dewald Roode; (Boston: Springer), pp. 101–112.

information technology interventions developed have a positive impact on the community in the MNE, maintain the highest level of quality and are effectively diffused in the community.

Existing software development methodologies have been applied in software development projects for MNEs with limited success. However, a number of essential unique needs of MNEs are not being addressed. As a consequence, design, development and diffusion of information technology in communities of MNEs in the developing world context often fail. Therefore, there is a gap in the literature describing a software development methodology that effectively addresses the unique needs encountered in software development projects for MNEs. The definition of methodologies is done by specifying discrete methodology elements that are instantiated during the use of the methodology on specific projects as needed [11].

Methodologies such as the Crystal family [8] and Multiview [4] have been described to allow a development team to adapt the methodology for each project, based on the problem area and the team composition. Various authors have proposed the combination of techniques from different methodologies, for example Avison and Taylor [3] state that many situations will "require parts of several methodologies to be used", and McCormick [19] pleads for a Reform Party between the extreme beliefs held by Extreme Programming (XP) supporters on the one hand and those who endorse Capability Maturity Model (CMM) assessment on the other hand. Similarly, we aim to combine appropriate components of other methodologies in order to compile a software development methodology for the effective application in MNEs.

The objectives of our research are: to pin down the unique problems experienced when developing for MNEs and to identify tools and methods needed in a software development methodology that addresses the problems in order to improve the diffusion of information technology in MNEs. This work is of particular interest to organisations developing software for MNEs looking for a more effective software methodology to follow as well as institutions interested in adapting existing software methodologies to include support for software development for MNEs and diffusion of information technology interventions in MNE communities.

The structure of the paper is as follows: Market neglect environments are briefly discussed in Section 2 and the theoretical foundation and research design is described in Section 3. This is followed by a description of the case study and the findings in Section 4. The requirements for a software development methodology for application in MNEs, extracted from the findings, are described in Section 5. The paper is concluded in Section 6.

2. Market Neglect Environments

A market neglect environment (MNE) is defined as an environment where the market has failed to make an impact because the prospect for return on investment or profit is low in the short or medium term. The phrase *market neglect* originates from the concept of *market failure* and includes activities in a *pre-competitive* space. Market failure occurs when, without intervention, a market does not allocate resources efficiently [9]. Martin and Scott [18] argue that in the case of market failure, government funded intervention is needed to stimulate innovative activities to enable new companies and Small and Medium Enterprises (SMEs) to bring socially useful products to the market. Pre-competitive activities refer to research and development (R&D) which is distanced from the market and cover a spectrum from applied research to near-market development [22]. Pre-competitive R&D projects generate real economic effects in terms of new products, processes, innovative capabilities and knowledge [13].

Market neglect areas may occur when the client base is marginalised, small or with low economic power. This is particularly applicable to developing countries where the average economic power of potential users is low or where only a small section of the population will benefit, such as women, youth, disability groups and other marginalised communities. Effective diffusion of information technology is needed in MNEs for the upliftment of marginalised communities, empowerment through technology, and addressing problems related to the digital divide.

3. Theoretical Foundation

This research was conducted within an interpretive qualitative research tradition. Our ontological perspective is relativist and subjective. We therefore presuppose that there are multiple realities [6] and that what is taken as reality is an output of human cognitive process [15]. We also assume a subjectivist epistemology as identified by Lincoln and Guba [17]. In essence, it means that researchers and participants co-create understanding. This model provides a theoretic basis and analytic lens with which we investigated and established an understanding of the experiences of teams who are involved in software development for MNEs.

The research method used was that of a case study [23]. The method of interpretive case study was used to enable the exploration of the contemporary adaptation of a software engineering methodology application due to the change of the target market from industry to a MNE. The principles suggested by Klein and Myers [16] were followed. The principle of contextualization was particularly appropriate since the aim was to reflect on the historic background of the development team and its application of traditional software methodologies as well as the reaction of the team to the emerging need for a new software development methodology for a MNE.

Data was obtained through semi-structured interviews conducted with a range of role players. The interviewees included project managers, business analysts, a systems architect, software developers and researchers working on projects aimed at MNEs. Their responses were recorded through note taking during the interviews. The responses were analysed and coded using qualitative content analysis to solicit latent content as described by Graneheim and Lundman [12]. Concepts were extracted through comparison analysis by distinguishing between similarities and differences of stated experiences [21]. 105 distinct concepts were identified. The identified concepts were grouped together into six higher, more abstract categories [10] describing the limitations experienced in applying the traditional software development methodology in a MNE. The defined categories, i.e. the limitations experienced, are described in the findings in Section 4.

4. Case Study and Findings

The case study is based on software development teams in the Meraka Institute, part of the Council for Scientific and Industrial Research (CSIR) in South Africa. The Meraka Institute was established in 2005. One of the major objectives of the Meraka Institute is to facilitate research, development and implementation of information and communication technology (ICT) applications to address problems related to the digital divide in developing countries. The institute focuses on the pre-competitive space in areas of market neglect. The software development teams in the institute were originally part of a division of the CSIR involved in software development for government and industry. The software development teams are well established and have extensive experience in developing software products using established software development methodologies based on the principles of the Unified Process (UP) [14].

Through projects conducted in MNEs, it became apparent that although the use case driven, architecture centric, iterative and incremental characteristics of the UP still proved effective, unique challenges encountered in MNEs were not supported by the traditional software development methodology. The limitations of the current methodology experienced by the team are described in the following subsections.

4.1 Needs Assessment and Requirements Elicitation

The biggest flaw in the current methodology application is the methods and processes used for needs assessment and requirements elicitation. This limitation was mentioned by all interviewees in the case study. Needs assessment is ineffective and too technology focused for an area where users cannot articulate their needs effectively in technical terms. One of the analysts commented:

> Currently we may want to 'force fit' their needs into something that is familiar for us. We need a structured process where the user is involved, feels empowered and is able to participate.

The requirements are mostly defined by analysts, based on the knowledge gained from the domain and needs assessment. Opportunity for user centric design or interaction design is low due to the inaccessibility of representation of actual users and this has a negative effect on the confidence in the accuracy of the defined requirements. Due to the fact that there is no concrete client that has the final say on the requirements, there is a lack of trust in the requirements produced by the analysts. This leads to conflict between analysts and development teams. As one developer commented:

> We don't always trust the requirements from the analysts because we also have our own ideas.

Developers will challenge the requirements, or simply implement it the way they think it should be. This adds to the pressure on the analysis team to constantly reassess and defend the requirements after it has been defined.

4.2 Design and Implementation

Due to the unknown domain, frequent changes and tight deadlines, design is done informally and is mostly communicated verbally between team members. Limited or no technical documentation is produced and the resulting technical design is not visible. This leads to situations where it only becomes apparent that the design does not support the requirements when it has already been implemented, leading to conflict in the team and unnecessary rework. In addition, the lack of technical documentation makes it difficult for industry partners to come on-board during or after development and makes outsourcing of maintenance of completed products virtually impossible. As one manager remarked:

> There is always a scuffle when a prospective industry partner is identified to develop the technical documentation after the fact.

The current development methodology is experienced by the development team as being too rigid and does not allow for creativeness in the implementation phase. Research into emerging technology enables the technical team to identify opportunities for the application these technologies to the benefit of the market. Due to the requirement driven characteristic of the current methodology, these opportunities are not addressed and the creativeness of the technical team is not supported. A developer remarked:

> The most innovative ideas are ignored because it does not fit in the current plan or deliverable.

Requirements change frequently due to continuous research input, feedback from communities and the changing nature of the MNE. The continuous changes imply that the system must be regularly changed. This has a negative impact on the morale of the development team. In the words of a developer:

> Please just confirm that we did achieve what we set out to do before you change the goal posts again!

4.3 Evaluation and Deployment

Due to the low confidence in the requirements, it is not clear if the developed software addresses the real needs of the community and will make an impact in the market. There is no formal method for the evaluation of the effectiveness of the products in the community. User evaluation of completed products is difficult due to the inaccessibility of representative members of the user community. Deployment of products to the community in the MNEs is ineffective. The community does not understand the benefits of the technology or products and therefore does not use it. Ineffective communication, involvement and feedback from the ultimate beneficiaries remain big obstacles. An analyst commented:

> It is very difficult to get user buy-in and participation after deployment.

4.4 Research Activities

Due to the unstructured environment and unknown domain, research is needed to ensure impact in the communities. The activities for development in MNEs are a fusion of structured software development and research. The emphasis of the current methodology is on the software development activities alone while the team finds it difficult to include the research activities in the process. The unstructured nature of research activities makes it difficult to manage. This leads to two separate processes: one for software development and one for research. It is important to have synergy between research and development since sometimes research is needed to enrich the development activities, while other times development is needed to evaluate or enable research activities. The current methodology does not support this need. A researcher commented:

> The timelines of research does not always correlate to that of a development project. It often takes longer to do research than to build something that is defined.

4.5 Team Composition

Due to the unique and sometimes unknown nature of MNEs, skills from disciplines other than those traditionally used in software development projects are needed. This includes disciplines such as social researchers, psychologists, domain experts, and other non-technical role players active in the domain. The coordination and integration of efforts over such a diverse group is a challenge that is not usually experienced in software projects. A technical resource remarked:

> The social researchers and domain experts are working in such a fuzzy, non definable space. I really struggle sometimes to understand where they are coming from and what their findings have to do with the real world with real deliverables.

On the other hand, a social researcher commented:

> The technical team does not always understand the deeper needs of the community, and I struggle to articulate it in such a way that they do.

4.6 Management and Sustainability

Developing software for a MNE requires activities on various levels, including research, development, partner management, funding and political issues. Effective management of these activities is not addressed in the current methodology. This is verbalised by one manager noting:

> You have this idea in your head and what emerges is totally different. You plan everything carefully, and then it becomes a bit chaotic. However, chaos is not necessarily a bad thing because that is where creativity lives. It is just, in the end you need to produce something with proven quality which makes management important.

The current methodology does not support effective management of role players in the market, collaboration, follow-ups and client relationships. Since the funding bodies are not the ultimate beneficiaries, expectation management and appreciation of benefits are experienced as challenging. As a project manager indicated:

> The person paying the money is not the person benefiting from the system. So, the guy with the cheque book wants to see results, but the results can only be reported by the community who did not request the intervention and may be hesitant to use it.

All products and services developed for MNEs must be sustainable to ensure an extended lifetime after the initial development and deployment. Currently, sustainability issues such as the inclusion of technology partners and SMEs in the design and development of products, securing of funding, business plans etc., are not effectively addressed.

All of the above limitations highlight requirements of a methodology for application in MNEs. These requirements are discussed in the next section.

5. Identified Requirements

The limitations experienced in applying a traditional software development methodology as described in Section 4 lead to the definition of a number of requirements for a software development methodology to make it suitable for application in a MNE. The defined requirements and the effectiveness of some existing popular methodologies in addressing these requirements are discussed in more detail in the following subsections.

5.1 Needs Assessment and Requirements Definition

The requirement for effective needs assessment and requirements definition is defined from the limitations described in Section 4.1. This is due to the nature of MNEs where there is usually no articulated preconceived need and the user base is not clearly defined, geographically distributed and possibly technologically unsophisticated. Needs assessment techniques must not be technology focused and can benefit by including techniques from social research disciplines. The techniques must be effective to capture the diverse needs within a MNE user base and ultimately ensure a positive impact on the lives of the community in the market. In the absence of a client that can affirm or negate the validity of the defined requirements, it is crucial that the requirements definition techniques are sufficiently rigorous and transparent to ensure trust in the validity of the requirements.

Needs assessment and requirements definition techniques of most methodologies are not sophisticated enough since they assume an organisational context for needs assessment. In a MNE this is not necessarily the case where you most often deal with a community rather than an organisation. In addition, most methodologies rely on client confirmation of the defined requirements which is not always possible in MNEs. Per contra, the Soft Systems Methodology (SSM) [7] has a holistic approach to needs assessment which is very appropriate for MNEs. Unfortunately, SSM does not address requirements definition. Multiview [2] includes the needs assessment techniques from SSM and also involves computer specialists and the users in the requirements definition process which may render Multiview as more applicable for MNEs.

5.2 Technical Design

The limitations described in Section 4.2 highlight the need for appropriate technical design and sufficient technical documentation for communication within the development team and ultimate hand-over to other technical teams for further development and maintenance. This is a universal requirement. However, some agile methodologies, such as eXtreme Programming (XP) [5], neglect its importance. ETHICS [1, 20] also fails since it only supports design in terms of data flow and human-computer interaction design which we deem inadequate for MNEs. Fortunately many methodologies such as UP, Rapid Application Development (RAD) [1] and Multiview include formal documented technical design.

5.3 Introduction of New Technology

The requirement for mechanisms to allow the development team to introduce new technology in the form of features in existing products, where emerging technology will benefit the community, is defined from the limitations described in Section 4.2. It appears to be the case that most software development methodologies fall short in supporting this requirement.

5.4 Include Research Activities and Methods

The limitations described in Section 4.4 indicate that the inclusion of research activities and methods is required. Development of information technology interventions for MNEs usually implies research. Coordination between development and research activities is problematic due to the differences in focus and pace. Research results must be fed into software development activities while research needs, identified during development, should inform the research. Both social and technical research must be supported. Due to the combination of research and development activities, success cannot be measured on successful implementation of information technology in communities alone. Success should also be measured in terms of impact on the community, as well as contribution to the research body of knowledge. Most existing methodologies concentrate only on the software development process and do not include phases for research as required for MNEs. Multiview seems to be the most applicable methodology since it is based on the action research process and includes investigations into socio-technical aspects through methods such as ethnographic approaches and analysis of political aspects.

5.5 Coordination of Multi-disciplinary Teams

The requirement for coordination of multi-disciplinary teams is defined from the limitations described in Section 4.5. For the successful diffusion of technology in MNEs, it is important to employ experts from different diverse disciplines such as social research, psychology, domain experts, human-computer interaction, development, architecture, and analysis. The methodology should provide processes and methods for experts from different disciplines to communicate and coordinate their activities toward a common goal. Existing popular methodologies address the integration of disciplines usually associated with software development, but do not specifically allow for inclusion of disciplines that are not normally associated with software development. The analysis phase in Multiview and SSM is aimed at different aspects such as social, political and technical views. This leads us to believe that multi-disciplinary teams are better supported by these methodologies than some of the other methodologies.

5.6 Involvement of a Loosely Defined User Base

The limitations described in Sections 4.1 and 4.3 indicate that techniques to effectively involve a loosely defined user base are required. In MNEs, the user base is not clearly defined and may be technologically unsophisticated. However, it remains essential to effectively reach and include members of the user base in the software development activities and to empower them to contribute. Users should ideally be involved in activities such as requirement definition, interface design, usability evaluation, and quality assurance. The identification of the correct users from an undefined user base, definition of user evaluation test cases, effective user feedback mechanisms and utilisation of community champions must be addressed. In addition, techniques for the effective communication of the benefits to the community are essential to ensure user involvement throughout the process, effective diffusion and ultimate buy-in and adoption of the resulting systems and products. Most popular software development methodologies fully acknowledge the need for user involvement. However, the difficulty experienced in MNEs (where the users are not clearly defined, are technologically unsophisticated, and may be geographically distributed) is not explicitly addressed by any of the methodologies we are aware of.

5.7 Support Clients who are not the Beneficiaries

The requirement to support clients who are no the ultimate beneficiaries are defined from the limitations described in Sections 4.3 and 4.6. In MNEs, clients or funding bodies provide funding as part of their social responsibility for the benefit of a community or group other than themselves. The client, therefore, is not the ultimate beneficiary. The methodology should define mechanisms to quantify results, such as proven impact in the market, new knowledge generation and research outputs, to be presented to funding parties. In addition, it must also define techniques to ensure that the beneficiaries buy into the project and value the resulting products even if they did not pay for it. None of the methodologies we investigated seem to support this requirement.

5.8 Sustainability

The limitation described in Section 4.6 indicates that mechanisms to ensure sustainability are required. After the successful completion and deployment of information technology interventions in a MNE, the funding body and the initial development agency may withdraw from the process. The developed products must therefore be self-sustained through partnerships with SMEs and champions in the community, or ongoing funding streams must be secured to ensure the continuous life of the intervention. The methodology should address issues of sustainability such as business models, partnerships, funding, hand-over to SMEs and industry. None of the methodologies we investigated seem to support this requirement.

6. Conclusion

Software development for MNEs has similar challenges to traditional software development projects, such as the need for accurate requirements; applicable architecture decisions; iterative and incremental development; effective evaluation; and delivery of quality products on time. However, from the case study it seems that the nature of a MNE also creates unique challenges that are not addressed by traditional software development methodologies. These challenges include understanding unknown domains; effective needs assessment and requirements elicitation techniques; management of multi-disciplinary teams; and the coordination and support of software development and research activities. The UP has been applied in projects for MNEs, but with limited success. There are needs that are not addressed which cause difficulties in the projects. These include a need for a structured process that: (1) allows for technical creativity, multi-disciplinary activities and support for research activities; (2) work for a user base that is not defined, not accessible and may be technologically unsophisticated; (3) embraces cultural, social and language differences; and (4) enables development teams to develop quality products that address the real needs of a community.

It is apparent from the study that existing methodologies support some of the requirements for application in MNEs, but not all. Multiview seems to be the closest fit, but it still does not fully address all the requirements defined, and it will be necessary to adapt it to address the requirements such as (1) the need for controlled introduction of new technology; (2) involvement of a loosely defined user base; (3) support of clients who are not the beneficiaries; and (4) sustainability in the face of the possible withdrawal of the funding body and/or the initial development agency. It is proposed to adapt existing methodologies and combine techniques from different methodologies to support the needs of a specific application area such as MNEs. In addition, methods and techniques from other disciplines, such as human-computer interaction, interaction design, social research, psychology, action research and design research, should also be included in the methodology since it is essential that the development process for MNEs include both development and research activities. The application of such an adapted methodology will improve the diffusion of information technology interventions in MNEs.

Further research will entail the definition, implementation and evaluation of an adapted software development methodology that supports the defined requirements for application in MNEs.

References

1. D. Avison and G. Fitzgerald. Information Systems Development: Methodologies, Techniques and Tools. McGraw-Hill Education, 3rd edition, 2003.
2. D. Avison, A. T. Wood-Harper, A. T. Vidgen, and J. R. G. Wood. A further exploration into information systems development: The evolution of multiview2. Information Technology & People, 11(2):124–139, 1998.
3. D. E. Avison and V. Taylor. Information systems development methodologies: A classification according to problem situation. Journal of Information Technology, 12(1):73–81, 1997.
4. D. E. Avison and A. T. Wood-Harper. Multiview - an exploration in information systems development. Australian Computer Journal, 18(4), 1986.
5. K. Beck. Extreme programming explained. Addison-Wesley, 2001.
6. D. Y. Borochowitz. Teaching a qualitative research seminar on sensitive issues an autoethnography. Qualitative Social Work, 4(3):347–362, 2005.
7. P. Checkland and J. Scholes. Soft Systems Methodology in action. John Wiley & Sons, 1990.
8. A. Cockburn. Crystal Clear: A Human Powered Methodology for Small Teams. Addison-Wesley, 2004.
9. Economist. Market failure. http://www.economist.com, Last accessed: 2007/04/30.
10. B. Glaser and A. Strauss. Discovery of Grounded Theory. Strategies for Qualitative Research. Sociology Press, 1967.
11. C. Gonzalez-Perez and B. Henderson-Sellers. Templates and resources in software development methodologies. Journal of Object Technology, 4(4):173–190, 2005.
12. U. H. Graneheim and B. Lundman. Qualitative content analysis in nursing research: concepts, procedures and measures to achieve trustworthiness. Nurse Education Today, 24(2):105–112, 2004.
13. R. Grimaldi and N. von Tunzelmann. Assessing collaborative, pre-competitive R&D projects: the case of the UK link scheme. R&D Management, 32(2):165–173, 2002.
14. I. Jacobson, G. Booch, and J. Rumbaugh. The unified software development process. Addison-Wesley, 1999.
15. P. Johnson and J. Duberley. Understanding management research. London: Sage, 2000.
16. H. K. Klein and M. D. Myers. A set of principles for conducting and evaluating interpretive field studies in information systems. MIS Quarterly, pages 67–93, 1999.
17. Y. Lincoln and E. Guba. Paradigmatic controversies, contradictions, and emerging confluences In Handbook of Qualitative Research, 2nd edn. Sage, 2000.
18. S. Martin and J. T. Scott. The nature of innovation market failure and the design of public support for private innovation. Research Policy, 29(4-5):437–447, 2000.
19. M. McCormick. Technical opinion: Programming extremism. Commun. ACM, 44(6):109–119, 2001.
20. E. Mumford. Designing Human Systems: The ETHICS Method. Manchester Business School, 1983.
21. P. L. Munhall. Nursing research: A qualitative perspective. Jones and Bartlett Publishers, 2001.
22. P. Quintas and K. Guy. Collaborative, pre-competitive R&D and the firm. Research Policy, 24(3):325–348, 1995.
23. G. Walsham. Interpretive case studies in is research: Nature and method. European Journal of Information Systems, 4(2):74–81, 1995.

'Driving' IS projects

Marta Fernández-Diego and Julián Marcelo-Cocho

Departamento de Organización de Empresas
Universidad Politécnica de Valencia, ES

Abstract Using a didactical car-driving metaphor, this paper deals with a proactive way of 'driving' projects with high uncertainty. The centrality of problem complexity and problem uncertainty are demonstrated, the mapping of these to human cognition is reviewed, and the car-driving metaphor as 'driving' project management is developed. The MadPRYX 'suite' develops didactic car-driving models and practical scoreboard metrics, looking for successful equilibrium of *effectiveness-efficiency*, conditioned by the levels and types of complexity and uncertainty in the project process and its environment

Keywords: Complexity, Effectiveness, Efficiency, Evolution, Project Management, Risk, Success, Uncertainty.

1. Complexity and Uncertainty in projects

Complexity X and uncertainty Y are mega-factors, threats and contributors to project risk (risk of no meeting the project objectives and results). Indeed, they are essential characteristics of any project and their consideration is a necessary step for any decisive advance in a taxonomy, causality, and resolution of risk, the same as in other relevant managerial duties (Fernandez 2008).

Furthermore, complexity X and uncertainty Y can be shown to be not only necessary but sufficient for describing the risk of a project situation and its evolution within its environment (see Appendix). The proof begins by clarifying the underlying reasoning of important papers about project risk management based on ambiguous or fuzzy meanings of X and Y.[1] Next, this paper contributes mainly to build some *Advances in IS Project Management Research, Education, and Practice,* showing didactic Models of Project Driving (Marcelo 1999), and the practical MadPRYX 'suite' of Methods for Adapting and Driving Projects by their Risks, Uncertainty Y, and Complexity X (Marcelo 2007).

Finally, the proof of sufficiency opens the use of both X and Y for an efficient generalization of the project concept in all sectors that currently study the *theory of complexity* (Wagensberg 1994) in the perspective of a *theory of mega-complexity* (combining the project complexity and the uncertainty born in its environment).

---

[1] The INSEAD model (De Meyer 2002a 2002b) e.g. assumes X and Y being necessary but non sufficient conditions, since it shows two other risk mega-factors, *ambiguity and chaos*. But other well-known authors (Klir 1988) believe that ambiguity and chaos are only two types of uncertainty.

Please use the following format when citing this chapter:

Fernández-Diego, M. and Marcelo-Cocho, J., 2008, in IFIP International Federation for Information Processing, Volume 274; *Advances in Information Systems Research, Education and Practice*; David Avison, George M. Kasper, Barbara Pernici, Isabel Ramos, Dewald Roode; (Boston: Springer), pp. 113–124.

2. 'Planning on the Left Side and Managing on the Right'

This classical figure of the brain (Mintzberg 1976) is based on the *Hall Project Management Risk Model* (Hall 1998).[2] The Hall model, linking basic organizational and intellectual functions located in specific areas of the brain, covers six disciplines, Plan, Produce, Measure, iMprove, Discover , and Design (PPMMDD), installed in the four brain quadrants, covering dynamic/static and long-term/short-term functions and knowledge (see figure 1):[3]

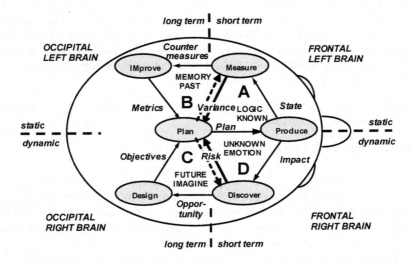

Fig. 1. Cerebral map showing 6 disciplines and 4 'circuits' (source: own development).

A. The *frontal left brain quadrant A* holds the *logic* of *known*, with influence on the 'circuit' PPM (Plan-Produce-Measure) which collects facts; analyses results; resolves problems in the short-term; reasons with the facts; understands the situation; and emphasizes the differences with respect to the plan.

---

[2] The use of brain maps for describing managerial functions has influential followers such as (Herrmann 1990) or (Webster 1999). In this paper, these maps have only been metaphorically taken, after confirmation of the level of support for the affirmations made by Hall by well known science publishers such as (Carter 1998). The quadrants indicate only complimentary functional areas in a brain totally interconnected, rather than tendencies or inclinations of any type.

[3] These four brain quadrants correspond to the four gnostic, temperamental and organizational 'circuits' MMP-PPM-PPD-DDP, related in this case to the driving of projects.

B. The *occipital left brain quadrant B* holds the *memory* of the *past*, with influence on the 'circuit' MMP (Measure-iMprove-Plan) which offers a long-term perspective to foresee prospects in a consistent and programmed manner.

C. The *occipital right brain quadrant C* supports *imagination* of the *future*, with influence on the 'circuit' DDP (Discover-Design-Plan) which provides long-term perspective on the circumstances; capitalizes on opportunities and develops a prospective vision based on own discovery.

D. The *frontal right brain quadrant D* holds a sense of *emotion* regarding the *unknown*, with influence on the 'circuit' PPD (Plan-Produce-Discover) which provides a short-term perspective regarding parts of the plan and production to be investigated; explores the requirements or technologies and its possible impacts on the plan; resolves problems intuitively; observes signs of imminent change; tolerates ambiguity; integrates ideas; and defies established policy.

3. Strategy for driving projects by their risks

The '*Project Driving*' concept (including Planning and Monitoring during Execution) goes a step further than the brain metaphor, using motor-racing metaphors when discussing the execution of project guidance: projects are vehicles, their development environment is a racing circuit, and project managers are drivers.

- In '*formula races*' we use delicate and complex machines with sophisticated features on specially prepared circuits with predictable risks (including perhaps a 'killer curve').
- In '*rallies*' we use robust vehicles on approximate and uncertain routes, with the boulevard and the crude animal path serving as road (such as the 'Paris-Dakar') full of predictable and unpredictable risks.

3.1. 'Formula' strategic model for driving projects

A single driver-manager can handle a highly complex project – providing the circuit only contains predictable variations (curves more or less risky), and providing that the environment does not contain unpredictable uncertainties (metaphorically, the circuit must be surrounded by an insurmountable crash barrier).

Although the driver uses all of his or her mental capabilities, he is basically using short-term frontal functions; whether to remember with the left hemisphere the logic of a 'known circuit'; or to anticipate an unknown factor in the curve ahead using the right hemisphere and adapt driving to the circuit (the predictable reference that structures the whole project). In this way he can focus all his attention on indicators of the vehicle's behaviour to guarantee the 'success' of the project (with policies and contingency plans to respond to predictable, but resolvable risk events such as breakdowns, punctures, fire, etc.).

3.2. 'Rally' strategic model for driving projects

Rally-style driving takes place on highly uncertain circuits and environments, with predictable and unpredictable risks, and requires two directors or at least, two functional directives (see figure 2).

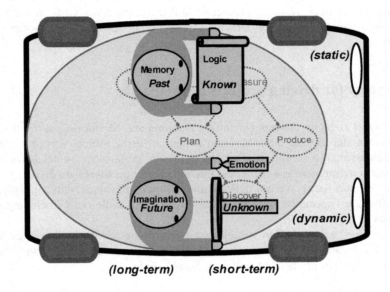

Fig. 2. 'Rally' driving, using both brain hemispheres (source: own development).

The co-driver monitors the circuit and its environment by reading a map. He tells the driver about the known risks on the circuit (predictable uncertainties) having acquired this information before the race as part of the planning process. In this way, he uses the functions of 'memory of the past' and 'logic of known' found in the left hemisphere of the brain.

The driver incorporates as 'imagination of the future' the preventive indications of the co-driver (predictable uncertainties); and performs the long-term manoeuvres (gear and speed changes). However, the driver uses the right cerebral hemisphere capabilities to handle the unknown (unpredictable uncertainties) that may arise, reacting with the brake and steering wheel.

Rally-style driving is best used in projects with great uncertainty, where the correlation of the functions of the driver and co-driver and the functions of both hemispheres are reflected and handled – according to the resources and capabilities available - by a team of specialist managers; or by a single manager with an uncommon ability to realize both functions, but capable of differentiating and combining the roles of driver and co-driver.

4. Proactive project driving

When confronted by risk from an incident generated by environmental uncertainty (a 'Murphy'), buffers of resources reserved for these risk situations allow the driver to continue. However, driving 'by sight' alone supposes not only a reactive step with respect to the project's environment, but a proactive step with respect to the project itself; learning to use a 'map' (project plan) when analyzing a situation, while resolving small and immediate incidents mechanically.

The *planning function*, in a situation of high uncertainty Y, is converted in a sense into a series of 'mappings' that; firstly, shortens the trip to the immediate 'journey' ahead with a certain and precise objective (meaning a sub-project or prototype, hereby baptised '*protoject*'); and secondly, virtually achieves the objective and so places the 'protoject' in the context of the project. The breakdown of the project in tasks changes, to becoming a set of iterations, or 'protojects', that are structured according to the most convenient segments and milestones from the point of view of the resolution of uncertainties (that is, predictable incidents). The 'danger map' establishes the most dangerous areas and the most adequate driving measures (for example, speed limits, extra resources to climb 'hills', environmental attention frequency, reviews, etc.).

The *monitoring function* is based on a comparison between what is indicated on the 'danger map' (performed by the co-driver function or something like an audio GPS system), and what is 'in sight' in each planned interval of the 'protoject'. This comparison requires the availability of a set of parameter measurers and measurement activators properly interrelated as a Balanced Scorecard; as well as interconnected between them (with measurement and action parameters adjustable as the project advances, in a similar way to automatic transmission or 'softness' of the suspension).

The 'by sight driver' must maintain global awareness of the project, as well as paying precise attention to the instruments and course, as suggested in the Theory of Constraints underlying the Critical Chain Project Management. The progressive depletion of the 'major resource reserve' (energy in the case of a vehicle) maintains a good level of efficiency in the project; while the 'small reserves' (including the activator's space-time margins) enable rapid rectifications required by the relevant contingencies.

5. Risk Management and Project Success Factors

The study of Critical Risk Factors of a project parallels the study of its Critical Success Factors, taken as a result of fulfilling the objective in a way that can be factorized and measured with two criteria:

- *Effectiveness* is an 'external' criterion of result comparison with the objective established outside of the development of the project; a qualitative criterion (client satisfaction, for example) that implies sub-criteria which are difficult to validate and rarely validated.
- *Efficiency* is an 'internal' criterion of result comparison with some reference related to the limitation of resources used in the project, or with the causes of its potential defects. Its measurement is quantitative or qualitative, and more or less subjective; but it can be referenced to the degree of advancement achieved by the project, which can, in turn, be determined by material and immaterial resources used by the participants.

These two criteria are not independent, but rather di-synergic or negatively synergic. *Efficiency* is more controllable, but impacts effectiveness when certain resources are unavailable. Strategic *ineffectiveness* (abortive shortages) conditions the interest of any tactic efficiency. Even in well organized projects without abortive shortages, a risk of minor non-fulfilment may produce an impact that always requires an increase in resources (meaning a controlled reduction in global *efficiency*) in order to redirect the project towards the objective.

In general, to achieve a certain level of *effectiveness* (or a threshold of risk represented by a limited distance between the result and objective), the level of *efficiency*, or used resource, depends on the levels of uncertainty Y in the development process, until the maximum level of *inefficiency* implied in abandoning of the project. Before arriving at such an unsatisfactory decision, the lowest possible consumption of resources will minimize waste and reduce inefficiency.

6. Basic characteristics of the MadPRYX method

The MadPRYX method collects the two project guidance strategies of 'formula' and 'rally' – and works by means of functions included in every project management, represented as a sequence of stages, as in PMBoK (ANSI 2004):

- *Initiating function* includes search and selection of all the possible information about the project and its environment and establishes an external objective for the project; assuring its viability (in clarity, scope, and resources).
- *Planning function* proactively prepares contingency plans and safeguard policies to prevent predictable risks, and responds to the appearance with necessary resources (including buffers).

- *Monitoring (of production) function* reacts to alerts (established in previous functions) with planned countermeasures (the policies deduced in the contingency plans for predictable uncertainties), and responds to the appearance of these risks with generic resources (buffers and others); and resolves unpredictable uncertainty. This function has the necessary flexibility to respond to unpredictable errors using adaptive buffers such as learning.
- *Executing function* includes the tasks reserved for the project manager – handled in parallel with his task of monitoring the production team operations.
- *Closing function* gathers experiences and project metrics to prepare for the application of new parameters to successive projects - as learning for predictable risks.

During the executing and monitoring stages, given the constructive necessities of the content of the project, the previously listed functions can, in the case of a high complexity X, be reiterated with respect to the itemised modules or the prototypes designed to reduce the high level of uncertainty Y.

7. Conclusion

This paper deals with a proactive way of 'driving' projects with high uncertainty, providing increased control by deviating from the reference (i.e., moving from a previous plan to one more adaptable to the evolving situation). The MadPRYX 'suite' develops didactic car-driving models and practical scoreboard metrics, looking for successful equilibrium of *effectiveness-efficiency*, conditioned by the levels and types of complexity X and uncertainty Y in the project process and its environment.

A second perspective deals with 'natural' systems evolution (that is, projects 'driven' by their environment, with high uncertainty Y due to weakness or lack of internal objectives): the system S evolves looking for its minor dependency of environment E for avoiding danger to the complexity X of system S by a 'catastrophic' deviation of the uncertainty Y due to environment E (not isolating system S, but increasing its capacity to anticipate and/or reducing the system S impact on its environment E).

Appendix A. Sufficiency of Complexity and Uncertainty as Project Management risk factors

Risk - defined as a variable related with change - in any project (seen as a dynamic *system S* interfacing with its *environment E*) needs two and only two mega-factors,

the complexity X of S and the uncertainty Y linked to relations between S and E. The proof will rely on two considerations:
1)   The characterization of both factors X and Y by two shapes of the same entropic variable in the two complementary sets S and E, embraceable by only one global entropic variable in the union ES of both sets, gathering both factors as instances of a *mega-complexity Z*.
2)   The exhaustive ecosystem ES of the 'universe' embraced by S and its E. That property is needed only for the boundary relations between S and E, where the 'distance' to the boundary would weaken, like in the gravitational models.

A.1 Complexity, uncertainty, entropy and information

The proof starts from the Shannon axiom about the conceptual identification between uncertainty and a kind of entropy, in order to extend this axiom to a new analogy between the complexity of the system and another type of entropy. If p(i) in the Shannon formula measures the probability that an individual belongs to the species i, the System Entropy or 'diversity' AI (the amount of average information of S) provides a measurement of its complexity. We can define both concepts of *System Complexity X* and *Environment Uncertainty Y* based on two different kinds of the same entropy; with S and E considered separately; or altogether, based on a combined entropy of the *combined ecosystem ES of S and E*.

In order to coordinate these three entropies, the *Information Theory* can be applied to ecosystem ES in its part referred to the source, alternatively or jointly with *Systems Theory*, reconstructing all the Shannon arguments on this combination of Information and Systems Theories. The 'ecomatic' model starts therefore from a structure of three sets (E, S, ES) with the three types of entropy that measure the different amounts of structural information needed to describe the system E, its environment S and the relation between both. The omission of any evolution parameter, like time t, does not imply that the situation can not be modified, but only that the regime is considered stationary or non transitory:
1)   The *complexity X of system S* is the entropy H of the structure (of states s_i) of S and measures in which degree its alternatives can be reached:

$$X[S] = H[S] = -\sum_n p(s_i)\log_2 p(s_i); X[S] \le \log_2 n; \tag{1}$$

$$S = \{p(s_i)\},$$

        where S is the set of probabilities of the n states s_i of S.
2)   The *uncertainty Y of environment E* is the entropy H of the structure (of states e_i) of E and measures in which degree its alternatives can be reached:

$$Y[E] = H[E] = -\sum_m p(e_j)\log_2 p(e_j); Y[E] \le \log_2 m; \tag{2}$$

$$E = \{p(e_j)\},$$

        where E is the set of probabilities of the m states e_j of E.

3) The *average entropy H[S/E]* of system S for a 'standard' state of environment E connects complexity and uncertainty in the ecosystem ES:

$$H[S/E] = \sum_m p(e_j)H[S/E = e_j]$$
$$= -\sum_m \sum_n p(e_j)p(s_i/e_j)\log_2 p(s_i/e_j) \qquad (3)$$

4) The *transmission T[S,E]* between S and E is the average amount of information trans-bordered, H[S] exits from S, but H[S/E] will not arrive to E:

$$T[S, E] = H[S] - H[S/E] = H[E] - H[E/S] = T[E, S] \qquad (4)$$

A.2 The internal complexity of the system, seen as a specialized connectivity

Reducing now the analysis to some structural parameters internal to the system S (out of its environment E), we define two probabilities of an 'informational' variable V (a concept that will appear latter) for each element or node i of S: the *probability p(Vr_i) of reception of V by i*; and the *probability p(Vd_i) of diffusion of V from i*. Each of them corresponds to this node i with respect to the n nodes of S:

$$p(Vr_i) = Vr_i/\sum_n Vr_i \,;\, p(Vd_i) = Vd_i/\sum_n Vd_i \qquad (5)$$

The connecting arcs between nodes (i,j) of S can be defined by the n^2 conditional probabilities $p(Vd_i/Vr_j)$, that is to say the part of all the V diffused from node i, whenever V would be received in node j, with respect to the whole reception in j. This *matrix of interaction $p(Vd_i/Vr_j)$* is related thus with the probabilities $p(Vd_i)$ and $p(Vr_j)$, where $p(Vd_i,Vr_j)$ is the probability of each connection (i,j).

$$p(Vd_i) = \sum_j p(Vd_i / Vr_j)p(Vr_j) = \sum_j p(Vd_i, Vr_j), \qquad (6)$$

Any flow graph of any type of variable V is considered like a transmission graph of V with arcs between two nodes, each one taken one time like a *source or global Diffuser $D_i\{Vd_i\}$* and another time like a *sink or global Receiver $R_j\{Vr_j\}$*.

The *entropy of the node i H[D_i]* is the amount of information diffused with respect to variable V and measured in bits:

$$H[D_i] = -\sum_i p(Vd_i) \log_2 p(Vd_i) \qquad (7)$$

H[D] can be considered like diversity of V exits; and H[R] like diversity of V entrances.

The *entropy of the connection between two nodes (i,j) $H[D_i,R_j]$* with respect to V can be represented by:

$$H[D_i, R_j] = \sum_i \sum_j p(Vd_i, Vr_j) \log_2 p(Vd_i, Vr_j) \qquad (8)$$

The *connectivity index $K[D_i,R_j]$* is the sum of the connection entropies between all the n nodes:

$$K[D_i, R_j] = \sum_n H[D_i, R_j] \tag{9}$$

The limit K_{min} corresponds to the less connected graph and K_{max} corresponds to the most connected or rigid graph, with n^2 equiprobable arcs, where n is the number of arcs or the number of nodes:

$$K_{min} = \log_2 n \tag{10}$$
$$K_{max} = 2K_{min}$$

K is thus a first complexity index of S that "measures uncertainty of the simultaneous events", according to [19]. In strict Information Theory and in the attainable domain of K:

$$K[D_i, R_j] = H[R_j] + H[D_i/R_j] = H[D_i] + H[R_j/D_i] \tag{11}$$

The *transmission of information* $T[D_i, R_j]$ by an arc (a 'noisy channel') with respect to V is also seen in strict Information Theory as:

$$T[D_i, R_j] = H[D_i] - H[D_i/R_j] = H[R_j] - H[R_j/D_i], \tag{12}$$

where

$$H[D_i/R_j] = -\sum_i \sum_j p(Vd_i)p(Vd_i, Vr_j)\log_2 p(Vd_i/Vr_j) \tag{13}$$

is also interpreted like a 'mistake'.

T carries on a specialization degree of interactions between nodes:

$$0 \prec T \prec \log_2 n, \tag{14}$$

that is the greatest specialization or transmissibility.

In the limit of a channel without noise, where

$$p(Vd_i/Vr_j) = p_{ij}, \tag{15}$$

the 'mistake' disappears; or it equals the value H of the source of information if the transmission is lost in the channel:

$$p(Vd_i/Vr_j) = p(Vd_i) \tag{16}$$

The *global 'mini-complexity' of system S* is a type of internal complexity resumed as the duple <K,T> of *connectivity K* and *specialization T* of the S graph. K and T are associated in several ways, as Venn diagram shows easily (see figure 3).

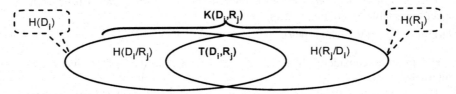

Fig. 3. Venn diagram for mini-complexity of system S (source: own development).

Thus:

$$K[D_i, R_j] + T[D_i, R_j] = H[D_i] + H[R_j] \leq 2\log_2 n \tag{17}$$

$$K[D_i, R_j] - T[D_i, R_j] = H[R_j/D_i] + H[D_i/R_j],$$

As $K - T \succ 0$; then $K \succ T$ \tag{18}

A.3 Interaction between the system S and its environment E

The partition of S into n components (or nodes) is initially arbitrary; but once conceived or made, the structural probabilities $\{p(Vd_i/Vr_j), p(Vr_j)\}$ remain completely defined. The real problem will only require adding some restrictions (inequations). E.g. we obtain stationary states related to activity V if the V flow disappears in each node of the graph (the node neither gains nor loses V); that is:

$$p(Vd_i) = p(Vr_i) \text{ for all } i = 1, ..., n \qquad (19)$$

All this can now be applied if the ecosystem ES is considered like an isolated system, taking the environment E like a node, *node '0'*. The uncertainty Y of E relating E (now node '0') to the other nodes of S can be considered in this case as a special type of complexity (or relation $<K,T>$ between nodes) included in a *'mega-complexity'* Z of ES seen as an isolated system (see figure 4).

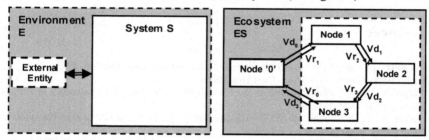

Fig. 4. Dual view of S+E or ES (source: own development).

Coming back to the modification scheme M of the ecosystem ES as the set of probabilities $\{p(s_i/e_j)\}$ and taking now the set of states of (E,S) as the variable V:

$$K[E, S] = H[E] + H[S/E] = K[S, E]$$
$$= -\sum_n \sum_m p(s_i, e_j) \log_2 p(s_i/e_j) = H[M] = Z[M] \qquad (20)$$

that is to say the 'mega-complexity' Z of the ecosystem ES.

The matrix of conditional probabilities $\{p(s_i/e_j)\}$ resumes the interaction between S and E, transmitted by a 'noisy virtual channel' acting as intermediate between two extreme values:

1) A 'permeable channel' where:

$$H[S/E] = 0 \Rightarrow T[S/E] = H[S]; \qquad (21)$$

that is: $p(s_i/e_j) = 0 \text{ if } i \prec j; p(s_i/e_j) = 1 \text{ if } i = j \qquad (22)$

2) A 'non permeable channel' where:

$$H[S/E] = H[S] \Rightarrow T[S/E] = 0; \qquad (23)$$

that is: $p(s_i/e_j) = p(s_i) \qquad (24)$

The conditional probability $\{p(s_i/e_j)\}$ means the probability that 'informational variable' s_i is seen in system S whenever environment E emits an 'activity' e_j; that is to say the capacity of system S to perceive what happens in its environment E and the capacity to answer to the state of E.

A.4 'Ecosistemics', evolution, adaptation and survival

Each type of System S (with its partition in an internal graph and related to its environment E) has some channel 'permeability' for each type of 'informational variable' V. The more interesting V is the 'auto-conscience' of the system S, that is to say the information about its own mini-complexity X or about its mega-complexity Z –if it includes uncertainty and its relations with its environment E.[4]

The 'adaptive' criterion is the core of the *Evolution Theory of complex systems* established experimentally with biological populations of ecosystems ES. In these ecosystems, some characteristics constitute tactics of *'differentiability'*, like camouflage into environment E (a prey changing to non attractive colors to survive) or detaching out of E (a male changing to attractive colors to reproduce).

References

ANSI (2004) *A Guide to the Project Management Body of Knowledge, PMBoK.* PMI
Carter R (1998) *Mapping the Mind.* The Orion Publishing Group Ltd.
De Meyer A, Loch C, Pich M (2002 a) *On Uncertainty, Ambiguity and Complexity in Project Management.* INSEAD
De Meyer A, Loch C, Pich M (2002 b) *Managing Project Uncertainty: From Variation to Chaos.* MIT Sloan Management Review
Fernandez M, Marcelo J (2008) *Project management, Complexity & Uncertainty.* WCC
Hall E (1998) *Managing Risk. Methods for Software Systems Development.* Software Engineering Series, Addison-Wesley Longman
Herrmann N (1990) *The Creative Brain.* Brain Books
Klir G, Folger T (1988) *Fuzzy sets, uncertainty and information.* Prentice Hall
Marcelo J (2001) *From Managing Risks in Projects to Managing Projects by their Risks [(RM ⊂ PM) ∧ (PM ⊂ RM)].* Tutorial imparted at QUATIC 2001, 4th Encuentro para la Calidad en las TIC, Instituto Superior Técnico, Lisbon
Marcelo J (2004) *Risk in Systems and Projects with High Complexity and/or Uncertainty.* Ph.D. dissertation. Universidad Politécnica de Valencia
Marcelo J (2007) *Driving projects by their risks.* Upgrade. CEPIS. http://www.upgrade-cepis.org/issues/2007/5/upgrade-vol-VIII-5.html. Accessed 1 December 2007
Mintzberg H (1976) *Planning on the Left Side and Managing on the Right.* Harvard Business Review, July-August, p. 49
Wagensberg J (1994) *Ideas about the complexity of the world.* Tusquets Editores, Spain
Webster G (1999) *Managing Projects at Work.* ISBN 0 566 07982 8

---

[4] The accepted additivity of the different entropies and other dimensionally similar operands follows the traditional Boltzmann-Gibbs formulation of energy and entropy. The needed generalization of this formulation can be seen in C. Tsallis and E. Cured, "Generalized statistical mechanics: Connections with thermodynamics", *Journal of Physics*, 1991.

Bridging the Gap Between Service-Oriented and Object-Oriented Architectures in Information Systems Development

Viera Rozinajová, Marek Braun, Pavol Návrat and Mária Bieliková

Slovak University of Technology, SK

Abstract: The most popular development methodologies in the last decade are based on object-oriented techniques. The goal of this paper is to investigate the possibilities of extending the object-oriented methodology of information systems development with a service-oriented approach and to examine the benefits of this extension. We propose an augmentation to an object-oriented methodology known as BORM that incorporates service-oriented techniques. To demonstrate the advantages of this combination, the extended methodology was applied and its features evaluated.

Keywords: Service Oriented Architecture, Business Process Modeling, Business Process Execution Language, Object-Oriented Methodology

1. Introduction

Service oriented architecture (SOA) is one of the most challenging concepts in information systems development. Indeed, there are reasons to believe that it brings flexibility, scalability and faster system development. Current information systems are not developed for quick and dynamic modifications. Changes in processes that can have an impact on the entire organization are often reflected in information systems that require long time horizons to modify. If the organization wants these changes, it must wait a long time for the modification.

In contrast, SOA systems consist of modular components with standardized interfaces through which components (services) deliver their functionality. To set up

Institute of Informatics and Software Engineering
Faculty of Informatics and Information Technologies
Slovak University of Technology, Ilkovicova 3, 842 16 Bratislava, Slovakia
{rozinajova, navrat, bielik}@fiit.stuba.sk

Please use the following format when citing this chapter:

Rozinajová, V., Braun, M., Návrat, P. and Bieliková, M., 2008, in IFIP International Federation for Information Processing, Volume 274; *Advances in Information Systems Research, Education and Practice*; David Avison, George M. Kasper, Barbara Pernici, Isabel Ramos, Dewald Roode; (Boston: Springer), pp. 125–134.

SOA, it is often necessary to concentrate on business processes, their modeling and management. According to Erl (2008), many of the services that will eventually be modeled and designed will be business services, responsible for accurately encapsulating and expressing business logic. Therefore, a comprehensive set of business models and specifications is needed. In this paper we focus our attention on the systems based on the business process-oriented approach to SOA, i.e. the systems consisting of the services that support business process realization.

These services express business logic as abstract representations of business capabilities that the business can compose into processes. Therefore, a well defined business process is a critical success factor for deploying SOA, and using a methodology based on business process modeling would be beneficial for systems reflecting business needs. This is one of the reasons why we have chosen BORM methodology (Business Object Relation Modeling) (Knott et al. 2000) - an object-oriented methodology for information system design and development based on the business process modeling. BORM itself focuses to modules from a reusability point of view and its focus is also to business process modeling. These aspects are similar to SOA principles, but BORM is pure object-oriented.

2.   BORM methodology

BORM, Business Object Relation Modeling, was originally developed in 1993 and was intended to provide seamless support for building object-oriented software systems based on pure object-oriented languages and environments such as Smalltalk and object databases. Subsequently, it has been realized that this method has also significant potential in business process modeling and other related business and user requirements issues.

Business Object Relation Modeling is an approach to both process modeling and the subsequent development of information systems. It provides a methodology that facilitates the description of how real business systems evolve, change and behave. It has been used successfully for developing a number of information systems in various areas of business activities. The BORM approach is based on each object having three independent attributes called dimensions. These dimensions are data, behavior, and history (a composition of states and transitions, i.e. the object lifecycle).

BORM is fundamentally an object-oriented development methodology, but differs from other such methodologies. In BORM, the extent of knowledge required to understand an object and use it effectively in the design process evolves throughout the development process in a clear, precise and consistent manner. Initially, objects are defined as business objects, where only knowledge of their activities, relationships, and intercommunications is required (Satzinger and Orvik 1996). Business objects during the design process are changed via a set of clearly defined and consistent techniques into conceptual objects. During the implementation phase, conceptual objects evolve in a similar structured and controlled manner into software objects. Thus at each stage of the development process, BORM requires some degree of knowledge about the object to proceed further.

Contrary to some other object-oriented methodologies, which start with a set of initial objects without providing any method for discovering them, the BORM development methodology starts from an informal problem specification and provides both methods and techniques to enable this informal specification to be transformed into an initial set of interacting objects. The main technique used here is BORM is modified Object Behavioral Analysis (BOBA).

BORM, similar to other object-oriented development methodologies, is based on the spiral model of the development life cycle (Boehm 1981). One loop of the object-oriented spiral model contains stages of strategic analysis, initial analysis (both work with business objects), advance analysis, initial design (conceptual objects), advanced design, implementation and testing (software objects):

1. The first three stages are collectively referred to as the expansion stages. Expansion ends with finalizing the detailed analysis, which fully describes the solution of the problem from the requirements point of view.
2. The remaining stages are called consolidation stages. These are concerned with the process of developing from 'expanded ideas' to a working application. During these stages, the conceptual model is step by step transformed into a software design.

3.   Extending BORM with SOA

Our goal was to examine if the object models created using BORM development can be utilized to support the design of service-oriented systems and to investigate under which conditions this procedure will work.

For the purpose of practical investigation, an experimental project from the domain of self-service DVD rental store was developed. This project consisted of three phases. In the first step, design via original BORM was performed. In the second step, the design using SOA principles was developed. And in the last step, consolidation of these two designs was completed.

BORM design was performed according to its six stages. The SOA design was built using SOA principles and Business Process Execution Language (BPEL). BPEL models were used for visualization of service orchestration. These models provide a complete view of service architecture.

Comparing BORM and BPEL showed a similarity in activities. BORM process models are comparable with UML activity and state diagrams whereas they combine both state and activity aspects of processes in a single diagram. Besides vertical relations they also capture horizontal ones, which describe communication among processes of various participants. The similarity between BORM and BPEL processes lies in identified services and in process mapping where the services are orchestrated in related way – in terms of nesting, cycling, branching, and so on. The differences between models are due to their special purpose. BORM models are created in the first stages of system development in order to describe the problem area whilst BPEL models are designed in the latter phases based on well-known user needs and expectations. But BORM's process models are a good foundation for building SOA and BPEL models, if the latter are desired. More generally, when comparing BORM and SOA, it was found that support of services identification as functional elements (for SOA) together with their forming into cooperative unit is absent in BORM. The cooperative unit of formed and also orchestrated services is called a "process layer" in this paper. It is necessary to realize that there is a difference between the process layer on one hand and a business layer, business process and process diagram/model on the other. They are considered as two different models.

The gap between BORM and SOA should be filled. BORM methodology does not provide all the necessary information. Some additional data must be added for recognition of relevant activities as services. Moreover, their classification and grouping should be performed. Into the original BORM's six phases the additional activities were added taking into account the nature of each phase as well as its overall purpose in the methodology.

First and second phase. The aim of the first two phases of BORM is to describe a problem area. The requirements of the future system are defined along with process diagrams. These phases include all the necessary activities – also for SOA. Hence an upgrading of these phases is not required. In relation to the experimental project, project objectives were defined, together with sets of required system functions and system scenarios. And also the business processes for operators (customer administration + movie administration) and customers (movie rent and return, movie reservation and canceling of reservation) were recognized.

Third phase. In the third phase, process diagrams are processed and information for an initial software specification is extracted. The following activities were added to this phase in order to support SOA: initial service identification (based on process models), their classification – grouping according to their logic and decomposition of services, if it is appropriate. In this phase of the system design, object diagram and class diagram with relationships between objects, resp. classes has been created together with its extension by objects' dynamic properties. To support the SOA approach, initial identification and classification of services based on business processes was completed. Example of business services for customer is shown in Table 1.

Table 1 Initial list of customer business services

Participant	Business services
Customer	person's identification and authentication
	person's log off
	administration of borrowings
	creation of list of rented movies
	creation of list of reserved movies
	finding a movie
	movie reservation
	canceling of movie reservation
	stock out of movies reserved on current branch store (in case of picking up the movies)
	receiving of movie (in case of returning borrowed movie)

Fourth phase. Design in the fourth phase proceeds to software implementation. The relationships among objects are improved and transformed. Design patterns are applied and reusable components identified. From an SOA point of view, the existing services are identified and the input and output parameters are specified.

Business services are considered as SOA operations and bundled into SOA services according to theirs functionality. In this phase analysts should consult with developers to identify services from an implementation point of view. This is important to ensure effective implementation (it should be appropriate for decomposition, consolidation, regrouping of services etc.). Outputs of this phase are object diagrams enriched by design patterns and a list of regrouped SOA operations bundled in services. An example of customer service with its operations is shown in Table 2.

Table 2 List of SOA services and theirs operations for customer service with input and output parameters

Service	Operation	Input parameters	Output parameters
Customer	person's identification and authentication	customer id, branch store id	1 – successful 0 – unsuccessful
	person's logging off	customer id	1 – logging off successful 0 – logging off unsuccessful
	registration of new customer	name, address	1 – registration successful 0 – registration unsuccessful

Service	Operation	*Input parameters*	*Output parameters*
	canceling of customer registration	customer id	1 – canceling successful 0 – canceling unsuccessful
	person's identification via identification card	card id	customer id and name
	modification of customer data	customer id, new data	1 – data modification successful 0 – data modification unsuccessful
	listing of customers	-	list of customers with their data

Fifth phase. In the fifth phase a transformation of conceptual objects closer to the concrete implementation environment is made. Besides adjusting the class and object diagrams, process models of services are prepared in order to form a process layer of implementation. Design of the process layer where services and relations among them are captured, is made for later implementation purposes. This produces an outline for implementation of previously orchestrated services. The process diagrams from the second phase are helpful in this phase and the process layer design can be based on them.

The process layer can be designed using workflow patterns, business process modeling notation (BPMN), or eventually BPEL. BPEL should be used in this phase to create a high level design of the process layer, in case the process layer is later implemented in this language.

In the experimental project the diagrams of software objects capturing a server side with relation database were created. Then a process layer was designed (see Fig. 1) using NetBeans BPEL notation.

Sixth phase. In the sixth and final phase, the physical implementation of the system including implementation of identified services using web service standards was performed. The process layer, which is used for services interconnection is also created.

A prototype of a self-service DVD rental store was implemented in Java with MySQL. The Java application consisted of the web service layer, in which single SOA operations was implemented, and of the process layer, which was bundled with a user interface implemented using Java Server Faces and MySQL database. Implementing the process layer using BPEL offers a flexible and scalable system as SOA asserts.

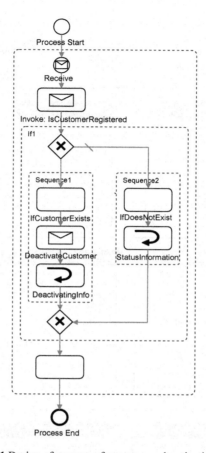

Fig. 1 Design of a process for customer deactivation

Our experiment has demonstrated that if the development of information systems according to BORM methodology is performed thoroughly, we can take advantage of the created models of business processes to support the system design while respecting the service oriented approach. Moreover, in addition to the benefits of models of business processes, the extended diagrams of objects and classes together with their relationships and dynamic properties from the BORM development can be beneficial when utilized in the process of service-oriented systems development.

An overall life cycle of extended BORM methodology is shown in Fig. 2 (BORM methodology is depicted with inspiration from (Molhanec 2008).

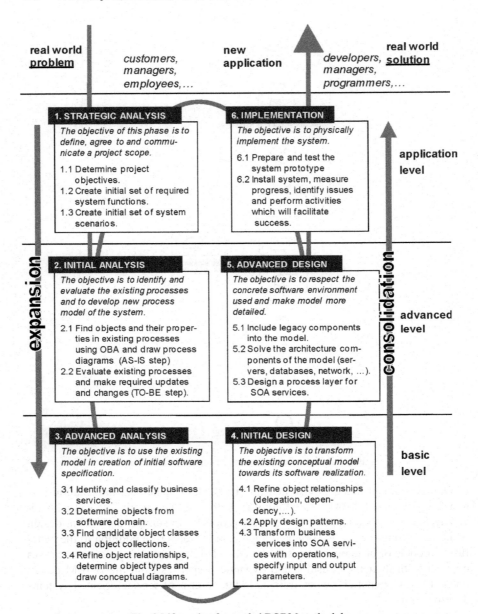

Fig. 2 Life cycle of extended BORM methodology

4.   Conclusions

This paper investigated the possibilities of extending the BORM methodology by incorporating the SOA approach. The development following all the steps of the original BORM sequence, augmented by activities allowing SOA principles to be a part of the design has shown to be viable – thus taking a step towards a new methodology for information system design and development.

We observed that good, quality design is possible using the BORM process models for initial service identification and the process layer implementation according to service oriented architecture. It is also possible to make use of other BORM diagrams from initial steps of system analysis and design. As a result of BORM extension, an adapted methodology with extended phases of the life cycle was created. This methodology is based on object-oriented approach taking into account requirements needed for service oriented principles. The extension is effective in the last four phases of the original BORM methodology. The new upgraded methodology allows smooth design of information systems, facilitating the building of systems that are service-oriented. An implementation of system prototype via extended BORM methodology served to evaluate the proposed extensions.

By extending the original BORM methodology with SOA, we achieve a methodology that enables identification and implementation of an information system process layer. The realization of the process layer can be done in several ways. If we choose BPEL, these changes can be performed at BPEL process model level using the BPEL engine. Thus we have the possibility of making fast and flexible modifications to information systems according to actual needs, and with flexibility among the most desirable attributes of information systems today, this is a step toward development of improved methodologies.

Acknowledgements This work was partially supported by the Slovak Research and Development Agency under the contracts No. APVV-0391-06 and No. APVT-20-007104.

References

1. Bell M.(2008). *Service-Oriented Modeling (SOA): Service Analysis, Design, and Architecture.* John Wiley & Sons, New Jersey.
2. Erl, T. (2008). *SOA: Principles of service design.* Prentice-Hall, Boston
3. Juric M., Mathew B., Poornachandra S. (2006). *Business Process Execution Language for Web Services,* Packt Publishing, Birmingham, UK
4. Knott R. P., Merunka V., Polak J. (2003). The BORM methodology: a third-generation fully object-oriented methodology. *Knowledge Based Systems*, 16 (2): 77–89.

5. Molhanec, M. (2004). An overview of Information Modelling for Manufacturing Systems In: 27th Int. Spring Seminar on Electronics Technology ISSE 2004. Sofia: IEEE, 2004, vol. 1, pp. 36-41.
6. Polášek,I., Chudá, D., Kristová, G. (2006). System dynamics modeling in the new version of UML 2.0 language. In: *System Integration 2006*, Žilina, University of Žilina, pp.311-317.
7. Satzinger J. W., Orvik T.U. (1996). *The Object-Oriented Approach - Concepts, Modeling and System Development*, Boyd&Fraser.

THE IFIP INTERNATIONAL PROFESSIONAL PRACTICE PARTNERSHIP

Transforming and Informing IT Professional Practice

Charles Hughes, Chair
International Professional Practice Partnership

Abstract: A global programme led by IFIP (The International Federation for Information Processing) to promote professionalism in IT, define international standards and create a global infrastructure that will encourage and support the development of both practitioners and employer organisations and give recognition to those who meet and maintain the required standards for knowledge, experience, competence and integrity.

1. The Vision

Our vision is the creation of an international IT profession, equivalent in prestige and structure to other established professions such as law, accountancy and medicine, that is:

- Focused on improving the ability of business and other organisations to exploit the potential of information technology effectively and consistently.
- Respected by its stakeholders – including employees, employers, customers, governments and key international bodies.
- A source of real pride and aspiration for IT practitioners.

2. The Background

The IT profession is at a critical point in its development. IT is now quite clearly an activity which is vital to the world economy and to the prosperity and quality of life of ordinary people across the world. At the same time it is marked by an almost complete absence of well established national or international standards to assure the essential requirements of a truly professional practitioner. While a confusing array of examination-based qualifications provide an indication of relevant knowledge, it is generally impossible to validate subjective judgements about the experience, competence or ethical standards of individuals – even where those judgements relate to

Please use the following format when citing this chapter:

Hughes, C., 2008, in IFIP International Federation for Information Processing, Volume 274; *Advances in Information Systems Research, Education and Practice*; David Avison, George M. Kasper, Barbara Pernici, Isabel Ramos, Dewald Roode; (Boston: Springer), pp. 135–138.

business-critical or even safety-critical positions. In a global industry in which practitioners are numbered in millions, this is very clearly unacceptable.

This lack of established national and international standards is a serious problem in a world in which everyone is now acutely aware of the need for IT professionalism - but it also provides a valuable opportunity. The IT profession stands on a cusp – sufficiently mature to recognise the importance of professionalism but not so far down the track that every nation has developed its own standards that would now require difficult and time consuming retrofitting to form an international standard. It is this unique and possibly short lived, opportunity that IFIP is determined to seize and exploit.

3. IP3 - Delivering the Vision

The IFIP *International Professional Practice Partnership* (IP3) is designed to deliver the vision set out above by the development of an overarching professional framework maintained and delivered through its network of over 90 national member societies.

The approach is essentially inclusive, intended neither to reinvent the wheel nor to supplant existing certifications. Rather the aim is to embrace and incorporate existing capabilities, strengthening and augmenting existing certification schemes by giving them a broader professional context and coherence, setting them in an architecture and generally promoting the value of standards, certifications and accreditations. The overriding aim is to develop, and to give recognition to individual practitioners and to IT employers who are ethical, experienced and competent and can be relied upon to form sound judgments and to make rational and principled decisions - qualities and capabilities that are especially important in our fast-moving business and rapidly changing technological world.

The profession reflected in the vision is one that has an extensive range of skills, encompassing not only the essential technical and engineering skills but also the key business focussed skills that ensure real business benefit. A vital role will be played by newer IT skills such as information management and business change management and it is particularly important that recognition is given to the growing importance of IT professionals in areas such as corporate governance and enterprise security

An essential feature of these arrangements will be encouraging and supporting development. Whilst certifications provide valuable markers on the path to full professionalism, it is equally important to provide the resources to support the development of knowledge, skills, competence and best professional practice for both individual practitioners and their employer organisations at all stages of that journey.

3.1 The Key Features of IP3 Certification

IP3 certification schemes, of which the first will be the 'gold standard' International IT Professional (IITP) certification, will be:

- Vendor independent;
- Operated by accredited IFIP member bodies;
- Available worldwide;
- Based on consistent global standards for professionals in all areas of IT activity;
- Built around a requirement for complete professional formation – including relevant knowledge, experience, competence and commitment to a code of professional ethics;
- Dependent on the maintenance of competence through a programme of continuing professional education and development;
- Supported by a disciplinary code with a process.

4. Why IFIP?

IFIP, with its UNESCO provenance, established reputation and existing infrastructure of over 90 independent, national member bodies and combined membership of around 1 million IT practitioners is uniquely qualified to lead this programme. There is no other organisation with the necessary independence, reputation and international reach that could contemplate the development, far less the delivery, of the proposed professionalism metaframework.

IFIP leadership also brings the advantage of significant and increasing national and international influence, both though IFIP itself and through its major member bodies. It also enables us to build on the very solid foundations established by a number of those bodies, including the British Computer Society the Australian Computer Society, the Canadian Information Processing Society and the IEEE Computer Society.

One of the key objectives for IP3 is to reach beyond the developed world, to encourage and facilitate the development of IT capability within the emerging nations. Here too the IFIP international infrastructure provides unique advantage.

5. Partners Organisations

Although IFIP is clearly the appropriate body to lead the development, delivery and management of the proposed professionalism framework, it needs the commitment, support and involvement of the industry. As the programme moves forward there will be opportunities for organisations of all kinds, both large and small, to associate themselves with the work. At this early stage we want to partner with a small group (probably no more than 4) of global organisations that share both our professionalism commitment and aspirations. For these *Platinum Sponsors* this involvement will provide opportunities to:

- Associate their brands with IT professionalism in a global context;

- Align their own IT professional development efforts with those of a global organization;

- Create and/or benchmark programs for the development of IT professionals;

- Participate in the development of standards for IT professionalism;

- Support and participate in building IT capability beyond the developed world.

6. Summary

We have a unique opportunity to put in place an urgently needed professional structure to underpin the competence and professionalism of IT practitioners and organisations on an international basis. IFIP, through the IP3 proposals outlined above, is committed to lead the development of that structure and invites support for a ground-breaking programme which will be of immense value to both the IT industry and to its stakeholders.

Requirements Elicitation in Data Mining for Business Intelligence Projects

Paola Britos[1], Oscar Dieste[2] and Ramón García-Martínez[3]

[1]Software and Knowledge Engineering Center. Buenos Aires Institute of Technology, AR
[2]Empirical Software Engineering Research Group, Polytechnic University of Madrid, ES
[3]Intelligent Systems Laboratory. Engineering School. University of Buenos Aires, AR
{pbritos, rgm}@itba.edu.ar, odieste@fi.upm.es

Abstract: There are data mining methodologies for business intelligence (DM-BI) projects that highlight the importance of planning an ordered, documented, consistent and traceable requirement's elicitation throughout the entire project. However, the classical software engineering approach is not completely suitable for DM-BI projects because it neglects the requirements specification aspects of projects. This article focuses on identifying concepts for understand DM-BI project domain from DM-BI field experience, including how requirements can be educed by a proposed DM-BI project requirements elicitation process and how they can be documented by a template set.

1. Introduction

A Data Mining for Business Intelligence (DM-BI) methodology seeks to organize the pattern discovery process in the data warehouse of an organization. These methodologies consider requirements specification as one of the early activities of the project (Chapman et al. 2000; Pyle 2003). Similarly, requirements are an important phase in software engineering methodologies (IEEE, 1993; Winter & Strauch 2004; Maiden et al. 2004, 2007; Solheim et al. 2005; Jiang & Eberlein 2007).

Several authors (Winter & Strauch 2002; Silva & Freire 2003; Yang and Wu, 2006) have addressed the need to improve DM-BI methodologies, but they focuses on DM-BI goals definition and DM-BI tasks specification as exploratory data analysis and develop tools for DM-BI process documentation, model-building, and pattern-finding. The DM-BI community has neglected the requirements specification aspects of projects, failing to identify any technique to elicit necessary knowledge or suggest any template for systematic documentation of requirements.

In order to explore how to minimize the impact of the presented problems this research focuses on an approach based on: understanding the DM-BI project's domain, knowing the DM-BI project's data domain, understanding the DM-BI project's scope, identifying the needed human resources, and selecting the appropriate DM-BI tool. The approach also looks to specify documentation tools for required information of DM-BI projects.

In this paper we present related research on DM methodologies addressing the problem (section 2); a solution approach is introduced (section 3); a proposed method for requirements engineering in DM-BI projects is developed (section 4); focusing on process and

---

Please use the following format when citing this chapter:

Britos, P., Dieste, O. and García-Martínez, R., 2008, in IFIP International Federation for Information Processing, Volume 274; *Advances in Information Systems Research, Education and Practice*; David Avison, George M. Kasper, Barbara Pernici, Isabel Ramos, Dewald Roode; (Boston: Springer), pp. 139–150.

products, an example of a real case based use of templates is drawn (section 5); a discussion of the strengths of the proposed process is presented (section 6); and some conclusions are drawn (section 7).

2. Current Methodologies for DM-BI

The DM-BI literature on requirements elicitation identifies concepts related to how to extract, transform, aggregate, and discover business patterns in organization data. Moreover, these activities should be performed based on a concise dimensional schema. In this context, stakeholders and requirements engineers work together to identify what and where to look within organization data sources, in order to provide the bases for discovering business patterns for business improvement. The requirement elicitation process is addressed by most commonly used data mining (DM) methodologies (Chapman et al, 2000; Pyle, 2003, SAS, 2008). DM methodologies state the necessity of business understanding as the starting point for any DM project.

The CRISP (cross industry standard for data mining) methodology (Chapman et al, 2000) consists of four levels of abstraction, hierarchically organized from general tasks to specific cases. The process is divided into six phases, each one having many general tasks of second level or sub phases. General tasks are projected to specific ones, where the actions that must be developed for specific situations are described. As a consequence, we find a general task "cleaning data" in second level; then in third level, those tasks that must be developed for a specific case, as for example "cleaning numerical data" or "cleaning categorical data". In the fourth level, groups of actions, decisions and results about the specific data mining project are collected. The CRISP-DM methodology presents two different documents as a tool for assisting during the development of the data mining project: the reference model and the user's guide. The document model of reference describes, in a general way, the phases, general tasks and exit-points of a data mining project. The user's guide brings detailed information about practical application of the model of reference to specific data mining projects; it also gives advices and check-lists about each phase's tasks.

The methodology P^3TQ (Product, Place, Price, Time, and Quantity) consists of two parts (Pyle, 2003): [a] Modeling (PI): provides a step-by-step guide to develop and to build a model to address a business problem or opportunity. Modeling depends very much on the business circumstances that prompt the modeling in the first place, as indicated by the five different entry scenarios to PI. Largely, PI provides lists of actions that must be completed, depending on circumstances; and [b] Data Mining (PII): provides a step-by-step guide to mining the data to produce the required model as identified in PI. Data Mining consists of a series of stages that have to be completed in order. Unlike modeling in which several tasks may take place at the same time, mining has to proceed from stage to stage. Each part is based on four types of "activity boxes"; action boxes: indicate one or more required "next steps" for you to take; discovery boxes: provide exploratory actions that you need to take to decide what to do next; technique boxes: provide supplemental information about the recommended steps to be described in the action or discovery boxes; and example boxes: gives a detailed description of how to use a specific technique, along with pointers to an excel worksheet.

SEMMA (Sample, Explore, Modify, Model and Assess) is a methodology oriented to select, explore and model a great amount of data; looking to discover business patterns in the data (SAS, 2008). The process begins with the extraction of sample data on which analysis is going to be applied. Once the sample is selected, the methodology proposes to explore the data in order to simplify the model. The third phase involves entailing data to DM tool. The fourth phase involves running the DM tool on the selected data. The last phase consists of evaluating results by analyzing the model by contrast with statistical models or new samples.

One assumption behind approaches to requirements engineering in DM-BI is that sufficient knowledge of the requirements already exits. It is quite well known that in normal situations, customers and users are 'speaking another language' than the development team (Maiden et al. 2007). The task of translating customers' and users' ideas into the development teams' language is done by requirements engineers and business-analysts using different notations (Jiang & Eberlein 2007). However, this is increasingly flawed because of the breadth of expertise that is needed to specify complex systems and the number of humans that may be involved in the process. Thus, current requirements elicitation methodologies fail in that they do not provide adequately coverage of concepts needed to elicit requirements, nor do they support corresponding documentation or cross referencing.

3. Framework for Requirements Elicitation in DM-BI

The need to adapt traditional requirements engineering process for DM-BI systems is based on the premise that the requirements analysis for these types of systems differ substantially from requirements analysis for conventional information systems. Evidence of this assertion is found in a wide range of DM-BI project domains: mobile telephony (Grosser *et al*, 2005), health policies (Felgaer *et al*, 2006), agro-industry (Cogliati *et al*, 2006), and criminal intelligence (Valenga *et al*, 2008). In each of these cases, the DM-BI methodologies had difficulty dealing with some common requirements problems, such as the customer doesn't understand the technical lexis used by DM-BI group, the customer were not clear about the goals and capabilities of the DM-BI project or what it could achieve, or the models defined by DM-BI group were different from the ones the customer envisioned. A complete list of the identified problems is shown in Fig. 1. This field experience has taught the authors the necessity of defining a list of concepts to be educed during the business understanding phase. The list of needed concepts and its relation to the detected problems is shown in Fig. 1.

PROBLEM	CONCEPTS TO BE EDUCED
[a] The customer doesn't understand the technical lexis used by DM-BI group [b] DM BI group can't understand the lexis of the customer's information domain [c] The DM-BI group found it hard to understand how they could help the customer because they didn't know the project domain	Definitions, acronyms and abbreviations
[d] The customer was not sure what the DM-BI project could do or achieve [e] Models defined by DM- BI group were different from the ones the customer envisioned	Project objectives Successful criteria of the project Project expectations Project suppositions
[f] The customer was an unpredictable group (not so concerned with the project)	Human resource involved
[g] The customer did not know the needed organizational information and its condition	Project restrictions Project risks Contingency planning
[h] Data identified by requirements were not the right ones	Requirements goal The requirement information or data source Attributes related on requirements

| [i] When DM-BI project was in modeling phase (requirements solutions) and DM-BI group detected problems in data, (i.e., data identified by requirements were not the right ones), it was necessary to redefine requirements | Requirement results suppositions
Requirement restrictions
Requirement risks
Requirement contingencies plan |
| [j] Requirements of DM-BI project misunderstandings resulted in selection of the wrong modeling tool | Evaluating DM-BI tools |

Fig. 1. Relation among identified problems in the field and the Concepts needed to be educed

To solve these problems, we have needed to educe specific information in each DM-BI project. This information may be modeled by a list of concepts that are educed in the listed below:

- *Definitions, acronyms and abbreviations:* It is necessary to identify definitions, acronyms and abbreviations for establishing lexis to be shared among all persons related to the DM-BI project. This addresses problems: [a], [b] and [c] (see Fig. 1).
- *Project objectives:* It is necessary to identify the objective of the DM-BI project and its motivation to characterize what customer needs. This addresses problems: [d] and [e].
- *Successful criteria of the project:* It is necessary to identify the criteria which turn the project into a successful one. The criteria must be described in terms of expected achievements of the DM-BI project. This addresses problems: [d] and [e].
- *Project expectations:* It is necessary to identify what is expected to be achieved by the DM-BI project and to confirm that they fulfill the customer's expectations. The expectations must be aligned with the objectives and the project success criteria. This addresses problems: [d] and [e].
- *Project's suppositions:* It is important to identify the suppositions that must be assumed as true ones in order to start the DM-BI project. The project's suppositions become the start point of the requirement elicitation process. This addresses problems: [d] and [e].
- *Project restrictions:* In order to specify the DM-BI project context, it is necessary to identify the limits previously established for the project: *related to organization:* political, legal and data quantity, *related to data:* to access sources of information, and data quality, *related to human and technical resources:* the size of the data sources related to hardware and software handlers, hardware and software limitations, human resources; and *related to the project:* those activities which affect the project and its security (access to documentation about the project, without any possibility of a backup). This address problem: [g].
- *Project risks:* Identify risks for the DM-BI project by looking continuously at what might be wrong in the organization (related to the DM-BI project) and determining which risks are important to be solved. Risks identification is needed to define contingency plans to be applied to mitigate risk. This address problem: [g].
- *Contingency plans:* It is necessary to define contingency plans to be applied to off-set risk. This address problem: [g].
- *Human resource involved:* It is important to identify the different roles in the DM-BI project and the human resources that will fill these roles. The roles are in the areas of exploring data and business domain expertise. This address problem: [f].
- *Requirement goals:* The project's objectives are decomposed in requirement goals. The requirement goals are needed in conjunction with project's suppositions to define the DM-BI processes to be applied. This address problem: [h].

- *The requirement information or data source*: It is necessary to establish which information or data source are going to be used and where is it in order to accomplish a requirement's goal. This address problem: [h].
- *Requirement results suppositions*: It is necessary to identify the suppositions about requirement results in order to have guidance to act to accomplish the requirement goal. It must be consistent with the project goal, its expectations and suppositions. This addresses problem: [i].
- *Requirements restrictions*: In order to specify each DM-BI project requirement context, it is necessary to identify requirement limits which must be consistent with those described in other parts of the elicitation document: *related to data*: to access sources of information, and data quality, *related to human and technical resources*: the size of the data sources related to hardware and software handlers, hardware and software limitations, human resources; and *related to the project security*. This address problem: [i].
- *Attributes related on requirements*: Establish which attributes are going to be used in order to accomplish a requirement goal. This address problem: [h].
- *Requirement risks*: It is important to identify DM-BI project requirement risks by looking continuously for what might be wrong in the requirement (related to the DM-BI project) and determining which risks are important to be solved. Requirement risks identification is needed to define contingency plans to be applied when needed. This address problem: [i].
- *Requirement contingency plans*: It is necessary to define contingency plans to be applied when an occurrence warrants. This address problem: [i].
- *Evaluating DM-BI tools*: It is necessary to evaluate available DM-BI tools to establish which are the best ones to accomplish the project's objectives. This address problem: [j].

Based on these concepts, to address the problems identified in Fig. 1, we propose a method for DM-BI project requirements elicitation process next.

4. Proposed Method

The proposed method of five steps is described in section 4.1, and the process products and their relation with the process steps is shown in section 4.2.

4.1. Process

Once the needed concepts have been identified, it is necessary to establish the steps to educe those concepts. The proposed structure is similar to those proposed by Software Engineering that allows progressing over the needed concepts to maintain their natural order. In the business understanding phase of any DM-BI methodology, we propose a DM-BI project requirements elicitation process of five steps that is shown in Fig. 2.

Fig. 2. Process of requirements elicitation

The purpose of the step "understand the project's domain" consists of establishing communication channels in ordinary language among persons involved into the DM-BI project. The purpose of the step "know the project's data domain" consists of establishing the project's requirements; the data needed for those requirements and its location, risks involved in the data and the requirements´ development, the data and requirements' restrictions, and finally its suppositions. The purpose of the step "understand the project's scope" is to achieve the DM-BI projects objective, its limitations, expectations and risks. The purpose of the step "identify the human resources needed skills" consists of knowing the list of human resources involved, its restrictions, risks and responsibilities. The purpose of the step "select the correct DM-BI tool" is to select an adequate tool according to the information obtained in the earlier steps.

To know the project's data domain in terms of requirements goal, the requirements information of data source information, requirements results suppositions, requirements restrictions, attributes involved in requirements, risks and contingency plans; it is necessary to understand the project's domain in terms of definitions, acronyms and abbreviations. To understand the project's scope in terms of project objectives, successful criteria of the project, project expectations, project suppositions, restrictions, risks, and contingency plans; it is necessary to know the project's data domain in terms of requirements goal, the requirements information of data source information, requirements results suppositions, requirements restrictions, attributes involved in requirements, requirements risks and requirements contingency plans. To identify the human resources needed in terms of defining human resources involved; it is necessary to understand the project's scope in terms of project objectives, project successful criteria, project expectations, project suppositions, project restrictions, project risks, and contingency plans. To identify the human resources needed skills in terms of defining human resources involved; it is necessary to select the correct DM-BI tool in terms of tools evaluation.

The conceptual dependency among the needed concept is shown in Fig. 3.

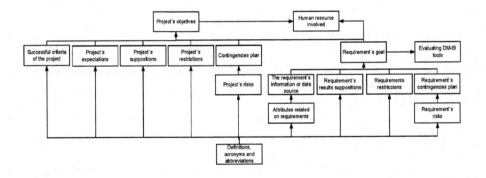

Fig. 3. Cross references of educed concepts represented by the templates

4.2 Products

We have defined a set of templates. Each template is associated to each concept. These templates have a detailed description of the concepts to be educed (see examples in section 5). The templates allow the concept evolution through the requirements elicitation process. The relation between the educed concepts as products and the steps of the proposed process (see section 4.1) to generate them is shown in Fig. 4.

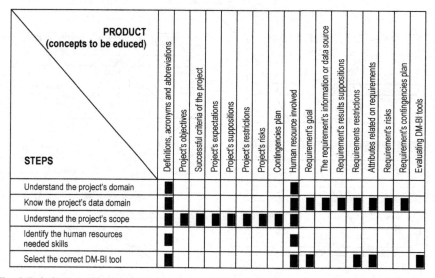

STEPS \ PRODUCT (concepts to be educed)	Definitions, acronyms and abbreviations	Project's objectives	Successful criteria of the project	Project's expectations	Project's suppositions	Project's restrictions	Project's risks	Contingencies plan	Human resource involved	Requirement's goal	The requirement's information or data source	Requirement's results suppositions	Requirements restrictions	Attributes related on requirements	Requirement's risks	Requirement's contingencies plan	Evaluating DM-BI tools
Understand the project's domain	■								■								
Know the project's data domain	■									■	■	■	■	■	■	■	■
Understand the project's scope	■	■	■	■	■	■	■	■									
Identify the human resources needed skills	■								■								
Select the correct DM-BI tool	■								■	■			■	■			■

Fig. 4. Relation among products (educed concepts) and process steps

5. Examples of Real Case Based Use of Templates

In this section we present a set of template examples based on a real DM-BI project (real case example) within the telecommunications industry. The case is centered on a company that scrutinizes the customers´ service closely, and the project objective is to show the relation between customer satisfaction (especially customers fidelity), and the company's products and qualities improvement initiatives. The DM-BI project requirements elicitation products and concept cross references are captured by the fulfillment and interaction among the different templates (i.e. for the real case example see Fig. 5 to Fig. 8).

Fig. 5 shows how the requirements objective: "causal evidence detection of the wide band service sign-off" (see Template "Report - Requirements Goal") needs supposition 1: "to identify causes of wide band service sign-off" (see Template "Report - Requirement's Results Supposition"), restriction 1: "amount of available identified wide band service sign-off cases" (see Template: "Report – Requirement's Restrictions"), attribute: "Service Sign-Off" (see Template: "Report - Attributes Related On Requirements"), contingency 1: "to identify the attributes more important for every requirement by means of brainstorming" (see Template: "Report – Requirement's Contingencies Plan"). The information origin for the attribute: "Service Sign-Off" (see Template: "Report - Attributes Related on Requirements") is in "Database of sign-off products and services transactions" (see Template "Report - The Requirement's Information of Data Source").

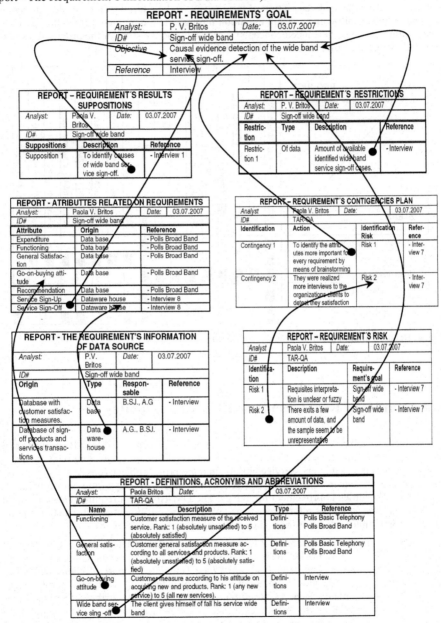

Fig. 5. Set of templates needed to define Requirements Goal

The information origin for the contingency 2: "they were realized more interviews to the organizations clients to detect their satisfaction" (see Template: "Report – Requirement's Contingencies Plan") is in risk 2: "there exits a few amount of data, and the sample seem to be unrepresentative" (see Tem plate: "Report – Requirement's Risk"). The definition of the concept: "go-on-buying attitude" (see Template: "Report - Definitions, Acronyms and Abbreviations") is used to understand the meaning of that attribute in Template: "Report - Attributes Related on Requirements". The definition of the concept: "wide band service sing - off" (see Template: "Report - Definitions, Acronyms and Abbreviations") is used to understand the requirements objective: "causal evidence detection of the wide band service sign-off" (see Template "Report - Requirements Goal").

Fig. 6 shows that the project's objective: "to determine indicators of correlation between investment and actions for quality improvement" (see Template "Report - Project's Objectives") needs criteria 1: " sign-Up and Sign-Off customer causes identification related to the described satisfaction measures." (See Template "Report – Successful Criteria of the Project"), expectation 1: "to identify variables

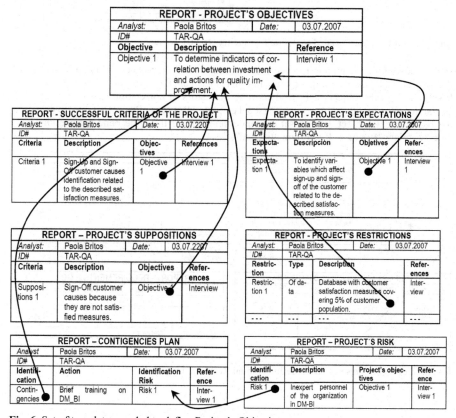

Fig. 6. Set of templates needed to define Project's Objectives

which affect sign-up and sign-off of the customer related to the described satisfaction measures" (see Template: "Report – Project's Expectations"), supposition 1: " sign-Off customer causes because they are not satisfied measures " (see Template: "Report – Project's Suppositions"), restriction 1: "Database with customer satisfaction measures covering 5% of customer population" (see Template: "Report – Project's Restrictions"), contingency 1: "brief training on DM_BI" (see training Template: "Report – Contingencies Plan"). The information origin for the contingency 1: "brief on DM_BI" (see Template: "Report – Contingencies Plan") is in risk 1: "inexpert personnel of the organization in DM-BI" (see Template: "Report – Project's Risk").

Fig. 7 shows that to evaluate DM-BI tools needs requirements objective: "causal evidence detection of the wide band service sign-off" (see Template "Report - Requirements Goal").

REPORT - REQUIREMENTS'S GOAL			
Analyst:	P. V. Britos	Date:	03.07.2007
ID#	Sign-off wide band		
Objective	Causal evidence detection of the wide band service sign-off.		
Reference	Interview		

REPORT – EVALUATING DM-NI TOOLS				
Analyst		Paola Britos	Date:	03.07.2007
ID#		TAR-QA		
Weighting for aspect/Tools		Clementine	MatLab	Weka
P1: Technical and functional	40%	148,4	129,6	98,0
P2: Of the supplier	25%	117,5	87,5	30,0
P3: Of the service	20%	70,0	NE	14,0
P4: Economic	- 15%	- 16,5	- 30,0	0,0
RESULT	100%	319,4	187,1	142

Fig. 7. Set of templates needed to define Evaluating DM-BI Tools

Fig. 8 shows how the human resources involved: "experts in business' domain", "leader of the project" and "data mining experts" in other (see Template "Report - Human Resource Involved") needs objective 1 "to determine indicators of correlation between investment and actions for quality improvement" (see Template "Report - Project's Objectives"), and the requirements objective: "causal evidence detection of the wide band service sign-off" (see Template "Report - Requirements Goal") .

REPORT – HUMAN RESOURCE INVOLVED						
Analyst:	Paola Britos		Date:	03.07.2007		
ID#	TAR-QA					
Position	Profile of the position		Belongs to:	Data:		
				Name	E-mail	TE
Experts in Business' domain	They are those who have experience in business' domain. They may be more than one.		The firm that was data	OA, DM, AG, BSJ	oa@itba.edu, dm@tar.com, ag@tar.com, bsj@tar.com	639
Leader of the Project	He is the one who leads the data mining project. He is part of the group. It is usually one person.		Consulting that completes the project	GG,RGM	gg@tar.com, rg@itba.edu	639 633
....	....		....	....	....	....
Datamining Experts	They are those who develop the data mining project and reach the goals. They may be more than one		Consulting that completes the project	PB,RGM	pb@itba.edu, rg@itba.edu	639 633

REPORT - PROJECT'S OBJECTIVES			
Analyst:	Paola Britos	Date:	03.07.2007
ID#	TAR-QA		
Objective	Description		Reference
Objective 1	To determine indicators of correlation between investment and actions for quality improvement.		Interview 1

REPORT - REQUIREMENTS'S GOAL			
Analyst:	P. V. Britos	Date:	03.07.2007
ID#	Sign-off wide band		
Objective	Causal evidence detection of the wide band service sign-off.		
Reference	Interview		

Fig. 8. Set of templates needed to define Human Resource Involved

6. Discussion

Current DM-BI methodologies fail to educe all the concepts (see section 3) needed during the business understanding phase of DM-BI (shown in Fig. 9). CRISP-DM educe on set of concepts, P3TQ another and SEMMA yet a third. In general, these methodologies attend to concepts related to determining business objectives and assess situations (at least for one methodology) and concepts related to determine data mining goals and project plan production are not attended. In this context, the proposed methodology is more robust than current ones, because it educes all the necessary concepts to model the DM-BI project's requirements.

Our consulting engagements in DM-BI projects have allowed us to test our ideas in the field, but we recognize the necessity for a formal research approach. So the next step will be to carry out experiments comparing the proposed DM-BI project requirements elicitation process with existing ones. The first step in the experiment will be to build a set of testing DM-BI project cases in which each case includes a case description K_i (description of case i) and the list of the requirements of the case R_i (requirements of case i) to be educed. Then two development groups will be considered, one trained in existing DM-BI business understanding phase (control group) and the other trained in our approach (testing group); both groups will be asked to identify and document DM-BI project requirement from the set of the previously defined DM-BI project cases (the set of K_i). The list of the requirements of the case will not be shown to any groups. Referees will compare the amount of well identified requirements from the control group with those identified by the testing group, and using statistical tests, differences between the groups will be compared. We expect to validate experimentally that the amount of correct requirements educed by the testing group (the one using the proposed process) is significantly better than the amount of correct requirements educed by the control group (current methodologies).

7. Conclusion

This paper presents an approach to educe the requirements for DM-BI project that addresses identified weaknesses in current data mining methodologies. The approach is based on a list of DM-BI project requirements, needed concepts that have to be educed, a set of templates to document its elicitation and the associated process.

The proposed process and set of templates have been tuned in field cases and their effectiveness has been demonstrated. To further verify the effectiveness of the proposed approach, a formal experiment is planned for the second semester 2008 with a population of advance students at the Software Engineering Bachelor Program, University of Buenos Aires.

The focus on DM-BI project requirements documentation enables the achievement of requisite, consistent, and traceable requirements specifications over the entire project. This documentation encourages beginning the modeling activities based on a common lexis and cross-referenced concepts related to the target business domain requirements.

8. References

Chapman P, Clinton J, Keber R, Khabaza T, Reinartz T, Shearer C, Wirth R (2000) CRISP-DM 1.0 Step by step BIguide Edited by SPSS. http://www.crisp-dm.org/CRISPWP-0800.pdf Accessed 14 September 2006.
Cogliati M, Britos P, García-Martínez R (2006) Patterns in Temporal Series of Meteorological Variables Using SOM & TDIDT In: Bramer M (ed) Artificial Intelligence in Theory and Practice, Boston, Springer, IFIP Series 217:305-314
Felgaer P, Britos P, and García-Martínez R, (2006) Prediction in Health Domain Using Bayesian Network Optimization Based on Induction Learning Techniques. Int. J. of Mod. Ph. C 17(3): 447-455
Grosser H, Britos P, García-Martínez R (2005) Detecting Fraud in Mobile Telephony Using Neural Networks. LNAI 3533:613-615
IEEE (1993) Standard IEEE 830-1993: Recommended Practice for Software Requirements Specifications. Institute of Electronic and Electrical Engineers Press.
IEEE (2004) Guide to the Software Engineering Body of Knowledge. IEEE Comp. Society Press
Jiang L, Eberlein A (2007) Selecting Requirements Engineering Techniques based on Project Attributes - A Case Study. 14th Annual IEEE ECBS: 269-278
Maiden N, Robertson S, Gizikis A (2004) Provoking Creativity: Imagine What Your Requirements Could be Like. IEEE Software 21(5): 68-75
Maiden N, Ncube C, Robertson S (2007) Can Requirements Be Creative? Experiences with an Enhanced Air Space Management System Proceedings 29th ICSE: 632-641
Pyle D (2003) Business Modeling and Business intelligence. Morgan Kaufmann
SAS (2008) SAS Enterprise Miner: SEMMA http://www.sas.com/technologies/analytics/ datamining/ miner/semma.html. Accessed 29 February 2008
Silva F, Freire J (2003) DWARF: An Approach for Requirements Definition and Management of Data Warehouse Systems. RE´03: 75-84
Solheim H, Lillehagen F, Petersen S, Jorgensen H, Anastasiou M (2005) Model-driven visual requirements engineering Proceedings RE´05:421-428
Valenga F, Fernández E, Merlino H, Rodríguez D, Procopio C, Britos P, García-Martínez R (2008) Minería de Datos Aplicada a la Detección de Patrones Delictivos en Argentina. VII JIISIC´08: 31-39
Winter R, Strauch B (2002) A Method for Demand-driven Information Requirements Analysis in Data Warehousing Projects. HICSS-36:231-239
Yang Q, Wu X (2006) 10 Challenging Problems in Data Mining Research. Int. J. Inf. Tech. & Decis. Mak. 5(4):597-604

Social Networks and KMS Use in US IT Services

William J. Dixon

Americas IT, Ernst & Young LLP, 1401 McKinney Street, Suite 1200, Houston, Texas, 77010, US, bill.dixon@ey.com

Abstract Little is known about how people, contexts, and tools impact decisions to use a Knowledge Management System (KMS). The purpose of this study was to better understand information retrieval when solving difficult problems. Key research questions focused on social structure, interpersonal relationships, and nature of the KMS. In this sequential exploratory study, semi-structured interviews were conducted and surveys were distributed to a purposive sample of 299 technology support personnel in a large accounting firm. Thematic analysis was applied against interview outcomes, and survey responses were analyzed using ANOVA and confirmed with the Kruskal-Wallis test. Social structure analysis showed fewer structural holes within networks among routine KMS users. Contrary to social resource theory, information was rarely sought from supervisors. Reciprocal information exchange accompanied asking for help, but not when information was retrieved from the KMS. In addition, formal designation of experts, electronic instant messaging (IM), and KMS minimized the impact of geographic disparity. The KMS facilitated the distribution of information and enabled learning but was not uniformly adopted. Recommendations for practice include the strategic designation of experts and refinement of mechanisms available for information retrieval.

1 Introduction

When a problem in the workplace is encountered, service providers make choices. Knowledge on which to base such decisions is imperfectly shared over time, and across people and organizations [10]. Employees often seek advice by asking their colleagues [14]. However, too much reliance on colleagues for advice may not result in an optimum outcome. People trying to solve a problem may not know who has the most pertinent expertise to help, resulting in an unconscious decision to settle for a less than optimum solution. The Knowledge Management (KM) literature abounds with descriptions of systems designed to guide decision makers [2,

Please use the following format when citing this chapter:

Dixon, W.J., 2008, in IFIP International Federation for Information Processing, Volume 274; *Advances in Information Systems Research, Education and Practice*; David Avison, George M. Kasper, Barbara Pernici, Isabel Ramos, Dewald Roode; (Boston: Springer), pp. 151–162.

15]. Most often, these systems include databases from which it is intended that decision makers will receive value. Value can be realized through shortened time to troubleshoot or better solutions to reoccurring problems. Designers of KM tools assume such systems will be used as they were intended. However, tools are often applied in practice differently than organizational leadership anticipated [2, 6]. This gap between organizationally-supported practice and actual behavior has been attributed to the "partial articulation of the espoused rules that govern behavior" [16, p. 601]. This research project examined the rules that govern the behavior of potential KMS users.

Borgatti and Cross supported the idea that "relationships are important for the acquisition of information and that the creation of knowledge is a social process" [5, p. 440]. Nevertheless, they concluded that little was known about the structural or interpersonal relationships that facilitated information exchange. Others have concluded "knowledge seeking and use, the employment of tools to support KM, and the outcomes of KM have yet to be carefully examined" [1, p. 197]. The problem examined in this study was this uncertainty around decisions to use a KMS. An extended literature review on these topics is available at http://home.comcast.net/~wm_dixon/. The following research questions framed this research:

1. How were the physical characteristics of the social networks of those who chose to use a KMS different than those who did not use a KMS?
2. How were the relational characteristics of the social networks of those who chose to use a KMS different than those who did not use a KMS?
3. What was the relationship between KMS utilization and the perceived accessibility of colleagues?
4. What was the relationship between KMS utilization and the perceived costs of asking colleagues for help?
5. What were the perceived benefits of KMS use?

2 Research Method

An exploratory, semi-structured interview strategy was used to first investigate how social context impacts decisions to use a KMS. Observations drawn from the interviews were then further examined and explored by conducting a census survey.

The behaviors of people associated with support services in the IT organization of a large accounting firm were examined in this study. The internal support organization maintained the IT infrastructure used by over 25,000 staff in the United States. Approximately 400 support technicians, spread between 72 offices, supported the day-to-day IT operations within the firm. All support technicians used the same call tracking and KMS to document their support activities. Technicians had the opportunity to both read support articles stored in the KMS and to recommend articles for inclusion. The article proposal process triggered a formal review of proposed support articles by specialists in each domain. Specialists then leveraged content managers and technical writers to publish a support article. Technicians were geographically dispersed throughout the continental U.S. and Hawaii. The sampling frame consisted of lists of login IDs from the call tracking system. A probability sample was drawn from this sampling frame. Stratification was employed, based on the concentration of support personnel in each office location. Three strata, each representing about 33% of the population, were established; offices in which 22 or more support personnel were based, where between 9 and 22 technicians were based, and where 8 or fewer technicians were based.

Participants of semi-structured interviews were identified using a proportionate stratified random sample. Five participants were randomly selected from each of the three strata to participate in face-to-face interviews which were conducted in the home office of the respondent. For the survey, a census sampling strategy was implemented. All members of the sampling frame were encouraged to complete an electronic self-administered questionnaire.

During the first phase of the study, semi-structured interviews were conducted to uncover attitudes toward KMS utilization and the social networks in which participants operated. The semi-structured interviews consisted of open-ended questions, and the topics were drawn from the literature. These questions focused on the quality of relationships, the nature of the KMS, and the nature of the information managed by participants. The objective of the interviews was to determine if there were particular concepts that were most important in deciding to use a KMS. Concepts in this category centered on trust, communication, relationships, job assignments, and individual predispositions. Data from the interviews was transcribed, coded, and compiled.

Subsequent to the interviewing process, a survey instrument was developed to determine the respondent's attitudes toward the outcomes of the interviews, physical structure of a respondent's social network, and relational structure of a respondent's network. The survey instrument used is available at http://home.comcast.net/~wm_dixon/. Demographic information sought included (a) employee tenure, (b) the professional rank, (c) how often the respondent used the KMS, and (d) the number of technicians based in their home office.

Descriptors of social network relationships, drawn from social network analysis (SNA), were calculated to compare the characteristics of social networks. The number of direct social linkages to each person named (agent or node) was calculated (vertex degree). Similarly, correlations between measures of network structure, relationships, and KMS use were sought. ANOVA of self-reported KMS utilization was compared between survey respondents from each of the three strata. The appropriate confirmatory tests were conducted in search of relationships between demonstrated KMS utilization and (a) vertex degree, (b) network centrality, (c) network density, (d) network cohesion, and (e) pertinent relationships that emerged from the interviews.

3 Results

Interviews were conducted with 15 technologists from 11 different office locations spread throughout the continental United States. During each interview, notes were taken by the interviewer. In addition, each session was recorded and transcribed. Information seeking behaviors were dependent on the circumstances. One respondent exhibited an innate tendency to think first about a person who had the information he sought and then to attempt to retrieve that information from the KMS.

> [My] first natural reaction is to think about who I think would know. That's my first
> natural reaction. What I really tend to do is look at the knowledge bases we have
> available. Depending on what the situation is. If it's a [Lotus] Notes issue, check out the
> Notes Knowledge Base. If it is something that is one of those general questions that I just
> forgot the answer, I know it's in there; I'll go into [the KMS] to find that information. (W.
> Dixon, personal communication, November 14, 2006)

The tendency to look for information in a KMS when the respondent was confident the information being sought was in the database was restated by participants from all strata. Furthermore, there was awareness among all interview participants of the professional rank of their information sources. Technical information was rarely sought from a participant's direct supervisor or person of senior rank.

Textual analysis was performed on the transcripts from the interviews. Respondents described their information retrieval protocol when being pushed to complete tasks quickly differently than when deadlines or heavy workloads were absent. Examples of why respondents preferred interpersonal interaction during information retrieval included (a) speed of information retrieval, (b) the ability to convey more specifically and completely what information was sought and (c) the opportunity to ask follow-up questions. The ability to engage in discussion with a knowledgeable colleague enhanced the learning process and helped the information seeker gain clarity on the information they needed. Two respondents indicated peer interaction facilitated KMS use when they were directed to a specific document in the KMS. Another interview participant described information retrieval from colleagues as a collaborative approach to the problem resolution process: "It is like having an extra set of hands. Two minds are better than one when trying to solve a problem."

There was greater consistency in terminology used by technologists who were from small offices than the medium and large offices. Technologists from small offices discussed direct interaction with their customers more often than their counterparts from larger offices. Peer interaction was discussed far more frequently by personnel in large offices and to a lesser extent by those who worked in medium-sized offices.

When in the presence of a client, respondents behaved differently than if they were on the telephone or if the client was not physically present. Information was sought from people when respondents knew a colleague had special information.

The KMS was often used when the respondent had sufficient information to formulate cohesive questions around the information being sought.

Individual communication styles were also criteria by which methods of information retrieval were determined. A respondent indicated interoffice conflicts had resulted from misconstrued messages among technologists. Consequently, some team members preferred face-to-face discussion over electronic instant messaging (IM) or e-mail.

Two classifications of affinity groups had been chartered by management as centers for information sharing. Members of these affinity groups were considered experts in their domains. One affinity group consisted of subject matter experts (SME teams) associated with selected products. Another was a group of people to whom problems were escalated by technologists once they had exhausted all troubleshooting resources, called the Virtual Technology Assistance Center (V-TAC). A respondent from a large office observed that many individuals who served in these expert roles were located in the same office location as he. Several kinds of IM sessions were discussed. More prevalent in small and medium-sized offices, some service managers had sanctioned IM sessions as information sharing mechanisms. One of the large offices had branded such sessions as *Tech Chat* and all technologists at that location where invited to participate.

Information retrieval strategies served multiple purposes. Relationships were nurtured as well as information obtained when respondents received information from colleagues. A participant mentioned she occasionally reached out to technologists outside of her area simply because she liked to meet new people. Another participant found the credibility of his peers reinforced through the information stored in the KMS.

Anchored to the research questions, four key operational themes emerged from the interview process and literature review: (a) preferences for information sources; (b) characteristics of a person as an information source; (c) information retrieval behaviors; and (d) situational nature of information retrieval.

The survey required the description of at least one interpersonal relationship. Respondents had the capability to complete a survey electronically for a two-week period. At that time, 299 technicians met the qualifications to complete the survey. Ultimately 129 surveys were completed and 17 additional respondents formally declined to participate. Those who reported weekly KMS use were labeled as routine KMS users (114). Non-routine KMS users were defined as those who self-reported having used the KMS on a quarterly basis or less, corresponding with the remaining 15 respondents.

Survey responses obtained from the routine KMS users were compared to responses from the non-routine KMS users. Both parametric and nonparametric statistical tests were used to mitigate the risks inherent in comparing unbalanced data, and assumptions regarding normal distributions, and similar variances [11].

Those who routinely used the KMS had worked for the firm for a shorter period of time than those who did not routinely use the KMS. The median number of years that routine KMS users had worked for the firm was 8.75 years, whereas the median tenure of those who reported they do not routinely use the KMS was 10 years. Similarly, the most recurrent response to the question regarding tenure with the firm was 7 years for KMS users and 11 years for non-routine KMS users.

3.1 Physical Characteristics of Social Networks

When describing their social networks, 700 unique descriptors were reported by respondents and linked to 1227 interpersonal relationships. The most recurrent person identified was named by 19 respondents. No statistical difference was found between the vertex degree of routine KMS users and respondents that did not routinely use the KMS.

Non-routine KMS users reported having known most of the members of their social networks longer than the routine KMS users. A statistical difference in how long KMS users had known the members of their networks was confirmed. The dispersion of years of employment was greatest for routine KMS users whereas the responses of non-routine KMS users were more heavily clustered at five or more years.

The frequency of interaction among network participants was most evenly distributed for routine KMS users. Non-KMS users interacted more frequently with their network members than those who routinely used the KMS. In Table 1, the characteristics of reported information networks are listed.

Table 1. General Social Network Characteristics

Strata/KMS Use	Nodes	Edges	Outsiders	Centrality	Density	Cohesion
Large Office/KMS User	35	44	0	4.5	0.0370	0
Med. Office/KMS User	158	236	4	9.5	0.0095	4
Med. Office/Non-User	14	11	0	2.8	0.0604	0
Small Office/KMS User	234	421	2	19.4	0.0077	6

Edges represented the number of relationships drawn between people. Outsiders were created when a respondent volunteered the names of their contacts, but that individual was not identified by other survey respondents. Centrality reflected the extent to which information in a network was distributed [4] and was lowest among those who did not routinely use the KMS. In Table 1, centrality was measured as relative entropy. Relative entropy accommodates the comparison of centrality between networks of differing sizes. The degree of connectedness of each network was represented by density and was highest for those who did not routinely use the KMS. Cohesion reflected the extent to which directed networks were symmetrical. Symmetry was greatest in networks with many nodes.

3.2 Relational Characteristics

Non-routine KMS users reported relationships with individuals in roles encompassing formalized expertise less often than did KMS users. Whereas non-routine KMS users reported relationships with V-TAC or SME team members in 37% of the relationships reported, KMS users reported that 63% of their relationships were with personnel in those formal roles. Personnel based in small offices leveraged those in formalized roles more often than their counterparts who were based in medium and large offices. Two respondents wrote comments indicating they also considered *prior* experience of information providers in formalized roles as an inducement to rely on those individuals for information.

Personnel who routinely used the KMS considered the legitimate roles of their contacts more important than the availability of that contact. In Table 2, the proportion of each population that reported any of these attributes of social relationships as most important is summarized. When seeking information, those who did not routinely use the KMS reported the availability of their contacts as more important than the legitimate role of that individual.

Table 2. Characteristics Reported as Most Important by KMS Use

Usage	Availability	Legitimate Role	Having Met	Face-to-Face Interaction	Supervisor
Routine KMS Users	32%	41%	5%	10%	1%
Non-routine KMS User	47%	27%	5%	11%	1%

Survey responses demonstrated a link between office size, the availability of an information source, and their legitimate role. In Table 3, the proportion for each stratum that reported relational criteria as most important is summarized. Personnel from small offices most often rated the legitimate role of information providers more important than their availability whereas personnel from the medium strata considered availability more important.

Table 3. Most Important Characteristics by Strata

Strata	N	Availability	Legitimate Role	Having Met	Face-to-Face Interaction	Supervisor
Large	9	22%	33%	11%	0	0
Medium	49	47%	31%	6%	10%	0
Small	71	25%	46%	3%	13%	1%

Contrary to the literature, supervisors were the least preferred information source for all respondents. Few survey respondents described information seeking relationships with their supervisors (10% of the relationships reported by non-routine KMS users and 6% of the relationships reported by routine KMS users).

3.3 Accessibility of Colleagues

Personnel who routinely used the KMS considered the legitimate roles of their contacts more important than the availability of that contact. Conversely, when seeking information, those who did not routinely use the KMS reported the availability of their contacts as more important than the legitimate role of that individual.

Interview participant's revealed accessibility could be obtained through direct interpersonal contact or by electronically mediated mechanisms. The majority of survey respondents participated in IM sessions with personnel from other offices to obtain support information. As detailed in Table 4, there was a higher incidence of IM participation among routine KMS users than those who did not routinely use the KMS.

Table 4. Participation in Electronic Chat (IM) Sessions

Usage	All	Large Office	Medium Office	Small Office
Routine KMS Users	77%	71%	70%	83%
Non-KMS Users	42%	67%	63%	25%

The availability of a colleague was a precursor to asking a colleague for information for those who did not routinely use the KMS. On average, routine KMS users did not agree that colleague availability led to asking him or her for information.

3.4 Costs of Asking for Help

Almost all respondents indicated they went out of their way to help a peer find information if a peer had provided information in the past. Claims of such reciprocity were not limited to any strata or contingent on KMS use. Few respondents agreed that asking a peer for help made the respondent appear less competent. There was no significant difference between cohorts in either of these areas.

Speed was a recurrent theme volunteered by those who participated in the interview process. Those who did not routinely use the KMS agreed information was most quickly retrieved from a colleague. In contrast, those who routinely used the KMS were indifferent to this idea.

3.5 Benefits of KMS Use

There was general agreement from both cohorts that asking a colleague for help was a mechanism by which interpersonal relationships were nurtured. In addition, there was general agreement among those who routinely used the KMS that the breadth of their knowledge in *existing areas* of knowledge and their knowledge in *new areas* were expanded as a consequence of KMS use. Those who did not routinely use the KMS agreed less frequently that KMS use broadened their breadth of technical knowledge.

4. Conclusions

Weak network ties were less prevalent among those who routinely used the KMS. A key difference between the physical characteristics of the networks of those who chose to use the KMS and those who did not was the level of network centrality. Behaviors indicative of information being concentrated with few individuals was lowest among non-routine KMS users (% of entropy = 3.5). Low measures of centrality are also indicative of weak ties. Granovetter claimed weak ties were a better source for innovative information than strong social ties [9]. The efficiency gained by having weak social ties enabled those who did not routinely use the KMS to achieve their goals without using the KMS. These behaviors may also reflect the longer tenure of respondents who indicated they did not routinely use the KMS. Having worked for the firm longer, respondents in this category developed information-seeking behaviors and interpersonal relationships which satisfied information requirements without the assistance of the KMS.

Information retrieval behaviors are shaped by geographic location. In addition, the legitimate role of potential information sources is a proxy for personal knowledge of others. Accordingly, respondents in medium and larger offices indicated they relied less on designations such as legitimate role in identifying potential information sources. In the absence of close physical proximity, the current and past role of an information source has the greatest impact on the information seeking behaviors where physical proximity constrains interaction.

Information seekers exclude potential information sources in efforts to improve information retrieval effectiveness. Contrary to social resource theory, few respondents sought information from their supervisors when solving an incident on behalf of their customers. In further contrast, actionable knowledge came from lower ranked individuals and was often obtained from organizationally-designated experts. Although a central premise of social resource theory was that those higher in the organizational hierarchy possessed better information [12], participants indicated they did not seek technical information from supervisors because they did not have current knowledge of the technologies supported by the firm.

The use of IM complements both KMS use and colleague access. IM has been described as a "critical real-time communications tool" by which distance and time were overcome [13, p.1]. IM enables rapid dissemination of information, rapid problem resolution, immediate contact with experts, and is ideally suited for environments fraught with time sensitivity and geographic dispersal [7]. A greater proportion of routine KMS users participated in IM sessions (77%) than those who did not routinely use the KMS (42%). As a synchronous tool, IM expanded access to colleagues as potential information sources. At the same time, those who had a propensity to use the KMS, an asynchronous tool, also tended to leverage IM. New technologies do not necessarily result in the abandonment of previous ones [8]. Instead, IM services complemented the KMS.

There is evidence that synchronous and asynchronous technologies are converging, with long term implications for the traditional architecture of a KMS. Robot technologies are currently offered by AOL and AIM which automatically return responses based on messages sent from IM. The extent to which organizations are successful in integrating these new technologies into their processes become more important as the demographics of the workforce shift. The age of those who use technologies may significantly influence the features actually used [8]. While longer tenure did not necessarily mean those who did not routinely use the KMS were older than those who routinely used the KMS, the literature suggests this may have been the case.

Regardless of a respondent's propensity to use the KMS, a perceived cost of asking colleagues for help was an obligation to reciprocate. Consistent with social resource theory, reciprocity in the provision of information was universal among all respondents. The emotion of gratitude encouraged reciprocation "even if such reciprocation will be costly to him or her in the short term" [3, p. 319]. An interview participant described attempts to attain help from people she did not know as an effort to build and nurture relationships. Reciprocal prosocial behavior helps build trust and preserves relationships.

Perceptions of the technical prowess of colleagues are enhanced through KMS use. When the identity of the information provider is included in the KMS, the KMS may act as a proxy for direct interaction between an information seeker and the information provider. However, the mechanism by which a KMS mediates the human emotion of gratitude and impacts the construction of ongoing relationships requires further study.

At the individual level, balance between gaining information from a colleague verses a KMS is shaped by available technologies and the physical environment. One information source does not necessarily replace another, as information was sometimes gained through the complementary use of colleague referral and the KMS. Respondents preferred to learn from their peers. Nevertheless, the breadth of knowledge and knowledge in new areas was expanded through KMS use. Consistent with those of Zander and Kogut [17], the written and teachable nature of KMS content facilitated knowledge transfer.

5 Limitations

The breadth of external validity of these conclusions needs to be established through further study. This study was conducted at multiple sites, within the same firm. It is unknown the extent to which conclusions drawn from the examination of one internal support organization can be generalized to other internal support organizations or in the open marketplace. Further consideration of organizational and geographic culture should be applied to related research in other contexts.

While efforts were made to encourage as much participation from potential participants as possible, ultimately responses to invitations for interviews or to complete surveys were voluntary. In addition, the author of this research conducted the interviews. Because he was associated with the KM tools being discussed, there is risk that the responses of respondents did not reflect their true feelings or perceptions.

6 Recommendations for Practice and Further Research

New tools do not necessarily replace old ones and the resultant levels of redundancy provide a mechanism by which all members of a community can participate in double-loop learning. Those responsible for encouraging collaboration within organizations should build redundancy into their knowledge sharing and learning platforms.

The acquisition of knowledge is not limited to the extraction of ideas from one source, such as a KMS, colleagues, or trial and error. Knowledge production can be facilitated through processes associated with social relationships, technologies, and direct experience. These processes may be organic or contrived in nature. Naturally occurring social networks or formalized knowledge refereeing and publication schemes are vehicles by which ideas are circulated within a work environment. Each methodology can contribute toward the integration of knowledge in the workplace. Those that influence or design such processes should be strategic when addressing the creation and propagation of these information paths.

Where great geographic disparity exists, information exchange is supported by relational structures that help people build and maintain ties along with corresponding mental directories. People in small offices recognized the expertise of others by virtue of formally designated roles; therefore, leaders in geographically dispersed organizations should consider purposeful and public designation of the expertise of members of the workforce when trying to build consistency across geographically-dispersed organizations.

Additional research is needed to understand the circumstances under which technologies can be leveraged to impact interpersonal network structure. Further research into the linkage between network centrality, social ties, and information exchange will provide guidance to practitioners seeking to improve the efficiency of information exchange across geographically-dispersed organizations. For both scholars and practitioners, the relevancy of further research in this area has expanded due to economic forces such as globalization, mergers, and acquisitions.

References

1. Alavi M, Kayworth T, Leidener D (2005) An empirical examination of the influence of organizational structure on knowledge management practices. J Management Inf Systems 22:191-224
2. Arnold V, Clark N, Collier P, Leech S, Sutton S (2006) The differential use and effect of knowledge-based system explanations in novice and expert judgment decisions. MIS Q 30:79-97
3. Bartlett M, DeSteno D (2006) Gratitude and proscocial behavior: Helping when it costs you. Psychological Science 17:319-325
4. Benta M (2005) Studying communication networks with Agna 2.1. Cognition, Brain, Behav 9:567-574
5. Borgatti S, Cross R (2003) A relational view of information seeking and learning in social networks. Management Science 49:432-445
6. Brown JS, Duguid P (1991) Organizational learning and communities-of-practice: Toward a unified view of working, learning, and innovation. Organizational Science 2:40-57
7. Cain M (2006) Justifying instant messaging investments. Technical Rep Gartner Res
8. Constantiou I, Damsgaard J, Knutsen L (2007) The four incremental steps toward advanced mobile service adoption. Communications of the ACM 50:51-55
9. Granovetter M (1973) The strength of weak ties. American J Sociology 78:1360-1380
10. Hargadon A, Sutton RI (1997) Technology brokering and innovation in a product development firm. Administrative Science Q 42:726-749
11. Keren G (1993) A balanced approach to unbalanced design. In: Keren G, Lewis C (eds) A handbook for data analysis in the behavior sciences. Lawrence Erlbaum Associates, Hillsdale, NJ
12. Lin N (2001) Social capital: A theory of social structure and action. Cambridge University Press, New York
13. Lundy J, Smith DM (2007) The top five uses for instant messaging. Technical Rep Gartner Res
14. Michailova S, Husted K (2003) Knowledge-sharing hostility in Russian firms. Calif Management Rev 43:59-77
15. Prince S (2006) HP's adaptive approach to enterprise content management. KM World 388:12-13
16. Szulanski G, Cappetta R, Jensen R (2004) When and how trustworthiness matters: Knowledge transfer and the moderating effect of causal ambiguity. Organizational Science 15:600-613
17. Zander U, Kogut B (1995) Knowledge and the speed of transfer and imitation of organizational capabilities: An empirical test. Organizational Science 6:76-92

Realizing the Value of Business Intelligence

Derek Smith and Maria Crossland

Department of Information Systems
University of Cape Town, ZA

Abstract: Business Intelligence (BI) remains one of the top priority issues for CIOs and investment in BI technologies continues to grow. This research attempted to understand how an organization can realize the business value derived from their investment in BI.

A single, in-depth case study was undertaken in a major South African financial services organization. An extended IT business value process model, derived from the research literature, was used as a framework.

The study found that the realization of business value from BI is highly dependent on activities that occur in all 5 stages of the process model – from the alignment of the BI strategy with that of the organization, through to the way in which the business benefits of BI are measured, but that the actual measurement of these remains challenging due to the delayed, indirect and intangible nature of many of the benefits.

Keywords: benefits realization, business intelligence, BI, business value

Please use the following format when citing this chapter:

Smith, D. and Crossland, M., 2008, in IFIP International Federation for Information Processing, Volume 274; *Advances in Information Systems Research, Education and Practice*; David Avison, George M. Kasper, Barbara Pernici, Isabel Ramos, Dewald Roode; (Boston: Springer), pp. 163–174.

1. Introduction

Whilst BI remains one of the top technology issues for CIOs, little research has been done regarding the actual business value realized as a result of BI investment (Bitterer, Rayner, Hostmann, Gassman, Schlegel, Beyer, Burton, Herschel, Friedman, Newman, Logan, Andrews, Sarner, White,& Radcliffe, 2006; Negash, 2004).

Measuring the business value attributable to investment in IT has been a challenge facing organizations for some time. Findings from past research into IT value have proposed a variety of solutions from calculations based solely on financial indicators to process models and scorecard-based models. However, many benefits associated with IT investment are often elusive.

In particular, it is difficult to determine actual value returned by investment in BI technologies as the business benefits can be indirect, intangible and difficult to measure and realize in different parts of the organization (Gartz, 2004).

This research aims to gain insights into how an organization realizes and measures the business value derived from investments in BI.

2. Measuring the Value of IT Investment

BI can be defined as a "collection of integrated operational as well as decision support applications and databases that provide the business community with easy access to business data" (Moss & Atre, 2003, p.4).

BI has no value of its own – value is created by acting on the information delivered to the organization (Brown, 2005; Lonnqvist & Pirttimaki, 2006). According to Pirttimaki, Lonngvist & Karjaluoto (2006), there is insufficient research on BI value measurement.

Several authors conclude that finding an accurate and reliable method to measure business value achieved as a result of IT investment remains elusive (Gibson & Arnott, 2005; Marshall, McKay, Prananto, 2004). Whilst studies have found that up to 86% of CFOs claim to use traditional, financial indicators such as Return on Investment (ROI) to evaluate IT investments, only 18% of CIOs reported using ROI as they acknowledged the need to consider factors such as reduced costs and improved productivity (Silvius, 2006). Criticism has been leveled at inflexible, financially-based evaluation models as this focus is deemed not wide enough (Gibson & Arnott, 2005). Intangible benefits often make a significant contribution to performance but even if they are measured (using instruments such as questionnaires), establishing the link between the benefit and organization performance is complex (Remenyi, 1999). Measuring the value of IT remains a complex task due to a lack of understanding of the processes responsible for realizing benefits (Jain, 2006).

A number of studies identified by Silvius (2006) conclude that a process model is appropriate for studying how IT adds business value. Many are based on the process model proposed by Soh and Markus (1995). This model, shown in Figure 1, identifies the relationship between IT investments and business value focusing on how, when and why IT creates value.

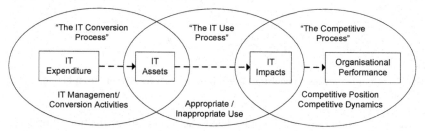

Figure 1 - How IT creates business value – a process model. Source: Soh & Markus (1995)

The IT Conversion Process addresses the acquisition of IT products and services and deployment of IT capability. Investment is necessary but not sufficient to ensure the conversion of expenditure into a usable asset (Soh & Markus, 1995). The outcome relies on the management of the IT Use Process and includes activities such as developing an IT strategy, ensuring the necessary organizational structures are available to support the strategy, focusing on the correct initiatives and the effective management of those IT projects.

The IT Use Process represents the activities that are necessary to ensure that IT assets are used appropriately in the organization. These activities result in new products, improved business processes and improved decision-making. Users need to have the necessary skills to use these IT assets appropriately for the benefits to be realized (Soh & Markus, 1995).

The IT Competitive Process examines the outcomes of the impacts achieved through investment in IT including improved products, services and business processes (Soh & Markus, 1995).

Marshall et al (2004) suggested a modified model which links the IT investments back to the business strategy. They proposed a fourth process (shown as the IT Alignment Process in figure 2) which recognizes a strategic focus for IT investment which aligns with business strategy and organizational performance.

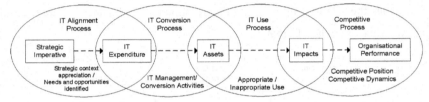

Figure 2 - Modified process model for the realization of business value from IT. Source: Marshall et al. (2004)

The IT alignment process includes tasks such as the identification of opportunities (both business and technical) and the development of a clear IT strategy which aligns with that of the organization (Marshall et al, 2004). This modified model was used by Marshall et al. (2004) to analyze how executives in Australian organizations ensured that IT investment resulted in increased organizational efficiency, effectiveness or competitiveness. They found that IT was seen to contribute to increased profitability and to business value. They identified the IT Alignment Process as the most critical process to reralize business value from IT investments.

3. The Value of Business Intelligence

Many of the benefits realized as a result of BI initiatives are non-financial and often intangible, such as timely delivery of information and improved product or
service quality, and whilst they should lead to financial, measurable benefits, a
time lag may make measurement difficult (Lonnqvist & Pirttimaki, 2006). These
intangible benefits are difficult to identify and this makes the process of evaluating
BI systems complex (Gibson & Arnott, 2005).

Many BI projects fail to deliver the expected benefits (Gartz, 2004). A user of
BI tools and process will perceive value related to the ease of use of the tools,
whereas at an organizational level, value would be based on benefits realized as a
result of the intelligence available (Pirttimaki et al., 2006).

The benefits related to enhanced knowledge availability often take time to
translate into returns which makes it difficult to connect the return to the information used to deliver it (Rouble-Flores & Kulkarni, 2005). It is therefore appropriate to use a process model which evaluates intermediate-level, business process
performance measures (such as efficiency and effectiveness) to connect individual
performance to that of the organization.

The modified Process Model together with the concept of benefits realization
management provided an Extended Process Model as shown in Figure 3.

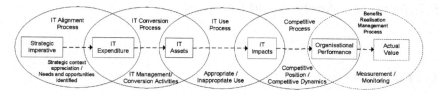

Figure 3 - Extended Process Model. Adapted from Soh & Markus (1995), Marshall et al.(2004)

The Benefits Realization Management process includes activities such as the
up-front estimation of expected benefits as well as ongoing monitoring to determine the actual benefit realized.

4. Research Methodology

The research approach was exploratory and deductive using an established model as a framework. A single case study approach was followed. Case studies are appropriate where there is limited amount of existing knowledge and when a phenomenon is broad and complex (Dube and Pare, 2003). A single case study fracilitiates an in-depth investigation.

The following research question was addressed:

What are the actions taken, challenges faced and measurement methodologies adopted by an organization in realizing and measuring the business value of BI investments?

Based on the extended process model, thirty-one open-ended questions were derived and qualitative data was collected using these questions in semi-structured interviews.

A sample of twelve senior IT and user managers responsible for BI were approached for interview. The instrument was pre-tested using a pilot interview with a BI executive.

The interview transcripts were analysed relative to the activities in each of the five processes in the model.

5. Information Analysis and Findings

5.1 IT Alignment Process

The bank's move from a product-centric strategy to a customer-centric approach is dependent on the bank being able to obtain a single view of data that is currently stored in a number of disparate systems. BI is often used to gain a customer-centric view of data as it makes it possible to build a single view based on data from multiple 'silo' source systems. There have been significant changes within the bank's IT architecture to align IT with the strategic goals – particularly the introduction of an ERP solution to provide a single view of a customer.

Whilst ZAFBank's business strategy is clear and the interviewees were aware of the organization's strategic goals, there was less clarity regarding BI strategy. The interviewees had quite different perceptions regarding the BI strategy depending on their roles and involvement in the BI process. The lack of clarity and understanding around BI strategy has led to disparate and duplicated data and effort.

ZAFBank has acknowledged the need for a more centralized, structured approach and three of the interviewees have recently moved into roles that have been created with a view to strengthening BI's contribution to towards the achievement of strategic goals. Without a clear BI strategy it is difficult to achieve alignment between BI and the overall business strategy and to ensure that all BI initiatives are driven by business goals (Venter & Tustin, 2006).

The need for change in budget ownership has been identified. The lack of clarity regarding the investment in BI and control of the BI budget can be attributed to the fact that the person currently responsible for the BI budget was not interviewed as budget ownership was unclear due to realignment of roles. The change to a charge-back system based on data usage rather than data volumes would be more in line with the BI process measurement indicators suggested by Howson (2006) and Pirttimaki et al. (2006).

5.2 IT Conversion Process

The Conversion Process in the model is used to address the acquisition of BI products and services and deployment of BI capability.

All participants shared the view that BI should be owned by the business and a business sponsor for BI projects is important. However, lack of a clear BI strategy and lack of business ownership has led to IT playing a driving role in the delivery of BI at times, resulting in solutions that often do not meet the business requirements.

A clearly defined BI strategy would also address the lack of consistency regarding BI architecture and limit the number of tactical solutions being created by business teams, a consequence predicted by Raab (2000). The concerns expressed regarding the need for a 'back-to-basics' approach to BI architecture indicate that the current design and platform may need to be reviewed. It will not be possible to put existing BI requirements on hold whilst a new BI environment is designed and implemented, however, the problems need to be addressed as the volumes of BI data stored outside of the EIW (such as the warehouse developed to meet Basel II requirements) may soon exceed the volumes in the EIW and the lack of governance around those solutions poses a risk to the business.

The importance of data quality and its impact on the overall success of BI initiatives is acknowledged, but whilst ZAFBank is consciously addressing data quality issues on its ERP platform, the BI environment does not yet have robust data governance processes and policies in place. Changes to the BI architecture to provide a *"single version of the truth"* would eliminate many of the data quality issues as all reports would be based on the same set of data. The recognition of the need for a person to take responsibility for information management indicates that there is commitment to addressing the data quality issues.

5.3 IT Use Process

The Use Process in the model represents the activities that are necessary to ensure that BI assets are used appropriately in the organization. The impacts of activities in this process may result in organizational impacts such as new products, improved business processes, improved decision making and the flexibility to take advantage of new opportunities. Users need to have the necessary skills to use the BI assets appropriately if the benefits are to be realized.

Various interviewees from the business area (BI teams and BI consumers) commented on the differences between data, information, intelligence and knowledge and share Williams and Williams (2007) view of their organization being data-rich but information-poor.

Involvement of business users in the entire BI process was viewed as critical an they need to play an increasingly significant role whereby they become owners and drivers of a BI strategy with IT playing a support role. Griffin (2007) identifies successful BI delivery to be dependent on a strong partnership between IT and business.

Interviewees involved in defining the strategic direction of BI within ZAFBank understand the concept of a Business Intelligence competency Centre (BICC). However, there are indications that a true BICC structure would not be possible within the organizational structures at ZAFBank as the EIW is owned by IT. A more centralized business BI team had been recently been established and was fulfilling some of the goals of a BICC.

5.4 IT Competitive Process

The IT Competitive process focuses on the benefit the organization achieves through improved products, services and business processes. The interviewees appreciated the importance of business involvement in BI which should the formal ownership of BI in the business. The positive views of all interviewees regarding the success of their BI initiatives should encourage increased use of BI to support business goals.

The interviewees view the current data quality levels and the BI architecture as weak. This implies that these basic issues need addressing to realize the full benefit of its investment in BI.

The BI activities of competitors are not currently of concern to ZAFBank. If the level of awareness of BI value is raised within the organization, more attention might be paid to competitors as BI could be seen as a means of achieving competitive advantage (O'Brien & Kok, 2006). ZAFBank already has competitive intelligence programs but the data resides outside of the formal BI environment. This information would add additional value if it was more easily accessible to BI users.

5.5 Benefits Realization Management Process

The concept of benefits realization management is understood in ZAFBank and ongoing measuring and monitoring is taking place in certain cases. Although the study undertaken by Lin and Pervan (2003) focused on benefits realization management linked to IT projects, similar situations appear in the BI environment at ZAFBank – indirect benefits are used to justify BI initiatives and there is confidence that the investment in BI is adding value. However there is little planning for benefits realization management and the measurement of actual value realized is almost non-existent.

The establishment of a formal benefits realization management process could make the prioritization of BI requests simpler and more effective as it would be possible to link priority to expected business benefits. The description of a project that had a strong business case but was later viewed as unnecessary was a good example of what Reiss et al. (2006, p250) refer to as "voodoo figures" being used to justify a BI initiative. Techniques and methods for estimating expected business value for those types of BI requests that are currently difficult to quantify are required (Pirttimaki et al., 2006).

The view that BI is adding value simply because it is being used contradicts the view of Lin & Pervan (2003) which states that unless measurable impacts of the implementation of IT investments can be identified, it is unlikely that any benefit has been realized.

6. Conclusion

This study concludes that the realization of business value from BI is highly dependent on activities that occur in all 5 stages of the process model – from the alignment of the BI strategy with that of the organization, through to the way in which the business benefits of BI are measured, but that the actual measurement of these remains challenging due to the delayed, indirect and intangible nature of many of the benefits. As the investment in BI grows, the requirement to realize the benefit will become more important.

In the organization studied, establishing clear ownership and responsibility for the BI budget led to an improvement in benefits estimation as expected benefits and business value became more significant in the project portfolio prioritization process. Clear, overall governance and ownership of a BI function also encourages the creation of a documented BI strategy. It seems unlikely that a single team could become responsible for both the technical and business BI functions within an organization. A strong partnership, established between the business and IT BI teams, is identified as the major reason for success.

Whilst there appears to be a general need for more robust value and benefit measurement processes, the organization studied appeared to be comfortable with the notion that BI adds value even if it cannot always be measured. From the study, it appears that much of the business value is derived from activities linked to the IT Use Process. There is considerable potential to derive even more business value with an increased focus on the activities across the entire process model and in particular on the IT Alignment and Conversion Process.

Although this study focused on one financial services organization, the conclusions relating to BI are supported by previous research findings with a broader IT focus covering a variety of business sectors.

References

Bitterer, A., Rayner, N., Hostmann, B., Gassman, B., Schlegel, K., Beyer, M.A., Burton, B., Herschel, G. Friedman, T., Newman, D., Logan, D., Andrews, W., Sarner, A., White, A.& Radcliffe, J. (2006). *Hype Cycle for Business Intelligence and Corporate Performance Management, 2006.* Retrieved 13 April 2007 from http://www.gartner.com ID G00140064.
Brown, A. (2005). IS Evaluation in Practice. *Electronic Journal of Information Systems Evaluation,* 8(3), 169-178. Retrieved 29 April 2007 from http://www.ejise.com
Dubé, L., & Paré, G. (2003). Rigor in Information Systems Positivist Case Research: Current Practices, Trends, and Recommendations, *MIS Quarterly,* 27(4), 597-636
Gartz, U. (2004). Enterprise Information Management, in Raisinghani, M. (Ed), *Business Intelligence in the Digital Economy: Opportunities, Limitations and Risks.* Hershey: Idea Group Publishing.

Gibson, M.& Arnott, D. (2005). The Evaluation of Business Intelligence: A Case Study in a Major Financial Institution. *Proceedings of the 16th Australasian Conference on Information Systems*, 29 Nov – 2 Dec 2005, Sydney.

Gonzales, M.L. (2004). Creating a BI Strategy Document. *DM Review* , 14(11), 24-51.

Griffiths, P.& Remenyi, D. (2003). Information Technology in Financial Services: A Model for Value Creation. *Electronic Journal of Systems Evaluation*, 6(2), 107 –116. Retrieved 29 April 2007 from http://www.ejise.com

Griffin, J. (2007). Putting the Business Back into Business Intelligence Initiatives. *DM Review*, 17(2), 15.

Howson, C. (2006). The Seven Pillars of BI Success. *Intelligent Enterprise*, 9(9), 33-37.

Kohli, R.& Sherer, S. A. (2006). Deriving Value from Information Technology: Role of Concordance Investments. *Proceedings of the 12th Americas Conference on Information Systems*, 4-6 Aug 2006, Acapulco.

Lin, C. & Pervan, G. (2003). The Practice of IS/IT Benefits Management in Large Australian Organizations. *Information and Management*, 41(1), 13-24.

Lonnqvist, A. & Pirttimaki, V (2006). The Measurement of Business Intelligence. *Information Systems Management Journal*, 23(1), 32-40. 1-3 Dec 2004, Hobart, Tasmania

Marshall, P., McKay, J. & Prananto, A. (2004). A Process Model of Business Value Creation from IT Investments. *Proceedings of the Fifteenth Australasian Conference on Information Systems*, 1-3 Dec 2004, Hobrt, Tasmania.

Moss, L.T. & Atre, S. (2003). *Business Intelligence Roadmap: The Complete Project Lifecycle for Decision Support Applications.* Boston: Addison Wesley.

Negash, S. (2004). Business Intelligence. *Communications of the Association for Information Systems* 13, 177-195.

O'Brien, J. & Kok, J.A. (2006). Business Intelligence and the Telecommunications Industry: Can Business Intelligence Lead to Higher Profits? South African Journal of Information Management, 8(3). . Retrieved 10 March 2007 from http://www.sajim.co.za

Peppard, J., Ward, J. & Daniel, E. (2007). Managing the Realization of Business Benefits from IT Investments. *MIS Quarterly Executive*, 6(1), 1 – 11.

Pirttimaki, V., Lonngvist, A. & Karjaluoto, A. (2006). Measurement of Business Intelligence in a Finnish Telecommunications Company. *The Electronic Journal of Knowledge Management*, 4(1), 83-90. Retrieved 29 April 2007 from http://www.ejkm.com

Raab, T. (2000). The Need for a Business Intelligence strategy: A Critical Analysis from the Insurance Industry. *DM Review*,10(6). Retrieved 9 September 2007 from http://www.dmreview.com/article_sub.cfm?articleId=2291

Reiss,G., Anthony, M., Chapman, J., Leigh, G., Pyne, A. & Rayner,P. (2006). *Gower Handbook of Programme Management.* Aldershot: Gower Publishing Limited.

Remenyi, D. (1999). The Elusive Nature of Delivering Benefits from IT Investment. *The Electronic Journal of Systems Evaluation*, 3(1). Retrieved 29 April 2007 from http://www.ejise.com

Robles-Flores. J.A. & Kulkarni, U. (2005). Knowledge Management Systemes: A Business Value Model. *Proceedings of the Ninth Pacific Asia Conference on Information Systems*, 7-10 July 2005, Bangkok.

Silvius, A.J.G. (2006). Does ROI Matter? Insights into the True Business Value of IT. *The Electronic Journal of Systems Evaluation* 9(2), 93 – 104. Retrieved 13 April 2007 from http://www.ejise.com.

Soh, C. & Markus, M. L. (1995). How IT Creates Business Value: A Process Theory Synthesis. *Proceedings of the Sixteenth International Conference on Information Systems*

Venter, P. & Tustin, D.H. (2006). *Business Intelligence in South Africa.* Pretoria: Bureau of Market research.

Ward, J. & Daniel, E. (2006). *Benefits Management – Delivering Value from IS and IT Investments.* Chichester: John Wiley & Sons. , Amsterdam, The Netherlands, 1995.

Williams, S. & Williams, N. (2007). *The Profit Impact of Business Intelligence.* San Francisco: Morgan Kaufmann.

AN RFID ADOPTION FRAMEWORK: A CONTAINER SUPPLY CHAIN ANALYSIS

Lisa F Seymour, Emma Lambert-Porter and Lars Willuweit

Information Systems Department
University of Cape Town, ZA

Abstract: While the benefits of RFID (radio frequency identification) in supply chains have had extensive press, publicised cases showing poor returns on investment and a relative lack of research into its adoption has left organisations feeling uncertain about the challenges to be managed when assessing RFID adoption. This qualitative study in the South African port community refines and extends an RFID adoption framework and provides insight into the factors potentially affecting the adoption of this new technology as well as the probability of adoption in that community. Four new factors not previously mentioned in research were identified: related initiatives; the integrated structure of the industry; organisational dominance with the supply chain and the supply chain culture. An argument for their validity within the RFID adoption framework is presented. The research reveals that cost, the absence of a universally-adopted standard and the supply chain culture are currently the major setbacks to RFID adoption in the South African port community.

Keywords: RFID, Container Supply Chain, technology adoption

1. Introduction

The increasingly competitive nature of global markets has forced supply chain organisations to increase collaboration and flexibility in their business processes. Yet, the extended integration of a large number of parties along global supply chains means that a number of inefficiencies such as delayed shipments, shrinkage and billing delays can be incurred at many points. The solution to these inefficiencies is deemed to be complete tracking of goods in a cost-effective manner (Nikam and Satpute 2006). Radio Frequency Identification (RFID) has been proposed as a tracking solution due to its ability to enhance efficiency and quality of information exchange. Yet, many companies have failed to achieve benefits from RFID adoption and a relative lack of research on RFID adoption has left organisations feeling uncertain about the challenges to be faced (Ranganathan and Jha 2005). This calls for research to address unresolved RFID adoption issues.

Therefore, the main objective of this research was to understand and identify factors potentially affecting RFID adoption through refining and extending the RFID adoption framework proposed by Seymour et al. (2007). We chose to analyse the South African (SA) port community perceptions on (RFID) adoption

Please use the following format when citing this chapter:

Seymour, L.F., Lambert-Porter, E. and Willuweit, L., 2008, in IFIP International Federation for Information Processing, Volume 274; *Advances in Information Systems Research, Education and Practice*; David Avison, George M. Kasper, Barbara Pernici, Isabel Ramos, Dewald Roode; (Boston: Springer), pp. 175–188.

within the container supply chain. Ports play a fundamental part in global trade and global supply chains. As increasing trade pressures put their throughput under pressure, they are turning to technology solutions. Jansen (2005) argues that there are drawbacks in many development frameworks as they do not allow for specific national contexts and priorities. Each nation has its unique geography, history and culture and research needs to take into consideration these specifics. A second objective was therefore to understand the context of RFID adoption within the SA container supply chain and obtain insight into the probability of adoption.

2.   RFID and other supply chain technologies

For RFID to yield supply chain visibility, it needs to be integrated with other supply chain technologies (SCTs). SCTs assist organisations with tracking and are classified as either informational; decision oriented, or transactional (Singh et al. 2007). Transactional systems include enterprise resource planning (ERP) systems and decision oriented systems include Advanced planning systems (APS) found in APS packages and in the supply chain management components of ERP systems. Informational technologies include Extranets, EDI and RFID. The three types of SCTs are integrated to enable tracking. RFID tags are placed on items which then pass through the reader's generated magnetic field, identifying the item. The information is communicated, filtered by middleware and transferred typically via an integration server to the transactional and decision-oriented systems.

3.   Factors influencing RFID adoption

Organisations need a systematic framework to assess the fit of new technologies with their organisation and to understand adoption implications. Bakry (2003) proposed the STOPE model which can assist in determining the readiness of organisations to adopt new technologies. The model introduces five basic elements of development used in e-readiness analyses: Strategy (with regards to the future development of the industry), Technology (upon which the industry is based), Organisations (related to the industry), People (concerned in the industry) and Environment (existing in the industry). With intra- and inter-organizational factors included, the model provides a comprehensive base for technology adoption across multiple organisations. Using this model as a lens Seymour et al. (2007) reviewed the literature and identified factors relevant to RFID adoption. Their framework was used in this study.

4.   Methodology and Data Collection

This study was, in essence, 'open-ended' with the goal of explaining factors, considering the influence of context on perceptions, and determining whether or not factors were relevant. For these reasons we used a qualitative approach which allowed for a deeper understanding of the themes influencing adoption and for the emergence of new themes. The research was conducted by interviewing nine members of the Cape Town port community (It1 to It9) during July 2006. We endeavoured to interview a full spread of representative organisations, but accept that the results would have been improved if interviews had been conducted with the likes of customs, trucking companies and individual exporters and importers but the range of interviews still provided useful results. The interviewees are detailed in Table 1 without interview codes so as to ensure their anonymity. To obtain a good understanding of the situation, we conducted semi-structured interviews, consisting of both set and open-ended questions. We used an electronic recording application and hand-written notes to record the interviews and full transcripts were produced. We edited the data to ensure that no omissions had been made and that the data was consistent and then coded the data by placing the interview responses into themes and categories, before being analysed for frequency to establish patterns in the given responses. As part of the literature review, data collection and during analysis we needed to gain an understanding of the context of the SA container supply chain into which the RFID technology could be deployed. The following section details the context.

Table 1. Organisations and job positions of the nine interviewees.

Container Terminal Marketing Manager	Shipping line Operations Manager
Container Terminal Operations Manager	Shipping line Logistics Manager
SA Port Operations IT Manager	Shipping line IT Manager
Container Depot e-Commerce Manager	An RFID Vendor and Expert
Shipping line Systems Administrator	-

5.   The South African Port Community

The SA (SA) port community consists of a number of integrated parties, namely the importers/exporters, container depots, customs, container terminals and shipping lines. All operations are governed and influenced by two Transnet subsidiaries, the SA Port Operations (SAPO) and the National Port Authority which both replaced Portnet in 2000. In 1990, Transnet changed from being government run to a public company with government as its only shareholder. The National Port Authority is responsible for regulations and policy formations, and SAPO provides operational services such as cargo-handling and logistics to the port community. Customs, a division of the SA Revenue Service (SARS), inspect and collect import duties on incoming containers and check that they meet government and legal regulations (It3). Spoornet, Transnet's freight rail division also influences the container supply chain.

The central purpose of the ports is to berth container vessels, and load or unload them. Container terminals also offer container storage for a limited amount of time (It1). In South Africa, all container terminals are government-owned and controlled (It1). Container depots are privately-owned and provide their customers (importers and exporters) with the service of container storage. Container depots that are registered with customs also offer their clients container packing and unpacking services (It7). The shipping lines are privately-owned, are run locally through agencies and transport containers for a service fee, own the containers and administer and manage the vessels and containers (It3). Shipping lines would be the direct implementers of RFID technology as it would be their duty to install RFID tags into the containers.

Information is passed between parties at various points. When exporting goods, exporters send a shipping instruction to the shipping line which then creates the manifest (a complete list of the containers on board and the contents thereof) and then the bill of loading. The shipping line gives the depot an instruction to release an empty container (It6). The manifest is sent physically with the vessel to the destination port and/or electronically before the ship departs (It6). In the case of exports to the US, the local port must send the electronic manifest and expected arrival time to the destination port at least 24 hours before the vessel departs (It6). To dispatch a container from a port, the shipping line needs to issue a container terminal order to the trucking company which can then collect the container.

6.   Analysis and Interpretation

In this section, we analysed the interviews according to the themes in the framework and new factors that were identified were incorporated into the relevant STOPE categories. These themes are contrasted with the literature and their implications to the SA container supply chain are discussed. As this is a short paper, the analysis of some themes which were not that relevant to the South African context was not included.

6.1   Strategy: Organisational strategies

If an organisation's strategy is to increase value or service quality, then this strategy acts indirectly as an enabler for adopting RFID. In this study strategies were both enablers and obstacles to adoption, with Governmental strategies dominating the supply chain. While global competitiveness and increased security are government strategies which enable adoption, the social responsibility to create jobs, a factor more dominant in developing countries was seen as an obstacle to adoption. It2 noted that while the mission of Transnet is to reduce the cost of business, they have a social responsibility to alleviate unemployment. The fit with employment strategies was not clear. While It2 stated with certainty that RFID might "kill jobs", It4 commented that "RFID creates higher level employment". A further obstacle appeared to be the strategy of shipping lines which was seen as merely following technological innovations proposed by other parties as opposed to being innovative.

6.2   Strategy: Related initiatives

While not mentioned in the literature, we found "related initiatives" to be a factor influencing RFID adoption. Three of the seven organisations interviewed referred to a recent initiative of Spoornet to move containers onto rail to relieve truck congestion on the roads. They stated that RFID would help to track containers on the railways and therefore would enable the move to rail (It9, It8 and It1). The benefits of RFID would complement the Spoornet initiative and therefore this initiative is indirectly an enabler to RFID adoption.

6.3 Technology: Cost / Resources

As if and Mandviwalla (2005) found cost to be a significant challenge to the adoption of RFID and this study found cost to be one of the most significant factors. All interviewees commented on cost and the high cost of infrastructure, information integration and the tags were all cited. It7 argued that equipping containers with RFID would not cost-effective unless a 'critical mass', of between 50 and 60 percent of the containers that pass to and from South Africa, were installed with tags. There was acknowledgment that all port community members needed to bear a portion of the total cost (It6, It7, It8). However, the probability of this when the benefits are realised in varying degrees by each member was seen as small. For instance, trucking companies would see great benefit in reducing the amount of time taken to enter and leave a port or depot (It4, It7, It8). However because they operate on low margins and compete only on price, benefits might not outweigh the costs (It6, It7, It8). For the shipping lines, it was felt that because the manual, non-automated work (that would be replaced with RFID) is shouldered by other parties in the port community, the reduction in shipping costs and human errors would probably not justify the investment (It8, It3). Interestingly, only one respondent referred to cost savings and the value added through efficiency and throughput gains. Hence perceived value needs to be considered in conjunction with cost.

6.4 Technology: Perceived value / Usefulness

The literature implies that all organisations within a supply chain stand to gain benefits from adopting RFID. The majority of respondents cited benefits. The tracking capabilities of the technology was seen as the core potential benefit, which is in line with the motivation for the RFID project in line the Rotterdam port (RFid Gazette 2005). The stated major benefit of RFID was knowing where a container is and when it entered the gate, was loaded onto a ship etc. (It4, It5, It6, It7, It8). Tracking would therefore improve planning and document flow (It6) and information sharing (It1, It2). The port community had "about ten separate systems", and RFID would help with "the gap of information between the port and the depot" (It3).

Some respondents referred to increased throughput and efficiency. "Tight [shipping line] deadlines might be a huge enabler for RFID" (It3). "Ports are very poor in terms of throughput... for example a trucker is standing in line for four hours to move a container from a port to a depot" (It7). "There is always a shortage of space... the quicker you can get containers out of your system, the better" (It6). Reduction in manual labour was also commented on. "It would really benefit [the container depots] to reduce some of the work in entering and exiting facilities" (It7). "The industry is very paper-based, people work 18-20 hours a day to meet manifest deadline" (It3). The value of RFID also seemed to be increasing in this area. "Global trade is increasing in excess of 10% per annum, you either have to employ more people or get the existing people to work more." "Manual input is increasing every year" (It6). Temperature control was also identified as a potential benefit (It8). RFID tags with encoding options allow for the monitoring of temperature, reducing spoilage (Ryzex Group 2005).

The organisations interviewed that considered RFID to be of great benefit/value to their organisation were more willing to consider it. As an observation there is a perception that other organisations might benefit from RFID and therefore it appears that benefits to their own organisations is not understood or that there is little understanding that individual benefits are only accrued with integrated implementation and community-wide efficiency gains. It1 and It2 both repeated that the container terminal would not really gain any benefits from RFID as it was only part of the supply chain. It4 and It5 stated that shipping lines would gain no competitive advantage from RFID because "all the manual work is done by other parties throughout the port community", and that the port authorities, truckers and depots would benefit more. The port operations also felt RFID was of little benefit to them (It8).

6.5   Technology: Complexity/Ease of use

Most (4 of the 7) organisations had concern over the complexity of RFID information and business processes. Concerns were raised on the amount of information. "You would need information from all customers for all cargo types within a container on the chip" (It7). A container is manufactured in Japan and "then it moves to America, South Africa, West Africa, South America and Europe" (It4). The tag needs to be scanned and updated upon import, leaving the port and on arrival at the customer and the reverse upon departure (It6). Three of the organisations referred specifically to the complexity of the technology implementation (configuring business rules) and not the technology itself. This obstacle is not that easily overcome, because of the global nature of the problem and the poor infrastructure of a number of members in the port community.

6.6   Technology: Accuracy

Many (4 of the 7) organisations interviewed felt that accuracy was a consideration. It4 and It6 noted that RFID might help reduce data entry errors. "When it's dark, when it's foggy, when it's rainy, the [manually recorded] information is sometimes incorrect" (It6). It7 spoke confidently of the RFID solution to difficulties in reading documents, mentioning that cases existed where containers had been stored on incorrect shipping lines and had been sent to, for instance, China when it should have served the American trade. In contrast to previous research by Wu et al. (2006), no organisation expressed concern that RFID might not be fully accurate, stressing instead its improved accuracy over current methods.

6.7   Technology: Infrastructure

Existing 'inflexible' IT infrastructure, that cannot easily be integrated with the RFID technology) has been cited to be an unavoidable challenge. In the SA port community the existence and lack of infrastructure was seen as an enabler and an obstacle respectively. The existence of EDI and other information sharing projects between SA port community members was seen as a strong enabler for adopting RFID; as such infrastructure would complement RFID use and ensure automation along the supply chain. In contrast It3 stated that some depots still have paper-based processes. It7 noted that "many of the smaller importers and exporters don't even have PCs". Therefore the state of infrastructure is seen as both an enabler and an obstacle.

6.8   Intra-Organisation: Training and support

Training and support has been cited as enablers for user adoption. However, these factors are not seen to be relevant in early adoption. In contrast, the amount of re-skilling is seen as an obstacle to adoption. It1 stated that manual work would have to be replaced with higher level skills and It6 mentioned that current systems are manual other than the use of hand held computers to enter seal numbers.

6.9   Intra-Organisation: Organisation-wide readiness

Comments were made on the readiness states of other but not their own organisations. It8 stated that "hardly any exporter and importers have the ability to send manifests electronically". It appears that the integrated and interconnected nature of the community reduces the effect of a single organisation's readiness.

6.10 Intra-Organisation: Organisation size

The literature suggests that organisation size can play a significant role in technology adoption as larger organisations are generally more innovative because of extra capacity and financial resources (Patterson et al. 2003). None of the interviewees referred to the size of their respective organisation or its impact on adoption. It5 noted that the size and employment legislature of the port authority was a potential obstacle. In this research the larger organisations are seen to be government controlled with less need for innovation than privately-owned organisations.

6.11 Inter-Organisation: Security

In contrast to published security concerns of competitors 'stealing' information with fraudulent scanners (Smith 2005), concerns and benefits focused around current security problems and looting of containers. It2 raised the concern that through the RF scanning of containers, container terminal employees would be able to ascertain container contents resulting in "targeting the containers with valuables and stealing the contents". It7 mentioned that Spoornet had incidents of people getting information from their system when preparing manifests, and then following containers and looting them. In contrast to this, It1 confidently argued with authority that the number of instances where security was breached through either lost or looted containers was minimal, eradicating the need for RFID for security.

It1 noted a security-related benefit that "implementing RFID might reduce the number of people on the yard". It3 also stressed that RFID would allow reallocation of resources from data inputting to security issues. A further RFID security benefit is the availability of seals with embedded RFID chips (It9). "The integrity of the seal is very important for us as a shipping line because we are responsible that the cargo gets from A to B intact" (It6). "[RFID vendors] can guarantee the customer that goods have left, show where they are in the supply chain, and show that they haven't been tampered with" (It9). It6 noted that the US security protocols demanding manifest information 24 hours before a shipment leaves would "give RFID a push". However, It8 added confidently that RFID would not play much role in satisfying what the US wants SA to do before containers get shipped, because the requirements for the US are more around pre-screening and x-ray scanning of containers.

There was ambiguity among the interviewees over whether or not the high security requirements required by the shipping industry makes RFID a suitable solution. From a physical security and data security perspective, it appears that RFID meets the security needs of the industry in the form of accurate seal readings, reliable tamper-detection, tracking of containers and international security standards.

6.12 Inter-Organisation: Customer needs/satisfaction

Effective supply chain management requires that organisations strive to meet the needs of the end customer and interviews showed that customer satisfaction is still fundamentally important in the SA port community. Overwhelmingly, customer benefits were mentioned by interviewees as a positive consequence of RFID adoption. The tracking benefit was seen as significant, RFID "can guarantee the customer that the goods have left, show where they are in the supply chain and show that they haven't been tampered with" (It9). It6 noted enthusiastically that locating containers via a website would replace the lengthy, hour-long process of the customer phoning the shipping line, the shipping line phoning the depot etc. RFID could also provide "more stages where the container is scanned and tracked". It7 noted that with some tracking information currently being available to customers, "people have been seeing the holes in information, and so they put more pressure on shipping lines" who in turn had put pressure on SA port authorities, thereby implying that customer needs would indirectly drive RFID adoption. A further benefit of RFID was seen as the ability to break back into the US market. It7 said that the US security restrictions have meant that many exporters had been cut from US market and that enforced RFID adoption or similar "external drives would give it [US exports] a push". Speaking from personal opinion, It8 countered the more positive views by saying that "the shipping line of customers would indirectly pay for RFID" through the spill-over increase in costs.

6.13 Inter-Organisation: Intensity of information exchange

According to Ranganathan and Jha (2005) the information intensity and demanding nature of the container supply chain makes the possibility of RFID adoption greater. Evidence was given to show that the industry is information-intensive and the ability of RFID to bridge information gaps would enable adoption. It3 noted the number of parties were involved in the information flow, giving an example of how a container terminal order moves from shipping line to port, to trucking company, to depot and to customer. It3 said that a lot of information is collected on manifests and other documents and only some of it electronically. It1 stressed that there were over ten separate systems and minimal [electronic] information sharing, and that connecting systems would benefit the whole community.

6.14 Inter-Organisation: Integrated structure of industry

While not mentioned in the literature, the interconnected nature of the container supply chain does play a large role in the adoption of RFID. During the interviews, all parties made allusions to the heavily-interconnected nature of the port community, highlighting the need for improved information sharing and buy-in from many parties. Six of the seven parties noted in some way that all parties within the port community would need to reach consensus to adopt RFID. "Everyone is interlinked; therefore no single organisation can make a decision on whether or not to implement RFID... depots, port authority, customs and shipping lines would need to meet consensus" (It4). It4 repeated very clearly, "If RFID is going to be used; everybody in the world needs to comply." "The complete supply chain would have to be taken into account. Otherwise you only get half the benefit" (It9).

6.15 Inter-Organisation: Organisational dominance within supply chain

A factor identified by the research and not found in previous research is organisational dominance within the supply chain and in this case it was the influence of Government on port operations. A strong majority (It1, It6, It7, It9, It5) felt that the policy of their organisation was governed by a higher body. It9 noted that decisions concerning new technology adoption were made at a national level from the "SAPO, Customs, and Department of Trade point of view". It5 alluding to government influence said that the RFID implementation in Japan would be easier because depots are owned by the shipping line, "but in South Africa, this is not the case". It5 also commented that government organisations have little experience with IT projects which contributes to their slowness to react to technologies such as RFID. It5 reiterated, "It is hard to change the way that people think in government monopolies, things move very slowly". The monopoly or perceived government control over the container terminal presents a number of issues. Less emphasis appears to be placed on improving competitive advantage. At the beginning of 2006 Transnet was acknowledged as being an unwieldy conglomerate (Ramos 2006) and ultimately the control over RFID adoption is seen to lie with government who is perceived as slow with change and inexperienced with IT projects. Organisational dominance within a supply chain is not unique to this case, the Wal-Mart RFID adoption could arguably be attributed to its dominance within its retail supply chain. In mid-2004 Wal-Mart required that its top suppliers attach RFID tags to all cases and pallets (Hartman 2004).

6.16 People: Resistance to change

A fear of change in the work environment has been reported as an obstacle to RFID adoption (Asif and Mandviwalla 2005). While interview analysis found that resistance to change was not a factor explicitly stated by interviewees, resistance by IT management to changing IT systems was a potential obstacle. Both It1 and It2 argued that "COSMOS (the container terminal legacy system) is good enough."

6.17 People: Expertise

The lack of RFID expertise within the supply chain community was noted. This obstacle is not insurmountable, as expertise is available in South Africa but at a cost. "There is the [necessary] intelligence in South Africa, but it comes down to funds from the industry" (It6).

6.18 Environment: Willingness to collaborate

The container terminal's willingness to support any RFID initiative, despite not being clear on its ability to bring benefits, implies willingness to collaborate. It7 noted with clarity that getting parties to agree to adopt RFID together is incredibly difficult as they want RFID advantages for themselves and "throw sticks and hurdles in the path of any progress". It took 7 years of discussions to reach some agreement on EDI" (It7). It was felt that without a driver from government, reaching consensus would be too slow.

6.19 Environment: Relative advantage

Most organisations invest in a new technology with the long-term view to obtaining a competitive advantage over competitors. In this case relative advantage is both an obstacle and enabler, because while shipping lines might view the lack of relative advantage over competitors as an obstacle, trucking companies might view the benefits as an enabler. The container terminal and port authority monopolies did not consider relative advantage a consideration in RFID adoption.

6.20 Environment: Standards

A minority (2 of 7) of the interviewees mentioned standards. They spoke authoritatively on the subject and cited the lack of a single universally-accepted RFID standard as a major obstacle. "If there was a standard technology and communication standard, then [the port authority] would be more than happy to adopt RFID, as long as there is a significant percentage of containers that have RFID built into them" (It8). It7 stated that "it will be a very long process to get a standard going that's internationally accepted by all shipping lines."

6.21 Environment: Supply chain culture

The structure and mindset of the industry as a whole was not mentioned in the literature and yet is an overriding feature and an important obstacle for the SA port community. Interviewees commented on the overall culture of the port community implying that it was inert, made up of monopolies, bureaucratic, not service-oriented enough and lacking initiative. It5 remarked that "the mindset in South Africa is not service-oriented enough to help with implementing RFID", implying that the overall culture of the industry is not suited to RFID adoption or process innovation. It5 compared the port authority to a monopoly and commented that it was inert, "things move so slowly, because of the red tape". It7 commented that "It would be very difficult to motivate anything like this from a SA perspective". While SAPO and the National Port Authority both replaced Portnet in 2000 and Transnet changed from being government run in 1990, some interviewees still referred to Portnet and government ownership of the Transnet subsidiaries.

7. RFID adoption within the South African container supply chain

The major issues surrounding the adoption of RFID into the SA port community are presented in Table 2. The high costs and complexity of the RFID technology was found to be partially offset by the improved accuracy and usefulness of the technology. The Infrastructural and integration costs are high requiring all players to shoulder the cost. The complexity of the technology is overshadowed by complexity of the implementation; a challenge made harder by the poor infrastructure of a number of members involved in the port community. While benefits to the overall supply chain were not well understood, improved throughput; productivity; tracking; information sharing and temperature monitoring were identified. In terms of strategy, the lack of innovation and social responsibility to increase jobs is offset by global competitiveness, increased security requirements and enabling the more environmental move from truck to rail transport. Inter-organisational factors were found to enable adoption, but these are partially offset by intra-organisational factors. The good fit of RFID for customer needs in terms of tracking benefits and the potential to enable US exports as well as the security benefits of accurate seal readings, reliable tamper-detection, tracking of containers, international security standards and reduction of manual work are all seen to enable adoption. The obstacles include the size and employment legislature of the port authority and the substantial re-skilling required. People factors did not appear to have a strong impact while environmental factors presented as obstacles. The multiple standards for RFID hardware, software, and data management are seen as seen as a major obstacle and interviewees implied that the port community culture was inert, made up of monopolies, bureaucratic, not service-oriented enough and lacking initiative.

Table 2. Categories and Themes Identified for the Assessment of RFID Adoption. New themes are indicated in bold.

Categories	Themes	SA case
Strategy	Organisational strategies	
	Related initiatives	Enabler
Technology	Cost / Resources	**Obstacle**
	Perceived value / Usefulness	**Enabler**
	Complexity / Ease of use	Obstacle
	Accuracy	Enabler
	Infrastructure	
Intra-Organisation	Organisation culture	
	Training and support	**Obstacle**
	Organisation-wide readiness	
	Organisation size	**Obstacle**
Inter-Organisation	Security	Enabler
	Customer needs / satisfaction	**Enabler**
	Intensity of information exchange	Enabler
	Integrated structure of industry	
	Organisational dominance within supply chain	
People	Management support / Authority	
	Resistance to change	
	Expertise	
Environment	Willingness to collaborate	
	Relative advantage	
	Standards	**Obstacle**
	Supply chain culture	**Obstacle**

8. Conclusion

Through a thorough qualitative assessment of the intricacies of the Cape Town port community, we have highlighted and discussed the major issues surrounding the adoption of RFID into the SA port community. In addition to this, a framework for the adoption of the technology, presented as the structure of Table 2, has been refined. The four themes revealed through interview analysis and not identified by the literature review are presented in bold. These factors could present themselves as either enablers or obstacles. The right hand column in Table 2 identifies factors we found to influence RFID adoption in the SA container supply chain. Overall, cost, the absence of a universally-adopted standard and the supply chain culture were revealed to be the major setbacks to RFID adoption in the port community. The bureaucratic and monopolistic nature of the supply chain community contributes to the creation of an environment that struggles to reach a position of consensus. These are partially offset by customer needs and usefulness. Other uniquely South African elaborations on factors were revealed, including the idea that South Africa is not 'service-oriented' enough. An interesting finding which needs future research.

References

Asif, Z., Mandviwalla, M. (2005). Integrating the Supply chain with RFID: A technical and business analysis, *Communications of the Association for Information Systems*, 15, 393-427.

Bakry, S. H. (2003). Toward the development of a standard e-readiness assessment policy, *International Journal of Network Management*,13(2), 129-137.

Hartman, L. R. (2004). *Walmart's on schedule with RFID revolution*. Retrieved from http://www.packagingdigest.com/articles/200407/36.php.

Jansen, A. (2005). Assessing E-government progress– why and what, Proceedings of NOKOBIT 2005. Retrieved from http://www.afin.uio.no/forskning/notater/7_05.pdf. Accessed 3 March 2008.

Nikam, M., Satpute, S. (2006). *RFID: Changing the face of supply chain management*, (Working Paper, Welingkar Institute of Management and Development Research). Retrieved from http://www.indiainfoline.com/content/bschool/Your_Journal/2006/05/30052006/Chan.pdf. Accessed 12 June 2007.

Patterson, K. A., Grimm, C. M., Corsi, T. M. (2003). Adopting new technologies for Supply Chain Management, Research Part E: *Logistics and Transportation Review*, 39(2), 95-121.

Ramos, M. (2006). *Group Chief Executive's review*. Retrieved from http://www.transnet.co.za/AR_2006/cor_groupCE.html. Accessed 16 July 2007.

Ranganathan, C., Jha, S. (2005). *Adoption of RFID Technology: An exploratory examination from supplier's perspective*, Proceedings of the Eleventh Americas Conference on Information Systems, August, Omaha. Retrieved from http://aisel.isworld.org/proceedings/amcis/2005/. Accessed 11 June 2007.

The Ryzex Group. (2005). *Guide to Understanding and Evaluating RFID: An Application White Paper*. Retrieved from http://www.rfidjournal.com/whitepapers/1/2. Accessed 3 April 2006.

Seymour, L., Lambert-Porter, E., Willuweit, L. (2007). *RFID Adoption into the Container Supply Chain: Proposing a framework*. Proceedings of the ISOneWorld Conference, April 2007, Las Vegas. ISBN: 0-9772107-6-6. Retrieved from http://www.information-quarterly.org/ISOWProc/2007ISOWCD/PDFs/55.pdf.

Singh, N., Lai, K., Cheng, T. (2007). Intra-Organizational Perspectives on IT-Enabled Supply Chains: Aligning technology decisions with relevant organizational practices and policies. *Communications of the ACM*, 50(1), 59 – 65.

Smith, A.D. (2005). Exploring radio frequency identification technology and its impact on business systems, *Information Management and Computer Security*, 13(1), 16-28.

Wu, N.C., Nystrom, M.A., Lin T. R., Yu, H.C. (2006). Challenges to global RFID adoption, *Technovation*, 26(12) 1317-1323.

Adoption of Service Oriented Computing from the IT Professionals' Perspective: An e-Government Case Study

Ilse Baumgartner and Peter Green
Business School
The University of Queensland, St Lucia QLD 4072, AU
I.Baumgartner@business.uq.edu.au
P.Green@business.uq.edu.au

Abstract: The case study reported in this paper focuses on the question: what are the critical factors that influence IT professionals' intention to adopt the Service Oriented Computing (SOC) paradigm? This work reports a case study examining the e-Government initiative in a middle-sized European city. It uses an initial SOC adoption model developed through a proceeding interview-based exploratory study [2]. The current study has two principle aims. The first aim is to "shed some light" on the IT professionals' acceptance of such complex technological approaches as Service Oriented Computing in the e-Government sector and to report key learning issues emerging from the case study. The second aim of the case study is to bring further credibility to the first study and to validate empirically its assertions. Some of the major findings of the study are the replacement of the complexity variable by the variable of maintainability, and the replacement of the trust and dependency variables (both of interpersonal rather than of technical nature) by the variable of external involvement. The results of the study also suggest the introduction of the "champion" of the approach variable. Theoretical and practical implications that follow are presented and discussed.

Keywords: e-Government; technology acceptance; acceptance of Service Oriented Computing

1. Introduction

Presently, public administration systems in many countries of the world are undergoing fundamental restructuring and reorganisation as a result of the emerging e-Government strategies. These new "online-e-Government" services are designed to change radically the experiences that citizens and businesses have in dealing with government. It is not surprising therefore that intensive discussion about the

Please use the following format when citing this chapter:

Baumgartner, I. and Green, P., 2008, in IFIP International Federation for Information Processing, Volume 274; *Advances in Information Systems Research, Education and Practice*; David Avison, George M. Kasper, Barbara Pernici, Isabel Ramos, Dewald Roode; (Boston: Springer), pp. 189–201.

most appropriate information systems architectures to deal with the introduction of online-delivered government services is unfolding amongst practitioners and researchers presently [e.g. 5, 12, 21].

Service oriented computing (SOC), together with the fundamental concept of web services, has a high potential to enable and support successfully the evolution of e-Government. While traditional software development approaches focused mainly on individual components, the SOC paradigm emphasises the role of interaction and collaboration defining services as crosscutting system properties. While relying on a set of well-known technologies (XML and HTTP, WSDL, SOAP and UDDI), SOC combines these technologies in a new and innovative way enabling the development of distributed, interoperable and extendable systems and applications. However, the adoption and practical use of the SOC paradigm is usually associated with very diverse problematic issues. What are the financial and technical risks of implementing an SOC-based solution? How will the enormous complexity of an SOC-based system be addressed? What skills are necessary to build and maintain an SOC-based system? How secure will this system be? Are there any reference resources available?

The most significant motivation for this research-in-progress work is the lack of studies examining the **adoption of new technologies, techniques, approaches or tools from the perspective of IT professionals**. While there is extensive research on technology acceptance from the end-end user perspective only very few studies (e.g. [1, 8, 18]) examine and analyse the individual-level acceptance of new technologies, tools or methodologies by IT professionals. In addition to that, almost all of these studies are focusing on the acceptance of technological approaches in commercial settings and the results produced by most of these studies are hardly generalisable to such a multidimensional and complex paradigm as Service Oriented Computing without additional and focused research.

This work argues that an *individual* decision on whether or not using the SOC paradigm is justified and meaningful in a particular context has to be made by every single IT professional to make an organisational adoption truly successful. Using an e-Government case study, this study examines a number of critical factors that influence the IT professionals' individual-level decision to adopt the Service Oriented Computing paradigm.

2. Initial research model

Due to the absence of an established theoretical framework in the domain of individual-level technology acceptance in the IT industry, an exploratory investigation [2] was carried out in a commercial setting to formulate an initial SOC adoption model (see Fig. 1).

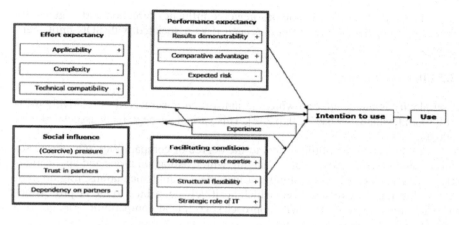

Figure 1. The initial SOC adoption model.

Short description of the constructs of the initial model follows.

2.1 Facilitating conditions

In the IS literature, the importance of integrating IT and business strategy has been extensively discussed pointing out that IT affects firm strategies and that strategies have IT implications. The strategic role of IT variable emerges from the connections between IT and the core objectives and propositions of an organisation and is primarily associated with the level of influence senior IT professionals have in an organisation. The higher is the influence level of the IT personnel the higher is the probability of the acceptance of such an approach as SOC.

The structural flexibility variable (having positive influence direction) complements the strategic role of IT variable and refers to the flexibility and efficiency of the IT-related decision-making process in an organisation.

The variable of adequate resources of expertise refers to existing and available external and internal resources (i.e. practical and theoretical knowledge, experience, existing successful/unsuccessful implementation references) which could be useful and supportive when implementing SOC-based systems and solutions. This variable is positively associated with the adoption intentions.

2.2 Performance expectancy

Result demonstrability is defined as the tangibility of the results of using the innovation including their observability and communicability [14, p.203]. This variable is positively associated with the intention to adopt the SOC paradigm.

Comparative (relative) advantage is understood as the "degree to which an idea is perceived as being better than the idea it supercedes" [20, p.212], and this variable is negatively associated with the adoption intentions.

The expected risk variable has negative influence direction and is generally representing technical and business-related risks associated with SOC implementations.

2.3 Effort expectancy

Complexity is the "degree to which an innovation is perceived as relatively difficult to understand and use" [20, p.242]. This variable is negatively associated with adoption intentions.

Technical compatibility refers to the degree of compatibility SOC-based solutions and systems are capable of having with existing solutions and applications (including issues such as possibility of incremental implementations, migration of assets, leverage of existing assets which positively contribute to the IT professionals' intentions to adopt the SOC approach). Technical compatibility has positive influence on the adoption intentions.

In the initial SOC adoption model, applicability refers to the extent to which business processes of a specific organisation are suitable to be implemented as "services".

2.4 Social factors

Trust and dependency represent two interrelated, but clearly distinguishable variables of interpersonal (rather than technical) nature. While the feeling of having trustworthy partners positively influence the intention of IT professionals to adopt the SOC paradigm, the degree of potential dependency on partners cause exactly the opposite effect.

The (coercive) pressure variable combines two different types of pressure – pressure from internal organisational structures and pressure from external entities (e.g. business partners, customers) – and is negatively associated with the intentions of IT professionals to adopt the SOC paradigm.

Moderating variable
The experience moderating variable refers to the adopter's general IT-related professional experience.

3. Research methodology

Our previous exploratory study [2] used interviews with senior IT professionals primarily working in commercial settings to formulate the initial SOC adoption model (Figure 1). In order to enhance the external validity of the emerging SOC adoption model and potentially gather new aspects from another setting, an e-Government initiative was selected for this case study.

An established case study method proposed by Yin [27] was followed in order to institute rigor in the methodology of this research work. The organisation for the case study reported in this paper was selected and the data collection protocol was developed. Due to the nature of the research question explored by the current study and due to a number of restrictions (access restrictions to archival records in a governmental agency, time restrictions regarding observations imposed by the subject organisation on the investigators), we decided to focus on three sources of evidence: documents provided by the subject organisation, focused interviews/informal discussions, and physical artefacts.

The primary data gathering was accomplished using focused interviews and informal discussions (three formal interviews and five informal discussions with senior IT professionals involved in the day-to-day e-Government environment development and support). In addition to that, physical artefacts were examined. The examination of supporting documentation provided by the subject organisation (such as protocols of internal meetings, documentation used in several external meetings and information sessions to present the e-Government initiative and other information) was performed after the interview process.

4. Data analysis

The research work used a data analysis method described by Miles and Huberman [13]. As suggested by them, three different activities were undertaken concurrently – data reduction, data display, and conclusion drawing/verification. The data segments resulting from selecting, simplifying, and abstracting the raw case study data were combined, summarised, grouped and then coded into categories derived from the initial theoretical framework of the study. Tables 1 and 2 show the high-level picture resulting from the analysis of the case study data. The detailed analysis leading to these results is explained subsequently.

Construct	Variables	Results
Facilitating conditions	Adequate resources of expertise (+)	Supported
	The strategic role of IT (+)	Supported
	Structural flexibility of the organisation (+)	Supported
Social influence	(Coercive) pressure (-)	Supported
	Dependency on partners (-)	Dependency and trust supported but mainly with a technical focus
	Trust in partners (+)	
Effort expectancy	Applicability (+)	Supported
	Complexity (-)	Supported but with a different focus
	Technical compatibility (+)	Supported
Performance expectancy	Results demonstrability (+)	Supported
	Comparative advantage (+)	No evidence available
	Expected risk (-)	Supported

Table 1: Constructs and Variables

Construct	Moderating variable	Results
Facilitating conditions	Experience	Supported
Social influence	Experience	Supported
Effort expectancy	Experience	Supported
Performance expectancy	-	-

Table 2: Constructs and moderating variable

4.1 Facilitating conditions

All three facilitating condition construct variables (strategic role of IT, adequate resources and structural flexibility) were strongly supported by the case study evidence material.

The advanced state of the project was primarily associated with the strong *strategic role of IT* and with the exceptionally *strong IT leadership*. The flat organisational structure and the remarkable mutual trust between the CIO and the leaders of other organisational structures apparently facilitate quick and unbureaucratic IT-related decisions.

Concerning the CIO's position in the subject organisation, one of the interviewed senior IT professionals, for example, noted:

"He [CIO] has an exceptionally strong position here in our organisation."

Regarding the structural flexibility of the organisation the same interviewee stated:

"We have senior management which is very open-minded towards new visions. Decisions are made very quickly."

Concerning the *adequate recourses of expertise*, all interviewees confirmed the importance of available and accessible external knowledge. They stressed the fact that there are several possibilities to access theoretical knowledge and expertise, however, the most important issue is lack of on-going reference projects enabling the exchange of first-hand practical experiences.

The CIO, for example, noted in this regard:

"There is a lot of [theoretical SOC] knowledge out there, but there are very few productive systems, successful systems, which could be looked at."

4.2 Social Influence

While one of the social influence construct variables ((coercive) pressure) was strongly supported by the case study evidence material, the dependency on and trust in partner's variables experienced major revision.

Very interesting insights appeared in relation to the *(coercive) pressure* variable within the social influence construct. Two different contexts were described by the interviewees: coercive pressure from higher-level government agencies on the subject organisation and coercive pressure on lower-level partners exerted by the subject organisation itself.

Contrary to the initial theoretical framework of the study both, the *dependency* variable and the *trust* variable, were mainly associated with technical rather than with interpersonal issues. As noted by the CIO:

> *"We use SOC at a very sensible point of the enterprise, namely, for supporting automated communication and transactions. And it is vital to be able to trust the technology that it will work exactly as required, because if it doesn't work you have a major problem."*

This effect might, however, be explainable when considering the difference between SOC-based environments implemented in a commercial organisation as opposed to an e-Government environment. In the context of trust and dependency the interviewees clearly confirmed that the level and intensity of "external" involvement will have direct influence on the SOC adoption intentions. This view is, indeed, congruent with the initial theoretical framework of the study – the interpersonal dependency and trust issues will become vital only in case of involvement of "external" and "unknown" partners. In the opposite case (involving only "internal" and "known" people, structures, partners) problems related to interpersonal dependency and trust will diminish radically, and they will not play any major role when considering the adoption of the SOC paradigm.

4.3 Effort Expectancy

In the context of the effort expectancy construct two of the variables (applicability and technical compatibility) were supported by the case study data, while the remaining variable of complexity experienced major revision.

The role of *complexity* was basically supported by the case study evidence material. SOC-based environments are clearly associated with complex implementations based on interrelation, collaboration and dependencies. However, two important issues should be mentioned in this context. First, it was remarkable that this potential complexity was not considered an issue that would have an exclusively negative influence on the intention to adopt and use SOC for building the e-Government-enabled environment. Second, in the context of this particular study, it became obvious that complexity is considered an "invariable feature" of SOC rather than a problem that has to be discussed and evaluated.

One of the interviewees noted in this context:

> *"We know that it will get very complex, and we know that there will be many dependencies. But at the very end, through segmentation and refinement, it will – ultimately – become simpler."*

Thus, in this context the complexity variable seems to be indirectly replaced by a variable like *"maintainability"* (i.e. the ease with which a software system can be modified to e.g. correct faults, improve performance, integrate new components or services or adapt to a changed environment).

While *applicability* (though supported by the case study data) did not represent a major issue for the interviewees, the *technical compatibility* appeared to have had a very strong influence on the decision to take an SOC-based approach when starting to implement the e-Government system.

As noted by one of the interviewees:

> *"[It is] a vision how to get the administrative system of our municipality which contains an extremely high number of very heterogeneous applica-*

tions, a highly distributed environment, towards a very strongly integrated solution, at the same time continuing to support this heterogeneity."

As shown by the case study, an e-Government-enabled environment does not exist in isolation. It coexists with many back-office applications that have been built using very different (and older) technologies. It will usually be impossible to rebuild these applications using state-of-the-art technologies and to seamlessly integrate them with the new SOC-based environment. Thus, the IT professionals will have to challenge the capability of SOC to enable integration of existing and very heterogeneous systems and applications. This issue (i.e. integration of existing – and extremely heterogeneous – systems and applications, migration of assets, leverage of existing assets) was also strongly supported by the documentation (especially architecture-related documentation) made available by the subject organisation.

4.4 Performance Expectancy

Finally, performance expectancy represents the least discussed construct of the theoretical framework of this study.

As far as the *comparative advantage* variable is concerned, none of the interviewees mentioned any other approach considered when discussing the basic architectural and technical implementation direction of the new e-Government initiative. Moreover, none of the interviewees mentioned any attempt to compare SOC with older and more conventional approaches, or to determine the advantages SOC has compared to conventional approaches.

As far as the *results demonstrability* variable is concerned, the most important issue discussed by the interviewees was the ability to demonstrate the progress of the SOC-based e-Government project to external interested parties (e.g. journalists, other government agencies) rather than to internal stakeholders.

The *expected risk* variable appears to have had substantial impact on the adoption decision process; however, similar to the complexity variable, this variable did not necessarily have an exclusively negative impact on the decision whether or not to adopt SOC. While admitting that the expected risk (technical as well as interpersonal) might be considerably high the interviewees regarded it both, a detriment as well as a challenge.

5. Summary and the refinement of the SOC adoption model

The case study evidence material does not suggest any changes to the existing three variables of the facilitating conditions construct (i.e. adequate resources of expertise, structural flexibility of the organisation, and the strategic role of IT in an organisation) and confirms the influence of the facilitating conditions construct on the intention to adopt the SOC paradigm. Additionally, the data analysis confirms the positive direction of influence of all three variables constituting the facilitating conditions construct.

In addition to the three existing variables for this construct, the data analysis suggests that a fourth variable should be added to the facilitating conditions construct – strong IT leader as a "champion" of the approach [16] (having strong positive influence). The role of a "champion" of an approach has been described by a large number of studies [e.g. 16, 17, 8]. As Palvia and Chervany note: "[...] the role of the project champion cannot be understated. In all stages this experimental factor produced the largest gains in the predictions that the system will succeed" [16, p 52]. Neither the strategic role of IT variable nor the structural flexibility variable cover the effect that derives from strong and influential IT leadership in an organisation. As shown by the current case, even considerable structural flexibility in the organisation and a strong strategic role of IT would not have been considered sufficient for taking an SOC-based approach if a strong and goal-oriented IT leadership – a "champion" of the approach – was missing.

As far as the effort expectancy construct is concerned, the current case study confirms the influence of this construct on the adoption intention. For two of the constituent variables, technical compatibility and applicability, the positive influence direction was clearly supported. The third variable, complexity – although discussed *in extenso* – did not show a clear influence direction. Moreover, the data analysis suggests that complexity is rather considered an "invariable" feature of SOC than an issue that has to be discussed and dealt with when deciding upon the adoption of SOC. Therefore, the variable of maintainability (having positive influence direction) replaces the variable of complexity in the refined SOC adoption model.

Within the performance expectancy construct, the influence of two variables – results demonstrability (positive) and expected risk – was confirmed by the data of the case study. Both constituent variables will be retained in the refined SOC adoption model with the same influence direction. Contrary to that, the influence of the comparative advantage variable could not be confirmed by the study as no data supporting the influence of this variable emerged from the case study. However, based on existing research in the field of technology acceptance in the IT industry, it can be assumed that the comparative (i.e. relative) advantage variable will have a certain impact on innovation adoptions, at least in commercial environments where the issues of investments and financial risk definitely have more severe impact than in public administration settings. (In a commercial environment, comparing existing conventional (and functioning) approaches with such an approach as SOC that requires a massive financial investment will most probably be a serious issue and will consequently influence the adoption decision). Based on this assumption, the comparative advantage variable will be retained in the refined SOC adoption model with the same influence direction.

The social influence construct has also been modified to a certain extent. The (coercive) pressure variable was clearly supported by the case study evidence material, and, thus, will be retained in the refined SOC adoption model with the same influence direction. The role of the trust and dependency variables (both being of interpersonal nature) seems to be partially neutralised by the effect of the (coercive) pressure variable, the issue of standardisation (which, to a considerable extent, is a result of coercive pressure), and the nature of the project environment (public administration/e-Government rather than commercial). However, the importance of avoiding or minimising "external" involvement in SOC-based solutions is strongly supported by the current study. Thus, both variables, interpersonal dependency and interpersonal trust, will be replaced by a single variable reflecting this issue – external involvement (having a negative influence direction).

Considering the above arguments as a whole, Figure 2 represents the refined SOC adoption model:

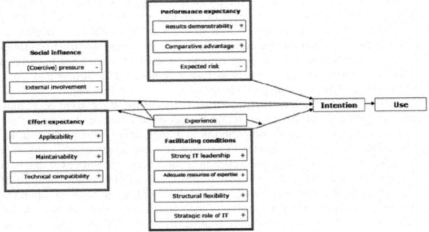

Figure 2. Refined SOC adoption model.

6. Conclusion, Limitations, and Further Work

In general, this study represents a step toward a better understanding of the adoption process of such complex innovations as Service Oriented Computing. The current study focuses on the individual-level perspective of IT professionals using this particular approach to support introduction and development of e-Government-enabled services.

The theoretical framework of this research work was initially developed through an exploratory interview-based study [2]. While the four major constructs exposed by this initial theoretical framework were confirmed the current study suggested several changes.

It is important to critically evaluate the study and its results. The present study has certain limitations that need to be taken into account when considering its contributions.

The refinement of the model is being performed using data from only one case. While every effort was taken to mitigate against selection bias in the subject organisation, the knowledge obtained from this study is necessarily bounded by the characteristics of the organisation and the characteristics of the interviewees. However, the e-Government initiative implemented by the selected subject organisation can be considered an exemplar and successful application of the SOC paradigm, the subject organisation plays a unique role in the Austrian e-Government standardisation process and the interviewed IT professionals have substantial work experience with SOC.

A concern with all qualitative inquiry methods (including interview-based case studies) is the propensity for the introduction of bias (e.g., researcher bias and expectation bias) into the data gathering and analysis stages. During the interview process, document and artefact examination, and the data analysis, every care was taken not to allow research biases to affect the direction of the interview, the observations recorded, and the analysis attained. In addition to that aspect, two of the three remedies proposed by Yin were used: multiple sources of evidence, and the revision of the basic structure of the case study report by the key informants.

In subsequent work, the refined SOC adoption model that has been presented in this paper will be validated using a survey instrument. Based on the results of this paper as well as on the results of the preceding study [2], a survey instrument will be developed, pilot-tested and then web-distributed to European IT experts who are utilising the Service Oriented Computing approach in their professional work or presently considering using it.

While carrying out the last validation step, it will be necessary to consider several additional aspects in order to enhance the quality of the results.

First, when collecting the respondents' demographic data it will be necessary to pay special attention to the type of the company the respondent is working for (i.e. commercial or public administration type of organisation). Second, it will be necessary to distinguish between two types of experience – experience with Service Oriented Computing and experience in the IT industry in general. Third, regarding the dependent variable, intention to use, it will be important to distinguish between the *intention to start using* the Service Oriented Computing paradigm and the *intention to continue using* it.

Ultimately, we expect to gain more knowledge of the determinants of IT professionals' intentions to adopt the Service Oriented Computing paradigm.

References

[1] R.Agarwal, J. Prasad, A field study of the adoption of software process innovations by information systems professionals, IEEE Transactions on Engineering Management 47:3 (2000) 295-308

[2] I.Baumgartner, P.Green, Service Oriented Computing: what do IT professionals think?, (2007) (currently under review)

[3] L. Carter, F. Belanger, The Influence of Perceived Characteristics of Innovating on e-Government Adoption, Electronic Journal of e-Government 2:1 (2003) 11-20

[4] J. D'Ambra, W. Huang, V. Bhalla, An empirical investigation of the adoption of e-Government by Australian citizens: some unexpected research findings, Journal of Computer Information Systems 3:1 (2002) 15 - 22

[5] Z. Ebrahim, Z. Irani, E-Government adoption: architecture and barriers, Business Process Management Journal 11:5 (2005) 589-611

[6] M. J. Gallivan, Organizational adoption and assimilation of complex technological innovations: development and application of a new framework, SIGMIS Database Special issue: Adoption, diffusion, and infusion of IT 32: 3 (2001) 51-85

[7] D. Gilbert, P. Balestrini, D. Littleboy, Barriers and benefits in the adoption of e-Government, The International Journal of Public Sector Management 17:4 (2004) 286-301

[8] R. A. Johnson, B. C. Hardgrave and, E. R. Doke, An industry analysis of developer beliefs about object-oriented systems development, SIGMIS Database 30:1 (1999) 47-64

[9] M. Khalifa, J.M. Verner, Drivers for software development method usage, IEEE Transactions on Engineering Management 47:3 (2000) 360-369

[10] B. Kitchenham, L. Pickard, S. L. Pfleeger, Case Studies for Method and Tool Evaluation, IEEE Software 12:4 (1995) 52-62

[11] A. Leigh, R. Atkinson, Breaking Down Bureaucratic Barriers: The Next Phase of Digital Government, Progressive Policy Institute, Technology & New Economy Project (2001)

[12] F. Li, Implementing E-Government strategy in Scotland: current situation and emerging issues, Journal of Electronic Commerce in Organisations 1:2 (2003) 44-65

[13] M.B. Miles, A.M. Humberman Qualitative Data Anaysis: A sourcebook of new methods, Sages Publications, Newsbury Park (1984)

[14] G.C. Moore, I.Benbasat, Development of an instrument to measure the perceptions of adopting an information technology innovation,. Information Systems Research 2:3 (1991) 192-222

[15] W.J. Orlikowski, D.C. Gash, Technological Frames: Making Sense of Information Technology in Organizations, ACM Transactions on Information Systems 2:2 (1994) 174-207

[16] S.C. Palvia, N.L. Chervany, An experimental investigation of factors influencing predicted success in DSS implementation, Information and Management 29:1 (1995) 43-53

[17] S.C. Palvia, N.L. Chervany, Effect of environmental and process variables on DSS implementation success: evidence from an experimental investigation for the moving stage of change, Decision Support and Knowledge Based Systems Track 3 (1989) 812-21

[18] C. K. Riemenschneider, B. C. Hardgrave, and F. D. Davis, Explaining Software Developer Acceptance of Methodologies: A Comparison of Five Theoretical Models, IEEE Transactions on Software Engineering 28:12 (2002) 1135-1145

[19] T.L. Roberts, M.L. Gibson, Jr., K.T. Fields, R.K. Rainer, Jr, Factors that impact implementing a system development methodology, IEEE Transactions on Software Engineering, 24:8 (1998) 640-649

[20] E.M. Rogers, Diffusion of Innovations (The Free Press, New York, 1995, 4th ed.)

[21] S. Smith, R. Jamieson, Determining key factors in e-Government information system security, Information Systems Management. Boston 23:2 (2006) 23-33

[22] R. Stake, The art of case research. Thousand Oaks, CA: Sage Publications (1995)

[23] F. Sultan, L. Chan, The adoption of new technology: the case of object-oriented computing in software companies, IEEE Transactions on Engineering Management 47:1 (2000) 106-126

[24] V. Venkatesh, M. G. Morris, G. B. Davis, and F. D. Davis, User Acceptance of Information Technology: Toward a Unified View, MIS Quarterly 27:3 (2003) 425-478

[25] M. Warkentin, D. Gefen, P. Pavlou, G. Rose, Encouraging Citizen Adoption of e-Government by Building Trust, Electronic Markets 12:3 (2002) 157-162

[26] X. Wei, J. Zhao, Citizens' requirement analysis in Chinese e-Government, Proceedings of the 7th international Conference on Electronic Commerce 113 (2005) 525 - 428

[27] R. Yin, Case study research: Design and methods, Beverly Hills, CA: Sage Publishing 2nd ed. (1994)

[28] M.V. Zelkowitz, D.R. Wallace, Experimental Models for Validating Technology, IEEE Computer 31:5 (1998) 23-31

[29] 2006 Online Availability of Public Services: How is Europe Progressing?, full Capgemini report available on http://www.capgemini.com/resources/thought_leadership /2006_online_availability_of_public_services/ (last access September 6, 2007)

[30] Platform "Digitales Österreich" (Digital Austria), available on http://reference.e-Government.gv.at/Digitales_OEsterreich.725.0.html (last access September 6, 2007)

Interview Questions

Have you ever experienced any type of pressure regarding the architectural and technical implementation direction of the new e-Government environment? If yes, would you describe this pressure?

What role, in your personal opinion, did the individual members of the IT department in general and the leader of the IT department in particular play when deciding upon the architectural and technical implementation direction of the new e-Government environment?

How did you acquire the technical and architectural SOC-related knowledge necessary to realise this particular project? Did you experience the need to consult external resources of SOC expertise in the course of the new e-Government project?

Did you experience any external control concerning the results of the new SOC-based e-Government initiative? Was it necessary – at any stage of the project – to prove the actual status/results of the project to external or internal stakeholders?

Was SOC the only approach you personally considered when arguing about the architectural and technical implementation direction of the new e-Government environment?

Did you consider any particular risks?

What issues would you associate with interpersonal trust and dependency in the context of the new SOC-based e-Government initiative?

What would you consider the most important problematic issues of the SOC approach?

What would you personally consider the most important advantages of the SOC approach?

Was the heterogeneity of the present environment an issue when deciding upon the architectural and technical implementation direction of the new e-Government environment?

Considering the present environment, do you think that all major business processes will be integrated into the new environment as "services"?

Introduction of a Public Sector e-Procurement Solution: Lessons Learned from Disappointing Adoption

John Krogstie

IDI, NTNU, Trondheim, NO
krogstie@idi.ntnu.no

Abstract: In this article, we look at the reasons why the introduction of the public sector Internet Marketplace – ehandel.no – has thus far not been a success in the County Municipality of Sør-Trøndelag (STFK), as compared to the original ambitions regarding usage volume for this channel. To look into the situation, we have interviewed users of ehandel.no in STFK, and in other public organizations which *are* seen as successful (given their usage volume objectives), such as Trondheim municipality. We have used various acceptance theories in order to analyze why the users accept the same system to different degrees. The theories were utilized prior to the interviews in order to formulate interview questions. Afterwards, we used the same theories to analyze the results. The results indicate that good product catalogues, motivated users, compulsory use of the system when possible, and renegotiation of contracts with the suppliers are some of the most important prerequisites in order to achieve success using ehandel.no.

Keywords: E-Business and E-Government Information Systems, transfer and diffusion of information technology

1. Introduction

An electronic marketplace is defined as: "An Internet-based solution that connects businesses that are interested in buying and selling goods or services to each other" (Lipis et al, 2000). This is also the purpose of the public sector marketplace ehandel.no. In 1999, under the auspices of the Ministry of Trade and Industry, the Program for Electronic Trade in the Public Sector was started. One of the primary goals of this project was to get a public sector marketplace established (E-Commerce Secretariat, 2001). A member of the public sector who wishes to make use of electronic commerce to purchase goods must subscribe to two services: an e-commerce platform and an end-user application. The e-commerce platform consists mainly of functionality for the distribution of the supplier product catalogues,

Please use the following format when citing this chapter:

Krogstie, J., 2008, in IFIP International Federation for Information Processing, Volume 274; *Advances in Information Systems Research, Education and Practice*; David Avison, George M. Kasper, Barbara Pernici, Isabel Ramos, Dewald Roode; (Boston: Springer), pp. 203–214.

searching these catalogues, retrieval of one's own purchase statistics, and transmission of purchase orders. The end-user application provides access to the functionality in order to place, accept and send orders, as per entered agreements. It also manages transfer of information regarding completed transactions to the economic and invoice systems.

Introducing electronic commerce does not need to be a complex process; everything depends upon the size of the organization, as well as the level of ambition one has. An important aspect of introducing electronic commerce is identifying the portion of the purchase volume and transactions that are suitable for e-commerce. Analyses show that it is possible to support approximately 30% of the operation purchases (money-value) with an electronic commerce solution. These purchases typically represent 50% of the total number of invoices (E-Commerce Secretariat, 2002).

The main objective of the public sector Marketplace is (E-Commerce Secretariat, 2001): "Use of electronic commerce in the public sector shall contribute to the considerable decline in acquisitions costs and to the raising of the quality of the public procurement processes. The freeing of resources shall contribute to allowing public offices to concentrate on their primary tasks to a greater degree."

It was originally an objective to sell for NOK 1 billion in the Marketplace by 2003. This figure was first reached in 2007. Simultaneously, sales in the public sector reach approximately NOK 120 billion every year.

In 2002, a pilot project for the establishment of the public sector Marketplace was started. The project had 14 participants, among them, the County Municipality of Sør-Trøndelag (STFK) and Trondheim Municipality[1]. The pilot project lasted from December 2001 to May 2002. At the end of the pilot project, both Trondheim Municipality and STFK concluded that they could receive substantial profits by subscribing to the solution on a permanent basis, and the solution was introduced for normal use. After the introduction of the solution, progress has gone slow up until today (winter 2008). Few buyers have used the system, and economic benefits have not yet been observed. On the other hand, in Trondheim Municipality, the use and acceptance of the system has been much higher.

In the next chapter, we describe the problems at hand and theory backgrounds, focusing on relevant theories regarding acceptance of new technology. Thereafter, the research method is described. Results from the interviews are analyzed, and we suggest what can be done to increase use and acceptance of the system. In the final chapter, we present a conclusion in which we discuss results, weaknesses in the method we have used, and suggest further work.

[1] Trondheim Municipality is part of the county municipality of Sør-Trøndelag. Municipalities and county municipalities have the responsibility of different public services, e.g. is it the County Municipality that has the responsibility for high schools, both in Trondheim and in the neighboring Municipalities. Primary schools in Trondheim on the other hand, is the responsibility of Trondheim Municipality

2. Problems and Theories

An analysis of the situation in the STFK on January 1, 2002 revealed a large improvement potential with the introduction of an e-commerce system. There were a large number of small and medium-sized purchases outside of the general agreements that involved considerable additional costs. 97% of the suppliers represented just 20% of the purchasing value. Approximately 80% of the invoices were derived from purchases under NOK 5000, and with an average administrative cost for the ordering, stock receipt and invoice process of NOK 450 per invoice, this involved considerable amounts each year. At that time, general agreements were drawn up for approximately 45% of the total purchases (the County Municipality of Sør-Trøndelag, 2006). Agreement loyalty was poor. Orders to suppliers were made independent of agreements, set prices, ordering terms and delivery terms.

Electronic ordering of products and invoice management showed a profit potential that STFK wanted to bring out. After an invitation from the Ministry of Trade and Industry (NHD), the Chief Administrative Officer decided that STFK should take part as a pilot in the e-commerce project. In addition to qualitative benefits, such as better information and communication, improved financial management and time freed up for service and professional focus, it was calculated that STFK could receive a profit of somewhere between NOK 8 and 11.5 million per year by introducing an e-commerce system (County Municipality of Sør-Trøndelag, 2006).

Our problem at hand was:

"What can explain STFK's lack of success with the introduction of the Marketplace, ehandel.no ?"

2.1 Acceptance Theories

In order for the introduction of a new IT system to be a success, it is necessary that potential users effectively use the system. Since we had witnessed that the use in Trondheim municipality first became widespread when the use of the system was enforced (on both the purchaser and supplier side), we wanted to investigate system acceptance. There are several models and technology acceptance theories, among them: Diffusion theory (Davis, 2003, Venkatesh et al, 2003), Theory of Reasoned Action (TRA) (Ajzen and Fishbein, 1980), Technology Acceptance Model (TAM and TAM2) (Davis, 1989, Davis, Bagozzi and Warshaw, 1989; Venkatesh et. al., 2003), and ITPOSMO (Heeks, 1999). The theories have roots in information systems, psychology, and sociology. In this work, we have chosen to use several of these in order to investigate our problem. Due to page limitations, these are only briefly described as part of the analysis.

2.2 Method

It has attempted to define the advantages and influences of electronic Market-places, but has not yet arrived at general theories that say anything about what makes an enterprise accept and use electronic marketplaces (Kioses, Pramatari, and Doukidis, 2006).

We assessed the evaluation methods questionnaires and interviews in order to collect data. Since we wished to go in-depth and we did not have a deep under-standing of the situation beforehand, we chose to collect the information via inter-viewing the purchasers (i.e. the potential primary users of the system). This also provided us with the possibility of being exploratory during the interviews, and made it possible for the informants to elaborate on their opinions. Therefore, we chose a semi-structured form of interview. 42 questions were formulated based on the different acceptance theories, but it wasn't necessary for us to slavishly follow wording or question sequence, as one does in a structured interview (Rogers, Preece and Sharp, 2002). Online interviews, for example utilizing email are a val-uable method to use when one wishes a quick response from users (Rogers, Preece and Sharp, 2002). We chose to carry out interviews in this way for those buyers that we did not have the opportunity of meeting personally. Due to the fact that we knew who the answers came from, we were able to pose follow-up questions.

The buyers in STFK can be roughly divided into three groups: schools, dental clinics, and management and administration. We have interviewed at least four people from each of these groups. We also interviewed those responsible for pur-chases at the local university (NTNU) and Trondheim municipality, both of which have been recognized as having success with the introduction of the marketplace. We interviewed both buyers who use the marketplace and those who do not (al-though they were expected to). In total, we interviewed 17 people, 6 of these in-terviews were face-to-face. The interviews took place in November 2006.

After an interview, we wrote a report and sent this back to the respondent so that he/she would have the opportunity to change, delete or add information.

3. Results and discussion

We here present the results from the study, structured according to the various ac-ceptance theories.

3.1 Diffusion Theory

Diffusion theory mentions five factors that influence whether or not a user accepts a system:

Relative advantage; to what degree the user regards the innovation as better than that which it replaces: Very few users perceive the marketplace as better than that which it replaces (telephone, telefax, and/or the suppliers own websites). No one we talked to thought that it was quicker to order products through the marketplace, not even those who eventually had received some experience making use of it. The dentists mainly have one supplier that they use – the Norwegian Dental Depot. This supplier has its own web shop. Several dentists mentioned that they prefer to purchase here because the products are placed, for them, in a logical, hierarchical structure. Consequently, one can navigate to a product, even though one doesn't know the name or article number, and thus would not have found it in an ordinary search.

A disadvantage that was mentioned is that the ordering must go through an approver before it is sent to the supplier, even though one has been authorized to send in orders. This additional element can result in delays since the approver can be out of town, or not have the time to approve the order right away.

Compatibility; to what degree an innovation is perceived as consistent with existing values, needs and experiences of potential users: We discovered that most employees were satisfied with the way in which they already ordered products. We were told from one of the administrative units that: "I have honestly never been into the marketplace... I have been issued a code or something, but I haven't had a use for it. (...) Sorry, that's just the way it is!" This reflects the attitude we saw with many. They don't see the need for a new system.

Something we discovered at a high school in the district, a problem the procurement service at STFK could confirm, was that two wishes they have in the districts cannot be fulfilled by the marketplace for the time being. Firstly, they want to support the local community by purchasing from the local suppliers. This is often not possible since these local suppliers are seldom a part of the marketplace. Secondly, the purchasers often need to receive the products on short notice, and the larger suppliers often deliver goods to the districts only once a week.

Complexity; to what degree an innovation is perceived as being difficult to understand and use: Many users think that the marketplace is difficult to understand and use. In particular, they think that it is difficult to find the products that they wish to buy. During the interviews, it was mentioned that it is frustrating that the product numbers are in different formats and that there are too few search criteria. The majority of users think that the product catalogues are not good enough, and that this is the biggest problem with using the marketplace. Many users are disappointed that the development of the marketplace has been so late and that it still has not become easier to find the products that they want. The supplier has given a free course in catalogue construction for suppliers, but very few showed up (County Municipality of Sør-Trøndelag, 2005).

Observability; to what degree the results of an innovation are visible to others: To a certain degree, one has attempted to influence this factor in STFK awarding those schools who had the greatest number of purchases on the marketplace (County Municipality of Sør-Trøndelag, 2005). A problem was that often it was the same schools that won every time. Further, several employees were displeased with the concept because, in a way, it was perceived that one was awarded for having used the most money.

Trialability; to what degree an innovation can be experimented with before it is finally used: Few users in STFK had the possibility of doing this.

3.2 TRA/TAM

Theory of Reasoned Action (TRA) is a model designed to explain human behavior (Ajzen and Fishbein, 1980). The model is based upon social psychology and the assumption that people use the information available to them in a reasonable manner when they make decisions. TRA's three components are behavioral intention, attitude and subjective norm (Davis, 2003). Technology Acceptance Model (TAM) (Davis, 1989) is based upon TRA, but is designed particularly in order to explain acceptance and use of information technology. The model can be used to foresee whether a system will be accepted by users, or in order to explain why a system is not adopted as it should be. They use two deciding factors in order to explain why people accept or reject information technology.

Perceived usefulness; the extent to which a person believes that a system will help them perform their job better. There are few positive feelings connected to the use of the Marketplace, meaning that perceived usefulness is small. Very few users in the County Municipality believe that the system will help them improve their job performance

Perceived ease of use; the degree to which a user believes the system to be free from effort. The user in STFK did not experience that the system is free from effort. Many think that they have to use a lot of time and energy on the system. As indicated also above, due to the poor product catalogue, other systems (e.g. the general web-shop of the supplier) were perceived to be easier to use than ehandel.no

3.3 TAM2

TAM 2 extend TAM on a number of areas. Here we present findings in light of the factors in TAM2.

Voluntariness; the extent to which the person perceives the decision to adopt an innovation as voluntary: The use of the marketplace is not voluntary. The decision to use electronic commerce in the County Municipality is taken and the users must comply. They are still not penalized if they do not make use of the marketplace, which can lead to many viewing the use as voluntary after all. For those operations that we interviewed, the number of purchasers who use the marketplace was low – nowhere was it over half. As mentioned above when discussing *observability* above, STFK had monthly awards to the school that relatively purchased the most via the Marketplace. This may have contributed to the schools viewing use of the Marketplace as voluntary, even though at the same time, they had received letters from the county executive stating that they must use the Marketplace for those suppliers that are associated with it (the County Municipality of Sør-Trøndelag, 2005).

Experience; how much experience one has using the system, or other similar systems: Among those who use electronic commerce in the high schools, a large number are cleaning personnel, cafeteria workers and janitors. These are occupational groups that often use computers very little in their daily duties. In addition, these can be people in an age group that seldom uses computers in their leisure time. When one is not very computer literate, one is often extra afraid of the consequences of doing something wrong. Consequently, one rather prefers to use more traditional methods of ordering, such as the telephone and telefax.

Many users in the County Municipality do not have much experience with similar systems. We received confirmation that the system functions much better for those who use the marketplace regularly than for those who seldom purchase products there.

Subjective Norm; the degree to which the person perceives that the people who are important to him think that he should or should not perform the action: If employees see that it is important for their managers that they use the Marketplace, this can lead to increased use. On the other hand, we saw that few managers had a positive attitude. Trondheim municipality has used a great deal of time and energy to motivate the managers, and they themselves see this as a critical factor for success (Trondheim municipality, 2006). This supports that the factor of subjective norm is important.

Image; the degree to which use of an innovation will promote one's status in the social system: Use of the marketplace does not promote any special status within the social system that users are a part of. This means that this factor is not included regarding acceptance of the system.

Job relevance; the degree to which a person perceives the system as useful and relevant to his or her job: For many buyers in STFK, the marketplace is not particularly useful or relevant to the job. Purchasing products is only a small part of their jobs. Several think that it is easier to order on the telephone since this is something that they are used to.

Output quality; how well a system performs the tasks that are relevant to the job: Several users in STFK are very displeased with the product catalogues. Searches often give either too many or too few hits. This results in the system not satisfactorily carrying out tasks that are relevant to the job.

Results demonstrability: No one we talked to clearly saw the positive results of using the marketplace. Users from several units told us that they had not noticed any financial profit using the marketplace, and didn't see that the prices had become lower either as a consequence of renegotiated general agreements. This was particularly true of the dentists, since they mainly use only one supplier. The contract with this supplier is renegotiated regularly in any case.

3.4 ITPOSMO

Here we analyze the results in light of the seven areas in ITPOSMO (Heeks, 1999).

Information: One condition necessary for a successful implementation of a reform is that the right amount of correct information reaches the users of the system. It was mentioned during interviews that some users received too much information during the first training session, so that it was difficult to extract what was essential in order to begin using the marketplace in an effective manner. Others remarked that they thought that they received too little training and that the information after the introduction had been lacking. Even if the users say that the catalogues are poor, it is difficult for the suppliers to know what they should change since the suppliers do not know how their own catalogues look for the users.

According to the one responsible for the marketplace in STFK, she seldom receives feedback from users regarding what they are displeased with, even though she encourages them to give it.

After having been in contact with purchasers at high schools, we see that the information regarding use of general agreements has not been sufficiently clear. Although users are obligated to use the suppliers on the marketplace, we have found several concrete examples in which other suppliers were used. Reasons for this are either that one receives lower prices from the supplier without a general agreement, or that one wishes to take local or timeliness considerations into account by using a local supplier. Some respondents said that they wanted more information regarding the use of general agreements.

One thing we found is that the majority of users used print catalogues to find the products that they wanted to buy. They go through and find the product, look at the picture, and make note of the product number. Afterwards, they search for the product on the marketplace. On the marketplace, the products are often poorly described and missing pictures. Therefore, it happens that users call the suppliers after they have found a product on the Marketplace. They do this to be sure that they have found the correct product.

Technology: Many users are displeased with the speed on the network connection, resulting in that product ordering takes a very long time. In addition, access to a computer can also be a problem. STFK has attempted to solve this by giving away computers, but due to lack of space, many declined the offer. In several dental clinics, the computer with an internet connection is in the lunch room. There are already computers in each office that do not have internet connections for security reasons. The fact that many have to share a computer means that the computer can often be in use when one has thought to order a product. If one does not have time to complete an order, something that is often the case in dental offices due to patient visits, someone else can take the computer in the meantime. Consequently, one must log in again to both the machine and the marketplace in order to continue with the order, and this is unnecessarily time-consuming.

Trondheim municipality saw to it that high-speed internet and all technical equipment was in place before they introduced electronic commerce.

Processes: A process that the ICT service in STFK works hard in order to improve is integration between the purchasing system and the economy system. Invoice amounts and orders shall be matched in the accounting system so that the invoices go straight into the data system. According to the original plan, this should have been finished a year ago. When this process is in place, it will free up time that can be used for the business operation's primary job tasks. The procurement process is also not fully mature, and many purchases still take place outside of the general agreements.

Objectives: A common feature among most of those we spoke with is that in the beginning, they did not have a particularly positive attitude towards electronic commerce. Many felt that this was just a new initiative in a series of orders from the County Municipality. We were told at a dental office that: "It is a wide-spread belief at the clinics that in the last several years, we have been given more and more administrative work that steals valuable time from our primary job tasks.. (...) When this comes in addition to other administrative routines, which in a busy day is viewed as hassle and annoyance, the threshold is very high in order to use systems that are seen as a local setback."

Skills: An enthusiastic person is a good starting point in order to have success with electronic commerce. We were in contact with an enthusiast who saw the meaning in this. She took time to sit down and show each person how to use the marketplace in order to make the purchasing process simpler. When other employees have a positive and helpful co-worker in the vicinity, the threshold to ask for help is low, and this leads to uncertainties being cleared up and irritation disappearing. The use of this kind of super-users/enthusiast was not pursued in any planned manner though. Several respondents maintained that they do not have time to sit down and learn how to use electronic commerce, because they have so much to do with their other work tasks. Others say that although they have been trained and know how to use electronic commerce, they use more time ordering from the Marketplace than via telephone/telefax.

Management structures: In each unit there is a leader who decides how many purchasers there will be. Our findings show that there is up to 20 purchasers in one unit in the County Municipality. One success factor Trondheim municipality brought up were good foundations in the leadership and relatively few purchasers that had this as a main part of their job. Both Trondheim Municipality and Sør-Trøndelag County Municipality have used much time and energy on this. Trondheim municipality gathered all 220 unit leaders on a half-day course in groups of 30 to create motivation.

Other resources: There was no particular remarks related to this part of the ITPOSMO framework.

4. Reflection and Conclusion

During this study, we have discovered many possible reasons for the lack of success with the introduction of the marketplace in STFK. The more important reasons are that users think they use too much time finding the products they wish to purchase, and that motivation among unit leaders and purchasers is low. In addition, many see the use of the marketplace as voluntary. We have shown that better product catalogues and search options are the most important things to tackle in order to improve user-friendliness. STFK will also most likely see an increase in purchases on the marketplace if they do what Trondheim Municipality did; enforce obligatory use. In Trondheim Municipality they require that the suppliers follow the agreement that buying and selling shall take place via the marketplace. At the same time, they should inform them that anything else will be seen as a breach of contract, and will lead to the cancellation of the agreement. In this connection, it is very important that employees remain loyal to the agreement. Although this appears to have been very effective in Trondheim Municipality, one should be cautious when introducing this kind of force and balance this with potentially negative side-effects. Introducing user support and ensuring that everyone has sufficiently high internet speed is also a good idea. STFK should use time to motivate the employees, and in particular, the unit leaders in addition to the purchasers. They should also renegotiate general agreements with suppliers and give electronic commerce the credit for the benefits this provides. It is important to inform employees about benefits since this will create motivation to use the Marketplace.

Theories we have used have pointed out factors we otherwise would not have been aware of such as the goal conflict in the district between supporting the local community vs. efficiency in the procurement processes, and they support that the findings we have made are real reasons that can explain lack of use.

4.1 Discussion on Research Method

We have been in contact with a total of 17 people. Thirteen of these are responsible for purchasing in STFK (i.e. they are actual purchaser and as such primary users of ehandel.no). We interviewed just 5 of the purchasers in STFK personally. This can be too few interviews to come to generally valid conclusions. In many of the email interviews, the responses were not as in-depth. Use of a broader survey would have perhaps been useful, providing us with more respondents. The response percent for the electronic interviews was approximately 60%, which is a good response percent for this type of inquiry (Rogers, Preece and Sharp, 2002). We chose to in addition to interview the Head of Purchasing of Trondheim municipality towards the conclusion of our work, rather than at an earlier stage, in order to take advantage of the possibility of being able to verify findings and measures we had arrived at.

We had a follow-up meeting with STFK's purchasing service in order to present the measures we had arrived at. This was useful because, among other things, we discovered that one of the measures we originally had landed on had several more disadvantages than first thought.

Because one of our main measures is that the supplier's product catalogues should be improved, it would have been appropriate to contact one or more suppliers on the Marketplace in order to get a better idea of their situation.

The frameworks we have used in order to understand acceptance of technology are diffusion theory, TRA/TAM, TAM2 and ITPOSMO. They have similarities, but emphasize slightly different things. They were used to form questions and to evaluate the information we collected. Since the TAM/TAM2 articles have a number of questions they have discovered useful to ask users, this model was a good start. The questions are a good starting point in order to ensure that one poses the most relevant questions when one is going to interview users regarding acceptance of a system, and in order to ensure that they are formulated in the correct manner. Regarding evaluation of the results, we think that TAM2 was a more complete model. Diffusion is the oldest acceptance theory, and this was also very useful. We see that all of the factors are involved in explaining lack of acceptance. TRA wasn't so relevant in our case, since this is a general model that can be used to explain almost all types of human behavior. Since TRA is built into TAM, it was not necessary to go in-depth into this. Diffusion, TRA, TAM and TAM2 have much in common. There is a reunified framework described in (Venkatesh et. al., 2003) called, Unified Theory of Acceptance and Use of Technology (UTAUT). It is claimed that this new model includes the factors that have shown to play the largest role concerning acceptance and use of new technology. We see in retrospect that this could have well been used instead of the four frameworks we used, but given the set of questions linked to the existing frameworks, we found it beneficial to use these. To cover the full UTAUT would probably also have resulted in a need to extend the survey form with additional questions, which might have resulted in lower response rate on the email interviews. ITPOSMO has a different slant than the others, which was very fitting since this focuses on the public sector in particular. This model alone would not have uncovered everything we have discovered though, so this, in combination with the diffusion theory and TAM2, provides the best explanation model in our situation.

4.2 Further Work

This is a qualitative study. It could be interesting to carry out an anonymous, quantitative study based upon the data we have collected. It might also be an idea to carry out a field study – that is, to observe the user in his/her daily work environment. One could then uncover information the user is unaware of or takes for granted. Tests for usability are a suitable method for identifying problems the user has with an application. Such tests can be completed and the results given to the supplier of the end-user application. It is also an idea to contact the suppliers. One should then find out what could motivate them to create good product catalogues.

In this work, we have gone in-depth into the introduction of the marketplace in the County Municipality of Sør-Trøndelag. It would also be interesting to take a closer look at other public sector operations, including those which have chosen not to introduce the marketplace. Electronic commerce is introduced in the public sectors of several countries. One possibility is to look closer at their systems, and compare these with the situation in Norway.

References

Ajzen, I. og Fishbein, M. (1980) Understanding attitudes and predicting social behaviour. Prentice-Hall.

County Municipality of Sør-Trøndelag (2005). Statusrapport (Status report) [Intern rapport utlånt av innkjøpstjenesten i Sør-Trøndelag Fylkeskommune] (Internal report loaned by the procurement service of the County Municipality of Sør-Trøndelag).

County Municipality of Sør-Trøndelag (2006). ESTER, e-handel i Sør-trøndelag fylkeskommune. status på innkjøp i fylkeskommunen. (ESTER: E-commerce in Sør-Trøndelag County Municipality. Status of purchases in the County Municipality). [Intern rapport utlånt av innkjøpstjenesten i Sør-Trøndelag Fylkeskommune]. (Internal report loaned by the procurement service of the County Municipality of Sør-Trøndelag).

Davis, C. (2003) Technologies and methodologies for evaluating information technology in business. IRM Press, 2003.

Davis, F. (1989) Perceived usefulness, perceived ease of use, and user acceptance of information technology. MIS Quarterly, 13(3).

Davis, F., Bagozzi, R. P. og Warshaw, P. R. User acceptance of information technology: A comparison of two theoretical models. Management Science, 35(8), 1989.

E-Commerce Secretariat (2001). "Elektronisk markedsplass for det offentlige: Sluttbrukerapplikasjon", (Electronic marketplace for the public sector: End-user application) http://www.ehandel.no/data/file/krav_sluttbrukerapplikasjon.pdf. Last visited 10.10.2007.

E-Commerce Secretariate (2002). "Veileder for forprosjekt - elektronisk markedsplass for det offentlige", (Guide to preliminary work – electronic Marketplace for the public sector) http://www.ehandel.no/data/file/file_110.pdf. Last visited 10.10.2007.

Heeks, R. (1999) Reinventing government in the information age. Routledge.

Kioses, E., Pramatari, K. og Doukidis, G. (2006) Factors affecting perceived impact of electronic marketplaces. Proceedings 19th Bled Electronic Commerce Conference, June 4-6, Bled, Slovenia.

Lipis, L. J., Byron, D., Villars, R. og Turner, V. (2000). "Putting markets into place: An e-marketplace definition and forecast", http://www.e-consultancy.com/knowledge/whitepapers/75/putting-markets-into-place-an-emarketplace-definition-and-forecast.html. Last visited 10.10.2007

Rogers, Y., Preece, J. and Sharp, H. (2002) Interaction Design. John Wiley.

Trondheim Municipality (2006) E-handel I Trondheim kommune Sluttrapport innføringsprosjekt. (E-commerce in Trondheim Municipality: Final report on introduction project) http://www.ehandel.no/data/file/file_308.pdf, Last visited 10.10.2007.

Venkatesh, V., Morris, M., Davis, G. og Davis, F. (2003) User acceptance of information technology: Toward a unified view. MIS Quarterly, 27(3). J. Krogstie